AMERICAN PERIOD INTERIORS IN MINIATURE

AMERICAN PERIOD INTERIORS IN MINIATURE

Kate Doordan Klavan

CHARLES SCRIBNER'S SONS / NEW YORK

Library of Congress Cataloging in Publication Data

Klavan, Kate Doordan.
 American period interiors in miniature.
 Bibliography: p.
 Includes index.
 1. Miniature rooms—United States. 2. Interior
decoration—United States. I. Title.
NK2117.M54K56 1984 747'.0228 83-22808
ISBN 0-684-18122-3

1 3 5 7 9 11 13 15 17 19 Q/C 20 18 16 14 12 10 8 6 4 2

Printed in the United States of America.

Unless otherwise indicated, all photographs
are by the author.
The section on the Southwest and California
in Chapter 6 was written by Nancy Doordan.

CONTENTS

A Word from the Author, ix

One **EARLY SETTLEMENT**: 1607–1690   3

Two **COLONIAL GLORY**: 1690–1790   26

Three **THE REPUBLIC**: 1780–1840   83

Four **VICTORIAN PERIODS**: 1830–1900   132

Five **AMERICAN KITCHENS AND BATHROOMS**   192

Six **SPECIAL CASES**   228

The New Century · Home on the Range
The Southwest and California · Shaker · The Farmhouse

A Quick Guide, 259
Bibliography, 263
Appendix, 268
Index, 274

ACKNOWLEDGMENTS

THERE are many people who helped me during this book's long preparation, and I came to know scores of people—artisans, collectors, dealers, and chroniclers—who are part of the miniatures community. I found them to be a friendly, interested, and generous group and I hope that those who are not mentioned here will not feel slighted if I draw special attention to some who were particularly helpful. I should like to acknowledge the friendship and encouragement of Terry Rogal, Catherine B. MacLaren, Marie Friedman, and especially Emily Good, whose hard work was integral to this book.

Among others who deserve special mention are Hermania Anslinger, Al Atkins, the Birkemeier Family in all its extensions, John M. and Ellen Krucker Blauer, Jack and Shirley Bloomfield, Rose Barell, Lee-Ann Chellis-Wessel, Mary Frances Cochran, Jim and Helen Dorsett, Rosemary Dyke, Rosemary Hansen, Howard Hartman, Don and Cindy Massie, Virginia Merrill, Robert S. Milne, Mary Grady O'Brien, Guy Roberts, Sylvia Rountree and her band of merrymakers, Kathy and Bill Sevebeck, Constance Simone, Vivian Stoddard, Susanne R. Strickland, Jean Stuart, Noel and Pat Thomas.

On the publishing side I wish to thank Harriet Rochman Bell, the Jay Acton Agency, Ann Ruble of *Nutshell News*, Rebecca Martin, Katherine Heintzelman, and Megan Schembre.

My family was extremely helpful. My mother, Nancy H. Doordan, put her expertise to work producing the chapter on Southwestern interiors. My father, John E. Doordan, drew a lively picture of his boyhood home, which was the key to understanding the family of the later years of the book (even though he himself came along later still). My grandfather, A. H. Hammond, Sr., delighted me with his wide-ranging and precise memories of growing up on a farm, and was my "technical" expert when I turned to the rural family of the turn of the century. My father-in-law, Gene Klavan, gave me some valuable lessons—and judgment—on photography.

Most important is my husband, Ross Klavan, who saw further than I—encouraging me to broaden the scope of what initially was a very tiny project—even taking some of the pictures himself. He has indulged my obsession with miniatures with understanding, enthusiasm, and humor, not to mention money. In the process he has become a very good judge of what's best in the world of miniatures—only one of the many happy worlds I share with him.

A WORD FROM
THE AUTHOR

THIS book is an attempt to rescue the befuddled collector who has tried to establish a dollhouse or scale rooms somewhere in the past 300 years of American history and has been interrupted along the way by frequent doubts about what *really* goes into a colonial kitchen or a Victorian drawing room

I, too, have been plagued by the questions about when a certain stove found its way into the kitchen or how long ago we traded in the chamber pot for its more modern substitute. I also wanted guidance on how to decorate the interior—wallpaper or whitewash; big window or little; Oriental rug or rag? I looked for a book that would help me, but I couldn't find one that was complete or concise enough. So I made an enjoyable journey through museums, books, restorations, and homes, and translated what I found into miniature.

My attention is focused primarily on the work of contemporary craftsmen and other producers rather than on antique miniatures although I believe collectors of antiques will find help and pleasure in these pages as well.

The book is divided into chapters treating specific decorative eras. The divisions are based on history, logic, convenience, and consensus—and consensus is hard to come by, which is why I tend to be rather generous with dating. After all, experts themselves do not always agree on absolute dates; formal furniture of one era often doesn't show up in its country version until the city slickers have laid the fashion to rest, and individual pieces frequently survive their stylistic dates because hardly anybody can afford to throw everything away every thirty years or so.

The text gives you the information about each period, discussing the things that go into making the interior look right and the furniture fit. I also treat some regional differences for the benefit of the collector who is interested in a Baltimore townhouse or a New England farm.

The pictures are meant as a catalogue and an inspiration. They show many commonly available pieces, some one-of-a-kind, some limited editions, and a few that are extraordinarily rare. The emphasis is always on the things that belong in a room to bring your favorite period to life.

The Quick Guide makes up a checklist to use against your current collection and give you a priority shopping plan for the future.

I strongly urge you not to confine yourself to the chapter that suits only your dollhouse or room settings. So often it happens that to understand one era you must learn something about those that preceded it—there are some surprises in these pages for many of you! I also urge you to make enjoying your collection your first priority. Do not feel you must be slavishly devoted to the prescriptions of this or any other book. Make historical authenticity a principle rather than a god that will only make you nervous.

Only the collector who loves miniatures and loves making them live together can lend the specialness that gives miniature rooms and dollhouses their real charm. This book is an attempt to help that collector.

American Period Interiors
in Miniature

ONE

EARLY SETTLEMENT

1607-1690

I N the 1580s Sir Walter Raleigh outfitted a series of ill-fated expeditions to the New World in an attempt to colonize Virginia. All that remains of these early efforts is the lingering romance of the adventure, from heroic beginning to tragic end. The first permanent English settlement was a commercial venture at Jamestown begun in 1607. But even there most of the colonists died from starvation, disease, or Indian arrows soon after they arrived.

Jamestown outlived its early difficulties, however, and by 1614 it was obvious that a strong future lay in raising tobacco, the crop that would bring prosperity before the end of the century. In 1620, encouraged by the promise of the golden leaf, England sent a ship carrying "maidens" to become wives to the colonists. Although the majority of them did not survive, they did introduce a more domestic note to the colony which had seen only a handful of European women. That same year the Pilgrims landed at Plymouth, having overshot their original destination by a hundred miles. The harsh winter literally froze them out of any help that might have been extended by their predecessors to the South.

The Pilgrims suffered mightily in their early years, though in general they fared better than did the first Jamestown settlers. They and the Massachusetts Bay colonists, who settled a decade later, encountered friendlier Indians. These natives taught the colonists how to grow new food in the new land. In 1621 they were doing well enough to hold a harvest festival, the first Thanksgiving. Events of subsequent years, including tragic Indian wars, would give both settlers and Indians reason to wonder if there really was anything for which to be thankful.

Against this background it is easy to understand why the first homes of both northern and southern settlers were not the cozy retreats we so often conjure up. Life was very hard in the New World, and home comforts were understandably far down on the list of priorities. The first settlers lived in willow-frame huts, shacks built against hollowed-out hillsides, and even in holes in the ground. In the North, a number of new arrivals moved into Indian dwellings which had been abandoned during a smallpox epidemic. As miniaturists we are more interested in the homes that followed, though even these were rude indeed.

The early houses were built out of timber and, more rarely, stone and brick and usually consisted of one square or rectangular all-purpose room. Sometimes there was a small anteroom attached. In the Plymouth Colony the average size of these houses was fifteen to twenty feet on each side, hardly spacious for the up to a dozen people who might live there. Excavations have also revealed long, narrow homes, ten feet wide by forty or sixty feet long, which presumably were divided into several rooms. The early homes had exposed oak beams, often chamfered or beveled, in the ceilings and walls. The main upper support, called the summer beam, was larger than the others and ran the length of the ceiling.

For much of the seventeenth century the homes of English settlers had walls no higher than seven or eight feet. These walls were often made of whitewashed plaster, although the wash might have been more brown than white. Some clapboard interior walls have also been noted.

The few windows the settlers had were glassless and were placed high up in the walls. They were covered with oiled cloth, thin horn sheets or wooden shutters.

The fireplace was the centerpiece of the house, since it not only functioned as the kitchen but also constituted the family's main source of heat and light. The earliest Jamestown fireplaces were nothing more than stone hearths placed under a hole in the ceiling, but they quickly grew into the more substantial form we recognize today.

Most fireplaces were made of brick, with stone fireplaces of an early date rarely found except in Connecticut and Rhode Island. A seven-foot-wide fireplace was common; one of ten feet or more in width was considered big. Many fireplaces were large enough, however, to accommodate two fires or a narrow ledge seat. The side walls of the fireplace generally were splayed, that is, slightly angled, and we know of a few examples of curved walls.

Among the Dutch, who despite losing their New World hold to England in 1664 made a lasting mark on the Delaware and Hudson River valleys, a fireplace with no side walls—or jambs—was the early rule. The Dutch fireplace had a raised hearth and a wide hood that was dropped about eighteen inches from the ceiling and resembled a molded cornice. It often had a ledge on

The typical jambless fireplace. This example, made by the author, is modeled after one in the Museum of the City of New York. Note the molded mantelpiece, raised hearth, pleated valance, and fireback with attached grate. The tiles were made by Marie Friedman after designs developed by Joe Hermes.

which colorful plates were displayed. Hanging from the hood was a valance or short fireplace curtain.

In the Middle Atlantic states, in areas of Scandinavian influence, there were some corner fireplaces with the front on a diagonal. Such fireplaces have even been found in log cabins, which were introduced to this country by the Scandinavians upon their arrival in the 1630s.

Over the opening of most fireplaces, three or four feet above the hearth floor, a massive timber called a lintel was sunk into the wall, primarily to support the masonry above the fireplace. As a rule, the fireplace did not have a shelflike mantelpiece, although there were exceptions.

The very earliest fireplaces did not have ovens, but by mid-century a square or beehive-shaped niche appeared in the back wall of the fireplace (ovens moved to the side and front walls during the eighteenth century). Below the oven there was another similar compartment called an ash pit. As the name implies, this was a place for storing ashes which were saved to be used in cooking and soapmaking, among other things. Ovens usually had removable iron or wood doors that looked like small shields with handles in the middle.

During the seventeenth century, cooking pots hung over the fire on trammels, long hook-ended poles which in turn were hung from a lug pole. The lug pole, made first of wood and later of metal, was positioned across the inside of the chimney parallel to the hearth. Cranes hanging from the side or back of the fireplace were not commonly used until the 1720s.

Some colonists inserted metal plates at the back of the fireplace to protect the masonry. The firebacks also served as heat reflectors and could be highly decorative. The earliest ones were square or rectangular but they later took on a tombstone shape with an arched top.

Some homes were equipped with ceiling hooks close to the fireplace. Poles were laid across the hooks so that herbs and vegetables and even clothes could be hung to dry.

A great many miniature fireplaces that were not built into dollhouses originally are very bulky because they must have depth for the hearth. If you are adding such a fireplace to your seventeenth-century dollhouse—and the room is large enough that you can afford to lose an inch or two—you can overcome the ungainly look of the fireplace jutting into the room by building a second parallel wall and sinking the fireplace into the space between it and the original wall. This also will cover the wide (and not entirely accurate) mantel shelf which tops most of them.

On a more drastic level you can cut a hole in the wall itself big enough for the fireplace and build an outside chimney to cover the fireplace. Chimneys built around fireplaces protruding from the exterior were common in the South.

Another alternative is simply to enjoy what you have and perhaps even capitalize on it, turning a disadvantage into a plus by pushing the fireplace to the corner and building a seat or cupboard onto the remaining exposed end.

Some chimneys at that time were made of wood covered with clay, which presented a fire hazard. Many local governments eventually outlawed wooden chimneys, just as they were forced to control the cutting of oak trees after the first burst of colonial building had felled so many.

Although many homes remained one-room affairs through the mid-1600s, that single room took on a more comfortable aspect. Glass was emplaced in the windows, usually as small diamond-shaped panes. Glass did not completely replace other window coverings but during the second half of the seventeenth century it became increasingly common, largely because of the development of American-based manufacturing. Houses in the cities were the most likely to use glass. For instance, in New Amsterdam glass production began around 1645; yet 100 years later glass was still rare in some rural areas.

Along with glass windows came wood, stone, and stucco floors to replace the earlier dirt floors. The dirt was mixed with ox-blood, sand, or clay and the floors were tamped to a rock-hard surface. Later, pine and oak floorboards were set in varying widths. Such floors with their familiar pegs are favorites in many dollhouses and scale rooms. For the closest match to the real thing, the pegs should be somewhat irregularly shaped because they were hand- rather than machine-made.

Despite these modest improvements, life was hardly genteel and in cold weather barnyard animals frequently shared the relative warmth of the human household. This may help explain why many homemakers spread their floors with fine sand. The sand picked up candle drippings, crumbs and other waste which was simply swept away on cleaning day. Women drew patterns in the sand, patterns destined to be ruined with the first footstep. Rugs were not used on the floors but were kept for tabletops.

As they had more time to devote to improving the interiors of their homes, colonists began to hide exposed beams, sometimes by building boxlike structures around ceiling timbers or covering wall supports with plaster or boards. At the same time, homebuilders and renovators turned with greater frequency to wall paneling—initially just simple sheathing with dressed oak boards. Often the fireplace wall was the only paneled wall and the other three had the more usual whitewash finish.

The single room was naturally bound to become two, then three and four rooms. The addition of rooms to the central core created the saltbox, a characteristically New England form that is found only rarely in the South. The saltbox was a house with a back roof sloping sharply almost to the ground. Under that slant was a low-ceilinged chamber that served as a bedroom, a new kitchen, a storage room, or a buttery. The buttery was a sort of dairy-pantry which might be lined with shelves. We also know that some homemakers put benches and shelves at the end of the main room opposite the fireplace in order to store food and utensils away from the heat of the fire.

One of the differences between homes that developed in the North and those in the South was the size of the rooms. Rooms in the South generally were larger, at least partly because large rooms were cooler in the summer.

Both Northern and Southern houses commonly featured a center hall with one or two rooms on either side. The four-room configuration which would become common in the eighteenth century was seldom seen during the seventeenth century except in the homes of the wealthy. In the South the center hall was more likely to run through the house, dividing it into two rooms, each with a fireplace in the exterior wall. In the North, one central chimney was the rule with the hall being more of an entryway. The hall often contained a ladder or narrow staircase leading to a sleeping loft. Alternatively, the stairway might be next to the fireplace, concealed by a door made of two or three boards fastened together with thin wooden strips called battens. All doors were made basically this way with rope or iron pulls.

One thing we do not find in seventeenth-century homes is a closet. Instead there sometimes was shelf or cupboard space, open or closed, beside or over the fireplace. Other storage was provided for in the loft, or in a few homes, in a cellar reached by a trap door. Pegs on the wall were the only built-in storage available for clothes.

FURNITURE

THE austerity of the seventeenth-century colonists' life naturally extended to the furnishings in the home. The most accurate observation we can make about the furniture of the earliest settlers is that there was not much of it. But despite the scarcity of furniture and the fact that practically nothing before 1640 has survived, what we do know of seventeenth-century American furniture indicates it has a very special charm. In fact, new research into the seventeenth century indicates that the colonists were not so pinched and pale as we have been led to believe. Their dual decorative tradition was partly medieval and, interestingly enough, partly Italian Renaissance strained through northern European craftsmen on its way to the New World. There was much more color and ornament than is popularly portrayed. The constraint on colonial production appears to have been more practical—they were living in the wilderness after all—than inspirational. It also appears that variety and workmanship picked up discernibly after midcentury because colonists then had more time and money to spend on home comforts.

Oak was the most common wood used in early furniture and usually had quite a bit of pine supporting it. Maple, ash, hickory, and other indigenous woods also were used and it was common to have more than one type of wood in a single piece of furniture.

Some miniature-craftsmen distress their pieces so that a seventeenth-century replica will look like a miniature antique after years of wear. Others point out that if the setting for the piece is to represent, for instance, 1670, it is unlikely that furniture in the original would have looked 200 years old! The choice is yours whether you want your miniatures to exhibit signs of *age* (like warping), but a compromise is possible if you concentrate on signs of *use* that would be obvious even early in the life of a piece of furniture: a dulling of the bright new finish, a few nicks on a chair leg, or a scratch on a tabletop. With the chest, one sign of use you can adapt is the charring of the finish because of constant exposure to the flames of candles and fireplace. Fire, in fact, probably destroyed more seventeenth-century furniture than did changing fashion.

Probably the most common piece of colonial furniture was the chest. It was important for storage, for seating, and sometimes for eating and sleeping. The simplest chest was the six-board version, which was literally six boards fastened together, one forming each of the four sides, one the bottom, and one the hinged lid.

More elaborate chests were carved or painted. During the second half of the seventeenth century the application of decorative turnings was especially popular. Turning refers to a woodworking technique done by hand or lathe that results in a decorative spindle. The finished spindle can be thick or thin, and at its most sophisticated can be described as resembling the balusters of a

staircase. A finely turned spindle was split in half (more precisely, two halves of a wooden block were glued, then turned and split again), and the flat side was fixed to the chest. Often these applied ornaments were painted black to imitate ebony which enjoyed a vogue in the seventeenth century. There also were some fancifully inlaid chests.

Among the most famous of the carved and painted chests were the Hartford and the Hadley. The Hartford chest had three front panels, two with stylized tulip carving and one in the center with a sunflower design. This is also called, understandably enough, a sunflower chest. A similar type with tulip and leaf designs in arcaded panels was popular during the third quarter of the seventeenth century and is known as an Ipswich chest.

The Hadley chest also was carved but the carving was shallow, like relief carving. It covered the entire chest in a pattern of flowers, tendrils, and other curving figures. Often the Hadley chest had a background of black and dark green with the carving outlined in red, all common colors for seventeenth-century furniture.

Around midcentury, chests added first one drawer and then another and another. The chest became the chest of drawers as the first bottom drawer was joined by others until the whole piece constituted drawers, at which point the top was fastened down. The chest of drawers did not, however, replace the chest which continued to be an important form well into the nineteenth century.

A similar metamorphosis can be traced with the desk. The

These two seventeenth-century pieces were made by Pierre Wallack. The Brewster chair is replete with spindles. Dates for a similar chair range from 1620 to 1660. The chest (1650–80) features turned (and then halved) spindles which were frequently applied as decoration. *Photo courtesy of Pierre Wallack*

A 1670 to 1680 heavy turned table with box stretcher and nicely carved skirt. The Bible boxes (c. 1670) are reminiscent of those in the Wadsworth Athenaeum. The one on the left is relief carved much in the manner of a Hadley chest. The box on the right has half-moon or lunette carving. Emily Good made the table and all accessories. *Photo by Emily Good*

desk's ancestor was the Bible box, a wooden box, often carved, in which rested the family Bible. Tradition says the Bible box, unlike some similar carved storage boxes, was not locked because it was considered dangerously blasphemous to steal a Bible. We may suppose that anybody not deterred from blaspheming would not be in the market for a Bible, so the lock would be doubly unnecessary.

Despite tradition, recent scholarship suggests that although family Bibles often came to rest in such receptacles, strictly speaking there was no such thing as a Bible box; there was instead a variety of lidded boxes with less specific purposes which stored documents, valuables, and, sometimes, Bibles.

All these boxes grew bigger as the years passed and quite early acquired a slanted lid which was a prop for books or paper. Sometimes they were covered by a cloth, as tabletops were covered by rugs. The slant-top box was destined to become the slant-top desk with the fall front, but not until the turn of the eighteenth century.

There are indications that these desk boxes sometimes were set on the tops of chests or mounted on their own frames, although the desk-on-frame itself—the piece that evolved from this—is now usually considered to be a development of the succeeding William and Mary era.

Besides the Bible box, another small storage item was the spice chest which also held other precious foodstuffs like sugar. It sometimes looked like a tiny chest of drawers or an apothecary chest and might be mounted on a wall.

Yet another form of storage piece was the cupboard of which

the early settlers had several different kinds including the court and press cupboards. These types were designed for both storage and display, with the court cupboard especially endowed with ample room to exhibit the family pewter or ceramic treasure. The only trouble for most seventeenth-century families was that there was not much treasure to display, although if a colonist could afford a court cupboard, there undoubtedly was something around the house worthy of exhibit. The court cupboard had an open bottom with a shelf; the top section featured either more shelf

Warren Dick made these two pieces of furniture in the style of the second half of the seventeenth century. Both the small chest and the court cupboard have typical applied turnings and ebonized highlights. The open bottom marks the larger piece as a court rather than a press cupboard.

Tom Poitras of Thomas Creations in Wood made this c. 1640 court cupboard based on an original found near the Maryland-Virginia border. *Photo courtesy of Tom Poitras*

Harry W. Smith made this press cupboard. Compare this with the court cupboard in plate (caption 499) for a clear illustration of the differences between the closed press cupboard which was designed primarily for storage and the open court cupboard which had storage space plus more room for display. Notice, too, the hanging corner ornaments, similar to those sometimes seen on building exteriors.
Photo courtesy of Coe-Kerr Gallery

This *kas* by Susanne Russo is decorated in *grisaille*—painting in shades of gray—which is typically Dutch and was popular in New York area homes. Although the *kas* appeared in seventeenth-century homes this particular piece was probably made later, set as it is on bracket feet.

space or an enclosed cabinet. The press cupboard was closely related, except that the bottom was enclosed. These cupboards ordinarily were five feet high or less.

Another kind of cupboard which appeared early in the era but which was only rarely seen was the livery cupboard. The livery cupboard sometimes was as simple as a box hung on the wall; at other times it was a larger piece like the court or press cupboard but with an important difference. The livery cupboard had a grilled front consisting of vertical spindles arranged close together. This allowed for air flow, and performed the same function as the pierced tin panels of the nineteenth-century pie safe and for much the same reason. In England, the livery cupboard stored the "livery" or small portion of food and drink that servants took to their quarters at night. There also were some standard dresser-type cupboards with open shelves above and doors below.

In areas of Dutch influence, a huge wardrobe called a *kas* was important from the middle of the century. The *kas* with its paneled doors sometimes had *grisaille* decoration. The term describes a drawing of fruits and vegetables in tones of gray shaded to give a three-dimensional effect.

The chair or hutch table combined storage with seating. This was a table with a top that swung up to form the back of a chair. Distinction is usually made between the chair table which might have a drawer beneath the seat, and the hutch table which had a bin in the seat. This versatile piece of furniture came in different sizes with square, oblong, or round tops. Long after 1800 it was still a fixture in many homes, especially in rural areas.

The settle was another piece that often combined storage with seating. It was usually found beside the fireplace and formed a windbreaker for the sitter. It was essentially a bench with a high solid back, sometimes curved or paneled, that extended to the floor. Some settles were equipped with small candlestands or

The curve-back settle of pine with a shelf was made by T. C. Cottrell, Jr. Displayed with it are a tall candlestand, betty lamp, and tin sconce by Studio B, and a rushlight holder by Jim Holmes. The rushlight holder bears a candle—the pincerslike apparatus that holds the rush is closed.

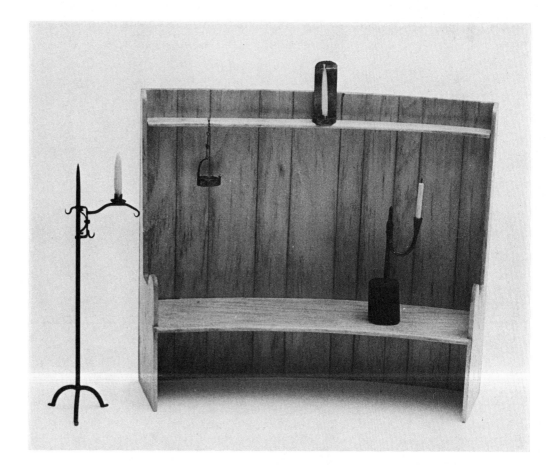

A turned triangular chair of the seventeenth century. It gives ample evidence of its medieval antecedents. From the collection of Robert Milne of Milne Miniatures.

Here is a Brewster chair made by Elena Lamb. The placement of spindles below the seat designates this as a Brewster rather than a Carver chair—and makes it much rarer.

holders either fixed on small protrusions or in the form of a little shelf attached to the back. Colonists used blankets, cushions, and pillows to make the settles more cozy and comfortable.

Although a number of elaborate chairs are known to have been brought from Europe, chairs as we know them were few in number during the early years of settlement. A scooped-out stump was often all the craftsmanship a colonist had time for. Among the earliest real chairs was the triangular turned chair with three legs and turned arms, supports, and spindles—a vestige of the medieval style. Another turned chair was the Brewster with a back consisting of vertical spindles, sometimes several rows of them. The spindles were also found under the arms and below the seat which was usually made of rush. The Carver chair, a related armchair, had the same spindle back but lacked the spindles below the seat. We often use "Carver" to designate any armchair, but it has a specific meaning when we are discussing the seventeenth century. The Brewster and Carver chairs were named for two of early New England's most honored citizens, Elder William Brewster and Governor John Carver. Some scholars say that the Brewster and Carver chairs appeared only in New England; but it is worth noting that several authorities indicate the Brewster had Dutch antecedents and of course the Dutch settled in the Middle Atlantic states. Even if the Brewster remained New England-bound, it may well be that the Carver wandered farther and wound up in homes somewhat south of New England.

One of the most impressive although relatively rare chairs of the seventeenth century was the wainscot chair. With its tall, wide, paneled or carved back, it looked like a rustic throne. Homemak-

A forthright Carver chair with sturdy stiles and nicely turned spindles and finials by Thayer Langworthy.

ers usually did not add a cushion to the flat wooden seat, except in the South, which probably reveals something about the role of creature comforts in New England.

Another traditional straight-backed chair was the farthingale chair, named because it accommodated a popular wide underskirt of that name. It was armless and upholstered in leather or turkey work—a carpetlike fabric—attached with metal studs. It had simply worked stretchers and legs, sometimes turned in a twist or rope design that points to a New York, New Jersey or Southern origin. This chair was also called a Cromwellian chair after Oliver Cromwell who brought a brief period of nonmonarchial government to England between 1649 and 1660, when the chair was popular. The bottom of the seat back did not touch the seat, a feature of most chairs until the eighteenth century and one we see in the Restoration or Charles II chair, which came with the restoration of the monarchy in 1660.

This Restoration chair was fancifully carved with a high back that was upholstered in leather, velvet, or other fabric. Seventeenth-century upholstery was often colorfully patterned; red, green and gold seem to have been the favored colors. The crest of the chair, the top piece of the back, rested between the upright back supports, another characteristic of chairs until the turn of the century when the crest rose to sit on top of the uprights.

This carved chair with its stern bearing was made by Tom Poitras of Thomas Creations in Wood. It has English antecedents in the Jacobean Lancashire–type chair. It dates to around 1641. *Photo courtesy of Tom Poitras*

This Carver chair is much like an example from about 1670 but it could be earlier. The difference between this and a Brewster chair is obvious. Pierre Wallack is the artisan. *Photo courtesy of Pierre Wallack*

Emily Good of Heirloom Replicas made these two pieces, a corner chair with spindles and a candlestand which is painted blue-green. Mrs. Good also made the hefty seventeenth-century candleholders which include two made with spikes which take reamed candles. *Photo by Emily Good*

A stocky splayed-leg stool sits in front of a typical turned-spindle chair. Both pieces are by Harry W. Smith of Barnstable Originals. *Photo courtesy of Harry W. Smith*

Chairs were special to the settlers and despite what may appear to be a wide, even luxurious variety of types, there were not many individual chairs in the average home. This is fortunate for miniature-collectors of limited means because they can furnish a room or house authentically without having to acquire a large number of pieces. Even *one* good chair can "make" a scale room setting and there are many to choose from being made by craftsmen and factories.

Remember that chairs like the wainscot or Restoration chair were rare, while slat-backs and plain backless benches (called forms) were perhaps the most common. The seventeenth-century slat-back was a heavy piece with a rush seat, bulky, turned legs and arms, and thick, straight, or only slightly curved horizontal slats in the back. Children hardly ever sat in chairs, which were reserved for more venerable family members or honored guests. Somewhat more their style was a piece allied to the bench called a joint stool. It looked like a little low table with turned legs and stretchers.

A small trestle table and a Carver chair with a rush seat by Warren Dick.

This is a very long mid-seventeenth-century trestle table from Jim Holmes. The stool was made with what's known as a box stretcher typical of the seventeenth century. Stretchers on later stools and tables generally come farther up from the floor.

Tom Latané made this table with a trestle support. As is the case with most trestle tables the top comes off. This one is different from most in that under the removable top is a shallow storage space. Notice the burn marks on the top where pots were carelessly set down. *Photo by Catherine Latané*

This sawbuck table from the Hoffman Collection has a drawer that opens conveniently from both sides. From the collection of Jack and Shirley Bloomfield.

Most seventeenth-century tables were stretcher tables, a term that refers to any table with supports stretched between the legs. Technically, such familiar types as the trestle and the sawback are stretcher tables although we usually reserve the term to describe tables with four turned legs at the corners joined by stretchers.

Because space was at such a premium, early trestle tabletops were detachable boards. Except when the table was in use for preparing or eating a meal, the top leaned against the wall out of the way, along with the trestle supports. Supports for the sawback were X-shaped and there is evidence that the sawback first appeared in Swedish settlements of the Delaware Valley.

A large stretcher table with an ancient lineage was the refectory table. There may have been a few here in this country following the sixteenth-century Elizabethan style—recognizable by big, bulbous, carved legs—but the legs were trimmer on most seventeenth-century Jacobean tables. Sometimes the refectory table was equipped with extensions that could be pulled up from its ends. In general, extension tables were called draw tables. It has been suggested that most large tables of the stretcher or refectory type would have been found in public buildings—particularly churches—rather than in private homes.

Seventeenth-century beds were varied and might be as fine as a four-poster with tester and heavy curtains and canopies, or as plain as a pallet with straw or old rags for a mattress. There were beds with turned posts, but most imposing, perhaps, was the wainscot, which like the wainscot chair had a paneled section, in this case the headboard, which was a solid high expanse of wood rising to a tester. At the foot of the bed were turned posts. Mattresses might be made with down, wool, or straw.

It was usual to find at least one bed in the main room of a house, even if there was a separate bedroom. Sometimes several people had to share one bed, just as more than one family might have to share the house.

Space considerations gave us the popular trundle bed, often the children's bed, that was slipped (on its own wheels) out of sight under the parents' bed during the day. Cradles for the youn-

A trundle bed on wooden wheels which could fit an interior from the seventeenth to the nineteenth century—the later periods finding this bed most frequently in rural homes. David White of White Mountain Woodworking is the craftsman.

Here is an enclosed box bed also known as a cupboard bed. It was associated particularly with the Dutch and, obviously, with a desire for privacy and warmth that transcends claustrophobia. The room setting with bed was made by Dusty Boynton of Country Rooms. *Photo courtesy of Dusty Boynton*

gest children were paneled and usually hooded. There were a few wicker cradles.

To add a note of privacy, some settlers, especially the Dutch, enclosed beds in a floor-to-ceiling box, literally building a room complete with door around the bed. These usually were built in corners and provided extra warmth and storage as well as privacy. Some low one-post beds were built into corners of rooms with the freestanding corner supported by a post. In most cases mattresses rested on cord or rope supports laced through the bed frame or on pegs attached to it.

ACCESSORIES

ACCESSORIES—the china and silver, the pots and pans—make miniature rooms come alive. They are fun to collect and are among the most interesting items produced by craftsmen. A personal selection gives a dollhouse or scale room a unique touch, and care in choosing and placing accessories can change an ordinary room with ordinary furniture into something quite outstanding. Accessories are also another test of authenticity. It is not unusual to find an otherwise perfect room marred by the inclusion of an unsuitable lamp, dish, rug, or picture. Picking the correct accessories requires as much attention as choosing the right furniture. We have already touched on some items in the discussion of the fireplace, and a more detailed treatment follows in Chapter Five, "American Kitchens and Bathrooms."

The well-lighted settler's home was not very well-lighted at all, depending as it did on the glow from the fireplace, flaming candles, and burning rags, reeds, tree slices, and grease. Among the myriad disadvantages of these light sources were danger from fire, unpleasant odor, insignificant illumination, and—all too significant—dirt.

One of the earliest forms of lighting was the rushlight. Colonists brought rushes in from the outside, dipped them in grease, stuck them in either a crack of the fireplace or a metal clamp, and set them afire. Rushlights are known to have been used in rural areas into the nineteenth century but apparently were not a part of the Dutch scene in this country. Pine or candlewood was also popular. Slivers and knots of pitchy pine were laid on stones or in dishes and burned satisfactorily by seventeenth-century standards. These tiny torches were used in rural areas through the eighteenth century and probably beyond in remote Southern and frontier regions.

Candles were not very common during the first years of settlement and although they did become more available once communities were established, they remained expensive throughout the period. While there were professional chandlers in Boston in 1634 and elsewhere in the 1680s, many people made their own. By one estimate the average home needed approximately 2,000 candles a year, which translates into a great deal of candlemaking.

The colonists' need for so many candles gives miniaturists an opportunity to build an effective vignette around the candlemaking process, which can be repeated in eighteenth-century dollhouses. Candles were sometimes made by handworking tallow around a string wick. Somewhat faster was the mold, constructed to make from one to four dozen candles. Molds were usually metal although some were glass or ceramic.

Candle dipping is the best procedure to use in creating a dollhouse scene. Dipping required a caldron of warm tallow and one or more thin poles over which the wicks were hung. The candlemaker would hold the pole over the caldron, dipping the wicks into the wax. The pole was set aside to cool, resting on the backs of two chairs. When the infant candles solidified, they were dipped again and the process was repeated until the build-up was thick enough. Drying candles were also hung from poles in the corner or suspended from chandelierlike hangers. If you set up such a scene, be sure to put a board or paper underneath the drying candles to catch the drippings as a colonial woman would. Extra candles were kept in a wood or metal box hung on the wall near the fireplace. Also kept close at hand were small tubes of rolled paper called spills which were used to light candles from the fire.

The colonists used a variety of candleholders and while most were made of metal (iron, pewter, brass, silver), some were made of wood or pottery. There were plain ones on tabletops, a few wall sconces, and some tall candleholders that were the seventeenth-century equivalent of the floor lamp. There also were occasional simple chandeliers. The famous hogscraper candlestick was another colonial device that served more than one purpose. It had a sharp-edged base that was used to scrape the tough bristles off hogs, and it usually had a handle that made it easy to hang the candleholder on the back of a chair.

The colonists also used saucer and boatlike lamps filled with oil or grease. Some of these lamps had tops and moss or rag wicks protruding from a tapered lip. As this basic lamp was refined it was called a betty lamp and either had its own stand or hung from a beam by a chain or from an adjustable trammel called a ratchet. Wooden stands for lamps and candles were cheaper and therefore more common than metal ones. No matter what the light source, it had to be lighted to begin with, and if the fire went out and all the candles were cold, the settlers resorted to a tinderbox. The tinderbox was a small metal container that held a flint, steel, and tinder. There were other ways to find fire, however, and one of them was to borrow it. Many settlers kept a piece of equipment that looked like the modern silent butler, with which they ferried hot embers from a neighbor's fireplace.

Embers and live coals were also held in long-handled warming pans. Warming pans were supposed to take the chill out of a cold bed, just as foot warmers kept damp and freezing toes from going numb. Before retiring, the colonial homemaker filled the warming pan and ran it over the sheets and covers of the bed to heat them to a comfortable state. Warming pans have been known to double as cooking pans in a pinch!

As indicated earlier, colonists were not so drab in their clothing and household fabrics as many grammar school textbooks suggest. Their homes often had several dyepots: earthenware containers of various sizes, rough on the outside and glazed on the inside. One of the dyepots, the one used for blue indigo, might best be kept on the hearth itself, convenient to the fire by which it was produced.

Throughout the colonial period, wooden barrels were important for food storage and every home had its supply. Buckets and pails were made of wood or metal and instead of the usual bail handle might simply have had a short pole thrust through holes in the top of the sides. Other containers you might consider for your seventeenth-century setting include bottles, of which there were a number made of pewter as well as of glass and ceramic, and a box for wood set near the fireplace.

In very early days colonists did not have great stores of tools. They were heavy for settlers to carry around from place to place and relatively expensive. The limitation on the variety of tools was a factor in the limited number and type of furniture and interior features. Nevertheless, there were enough tools being used in the colonies to satisfy any miniaturist's collecting instincts, among them axes, spades, chisels, augers, shovels, scythes, anvils, grinding stones and saws.

Despite the fact that American silver production dates from the second quarter of the century, silver was too rare and expensive for most people and it is not found very often in the earliest homes. However, some exceptionally fine and quite fancy silver artifacts—goblets to sugar dishes—have survived. More frequently we find woodenware and earthenware being used. Wooden trenchers were used in the colonies through the seventeenth century and much of the eighteenth, especially in the country. Pewter plates were also common though not every family was affluent enough to have one plate per person. Both plates and tankards were shared in many homes. The spoon was the most common item of flatware, while knives—and particularly forks—were much scarcer. Seventeenth-century knives had pointed tips—the better to spear food with. They became rounded in the eighteenth century when forks were more common.

Redware pottery was the most common type produced here and dates from early in the period. There also were some stonewares like the more common earthenware. Most of these were

These European pieces by Lee-Ann Chellis-Wessel could have come to this country with the early settlers. The plate is a British delft piece dated 1600. The jugs are German; the Frankfort jug with castle and lion arms is dated 1643 and the Westerwald jug in blue and gray is early seventeenth century.

utilitarian in nature but some, for instance German imports, were remarkably decorated. There even were some local Indian pottery pieces in colonial homes. Ceramic plates apparently were considered display pieces along with the best pewter and were exhibited on cupboards, often resting on cloths over the tops. (For more on the development of ceramics see Chapter Five.)

In the seventeenth century rugs were quite precious and they were usually laid over a table or used to warm a bed rather than laid underfoot. Early colonists were most likely to have animal skins spread on the floor if they had anything at all. The first rugs of local make that occur in any number were braided mats, perhaps of straw. There also were painted canvas floorcloths. These varied in size and whereas some might cover the whole floor, many floorcloths were made to fit under the table. The look of a black and white marble floor became fashionable around 1675, and floorcloths were painted to imitate that pattern. Those who could not afford a floorcloth might paint the floor directly.

Most colonists told time by the position of the sun and until around 1670 clocks and watches had only one hand, which might tell us something about the colonists' need for precision. The first pendulum clocks appeared in the late 1650s and by 1680 there was a rush to convert all clocks to pendulum clocks, from which developed the tall case clock which came to be known as the grandfather clock in the nineteenth century. Before the emergence of the tall case clock, which we shall discuss in more detail in the next chapter, the bracket clock prevailed. The family clock was usually hung on the wall or placed on the wall shelf.

The few available mirrors were also hung on the wall. Mirror glass was almost always imported and the high cost of glass meant that most were very small. The frames, which might have been made here, were typically wooden, sometimes with inlay, and frequently rectangular with a crest on the top. Interestingly enough, during this period there were more mirrors here per capita than in England, but given that there were so few people in this country, that still does not mean very many mirrors. Some colonists made do with polished metal rather than silvered glass, and even small fragments of a broken mirror, no matter how jagged, were saved and framed.

ALTHOUGH we now see old samplers hung on the walls of antique shops and restored houses, most seventeenth-century samplers were not made for decoration but as catalogues of stitches perfected by the homemaker. They were generally long, narrow cloths that were rolled up when not being consulted. In addition to samplers, colonial seamstresses made clothing and whatever was needed in the way of bedclothes and table linens. Early inventories do mention cloth napkins which along with tablecloths were considered an investment by affluent colonists who counted their wealth in possessions as often as in currency. The wealthy might import their linens rather than toil over a loom, but a loom and a spinning wheel are good additions to seventeenth-century dollhouses, especially the spinning wheel, which is made in all price ranges for miniaturists. Like most other pieces of substance, the spinning wheel was common only after the midcentury. To go with your spinning wheel you may want to add a yarn winder and "cards." Cards were small hand-held wooden paddles used to prepare the wool for spinning. They were stuck with metal spikes set in a brushlike arrangement.

Seventeenth-century bedspreads often were woven in two pieces instead of one because of the size limitations of the looms. Colors included red, black, blue, yellow, pink, green, and brown. Sometimes bedspreads were hung over windows as protection from drafts. More formal curtains began as single narrow panels, commonly purple or red, hung on a string or pole unceremoniously nailed to the window. Curtains were hung inside the window frame with string tiebacks. Wooden pegs were also used to hold curtains back during the day although some homemakers simply knotted their curtains to get them out of the way. As interest in more formal decoration grew so did the sophistication of the window dressing and by midcentury we see a few valances installed.

Bed curtains were made of calico, linen, serge, wool, and wool combined with other materials and there were some prints and embroidered fabrics. Bed hangings did not always match and the hangings on one bed might be of two or three different colors. When dressing miniature beds, remember that the curtains were meant to be drawn, so be sure you allow enough material to enclose the bed, even if you plan to leave the curtains open.

While the seventeenth-century home was distinctive it was ordinarily quite plain. There are exceptions, however, and part of the fun of exploring old homes through books or in person is discovering the oddities. One example is the Wanton-Lyman-Hazard House built in 1675 in Newport, which sports walls painted with red stripes in a diamond pattern. There is no reason why you cannot take some license with your dollhouse, perhaps devising your own delightful peculiarity.

COLONIAL GLORY

1690-1790

As we slip into the eighteenth century, please remember that the dates given for various periods are not absolute. I chose to close the period of early settlement at 1690 for several reasons: historical tradition; the assumption of the British throne by William and Mary in 1689; and the issuance by the Crown in 1691 of a new Massachusetts Bay charter under which that colony absorbed, in fact as it had in practice, the Plymouth Colony. It seems clear that a new colonial life was building.

As you go through this section bear in mind the overlapping of styles. Queen Anne furniture, for instance, was still being made in the Chippendale period and Chippendale lasted well into the Federal era. In researching American decorative arts it's interesting to see how *late* some styles developed and how *long* they prevailed. Many people lump together everything up to the Civil War as indefinably "Early American," believing that Windsor chairs and sideboards and Hartford chests emerged together; but although you might have found all three in the same room in 1790, you certainly would not have done so in 1700.

There are very clear distinctions in colonial decorative arts and to ignore them obscures the rich and varied history of how people learned to live in this country and what they lived with in terms of household goods and furniture.

With that warning, here is a table to acquaint you with the conventional wisdom regarding the dating of the styles that will be detailed in this chapter.

William and Mary	1690–1730
Queen Anne	1720–1765
Chippendale	1750–1790

The Georgian tradition is as follows.

Early Georgian	1714–1740
Mid-Georgian	1740–1770
Late Georgian	1770–1820

The Georgian designation refers, of course, to the several King Georges of England up through the beginning of the Republic. The dating is provided here strictly for convenience because many collectors and dealers use it.

THIS era brought a considerable change in the homes of colonists, at least those of some means. It is important to remember that even though many houses constructed in the eighteenth century were much more refined than those erected during the previous century, typical seventeenth-century-style homes still were occupied and were even being newly built after 1700. For instance, to make note that support beams were frequently concealed during the eighteenth century does not mean there were no exposed beams in later colonial homes.

Agricultural wealth grew in the South as did a new kind of mercantile wealth in the North. Much of the first half of the century was spent preparing for the reward of that growth: during the second half there was a notable surge in luxury as all the economic elements congealed into general prosperity in the colonies.

The four-room house became the norm during the early years of the era, and as the century passed, more rooms were added. Even during the William and Mary period, servants' halls and stair halls made their appearance. In the homes of the wealthy it was common to find four or five rooms to a floor. Rooms were taller, too, with ceilings of ten to twelve feet not uncommon. In very fine homes ceilings sometimes reached as high as eighteen feet. These figures reflect the height of first-floor ceilings; many second stories were shorter by three or four feet.

Especially after 1740 the central hallway became a dominant feature. The hallway might run the length of the house and, if wide enough, could be used as a sitting room in summer with front and back doors open to generate a breeze. In winter the same hallway might become a mudroom—in those days there was a good deal more mud!

Many German and Swiss homes had a three-room configuration that put a big kitchen on one side of the house and a parlor and bedroom on the other. In some areas, particularly the Hudson Valley, many homes had partially exposed basements, that is, basement levels that were not completely underground built into a hillside. Often the kitchen was in this basement which had its own outside door.

In the eighteenth century, the bedchamber became something more than a luxury. In larger homes it might have a small ante-

This is a reproduction by Kupjack studios of Park Ridge, Illinois, of the Queen Anne dining room at the Winterthur Museum. The Winterthur room might be called everybody's favorite room (certainly it's mine) because so many people are charmed by it. Current scholarship challenges its authenticity, however, and some modern observers say it reflects more the style of mid-twentieth-century collecting—specifically that of Henry F. DuPont—than mid-eighteenth-century reality. But it's still one of the warmest, most inviting rooms ever created—owing in part to its worn greenish-blue paneling and mauve and blue china, tiles, and upholstery. There is a substantial *kas* against the left wall along with a tea table. Less noticeable in the photograph are the table and chairs against the right wall. The dining table is a Queen Anne gateleg. The china on the table, in the cupboards, on the *kas,* and on the walls is a combination of English and Dutch glazed earthenware. Combined with the heavy, wide tankards it's obvious that this room was most likely from a New York home. All the furniture is from New York families and dated 1730–50. Even the heavy wide tankards bespeak a New York regional style. The marvelous brass chandelier is an English import. The room itself, with its clean paneling, is built from paneling in a New Hampshire home c. 1760. *Courtesy of the Henry Francis DuPont Winterthur Museum*

room serving as a wardrobe or servant's quarters. Nevertheless, throughout the century there were many houses in which the main bedchamber, the one used by the parents, remained on the first floor and was also a parlor. In these cases the upstairs bedrooms often were nothing more than lofts. Where there are definite staircases (not just ladders), it's worth remembering that not all colonial stairs were uniform. There might be very high and very low risers used on different sets of stairs even within the same house.

Closets appeared in colonial homes during the first quarter of the century, although pegs on the wall—perhaps curtained off—still served as the usual "closet" with chests being the most common form of storage. In the Corbit-Sharp House in Odessa, Delaware, for instance, there were quite "modern" closets built in next to the fireplace and equipped with shelves and pegs. There are also examples of small triangular closets that were built-in by closing off a corner of a room with a partition, and some that were built behind fireplaces. You can adapt the end of the fireplace by putting a closet door on it; that could help solve the problem of the miniature fireplace that projects unattractively into the room (see Chapter One).

By midcentury, large houses had butler's pantries for linen and china, as well as warming pantries which, especially in the South, were the last stop between the kitchen and the dining table. Warming pantries usually had fireplaces and were equipped almost like a kitchen.

Except in the South, dining rooms were not common until the Federal era but might be seen in more lavish homes, which might also have separate servants' dining facilities and a nursery.

During this period, architectural details came inside. Columns, pilasters, molded cornices, and entablatures appeared as interior appointments. This was particularly the case after the 1720s when staircases also took on greater importance, and became more varied in form and more finely decorated.

Cupboards were sometimes built-in and the corner cupboard reigned over many rooms. Around midcentury, smaller, curved-top niches also appeared in many colonial walls.

Interior doors were paneled in formal rooms. The molding was plain, usually a quarter round without any beading or scored embellishment. Rougher doors, for instance in the kitchen, were of the batten type with rope or simple wrought-iron latches and hinges, locked by a crossbar set in hangers on either side. Box locks were reserved for the wealthy and for blacksmiths who could make them for themselves. In general, the hardware on doors was left in its original state unless the door was painted, in which case the latch was painted the same color.

As mentioned before, eighteenth-century builders enclosed the ceiling and wall support beams. Paneling, which was limited during the previous era, spread to many homes, although it was still not unusual to find a room with only one or two paneled walls, the others left plain. By 1720 pine had supplanted oak as the ordinary wood for paneling. Paneling ran either floor to ceiling or took the form of wainscoting. Wainscoting covered roughly the bottom thirty inches of the wall and was topped by a strip of molding called a chair rail, which might be very thin or as thick as four inches. This lower area of the wall is called the dado. Walls or portions of walls that were not paneled were covered in plaster.

Beginning around 1725 it became popular to paint interiors and before the century ended, color choices for walls or trim included white, ochre, blue, green, cream, Indian red, brown, Prussian blue, raw umber, olive, vermillion, gray, mustard, ivory, and yellow in various combinations and intensities. Preservationists have been doing a good deal of rethinking about the colors the colonists used and the general, though not universal, consensus favors brighter colors than we have traditionally considered appropriate. Some colonists painted their wall paneling in a solid color while others took a two-tone approach using two shades of one color or perhaps even contrasting colors. Accent areas, for instance the inside of built-in cupboards, sometimes wore bold colors like red to contrast with quieter walls. A few eighteenth-century walls were covered in leather.

Fortunately for many miniaturists who have bought paper that has paneling printed on it, that was a device used by a number of colonial decorators whose cornice molding, wainscoting, and chair rails were nothing more than pieces of paper done up to imitate the real thing.

Wallpaper itself was known to have been imported from Europe as early as 1700 and was produced in America by 1739; but it was not until midcentury that it was practically available and then only to the relatively affluent. Early wallpaper came in pieces roughly measuring sixteen by twenty inches; by 1780 the dimensions grew to thirty by forty inches. Strips of wallpaper were developed about 1760. Interestingly, wallpaper was sometimes nailed rather than pasted to the wall.

All this is to be considered when you paper a dollhouse or a

This elegant room from the Thorne Rooms Collection is dated c. 1710 but has many earlier features which go back as far as Elizabethan times, most notably the spiral-twist turnings in the table and stool and the chair in the center covered in turkey-work upholstery. Among the especially fine pieces in this room are the impressive press cupboard on the left wall, the daybed in the right corner, and the intricately carved wainscot chair next to the fireplace. The room is adapted from one in the Samuel Wentworth House in Portsmouth, New Hampshire. Note its wide-board floor so typical of the era. Other elements true to the times are the single paneled wall surrounded by plastered walls, the side-hanging crane, the enclosed beams, and the new sash windows. *Courtesy of the Art Institute of Chicago, Gift of Mrs. James Ward Thorne*

miniature room. To be accurate the paper should be in strips or pieces but you should also take into account simply how it *looks*. Depending on the type of wallpaper you use, lines of demarcation may show up too harshly if you cut scale paper into strips. The full-size effect was of one solid wall of paper and it may better be achieved in miniature by using one sheet to paper a whole wall as most people do now. A test run with wallpaper is a wise step.

During the first half of the eighteenth century, flocked papers and pictorial and all-over figures or florals were fashionable. During the Chippendale era and beyond, hand-painted Chinese pastoral wallpaper was much desired. The wealthy could afford the genuine item while the less well-to-do resorted to imitations that had become much easier to produce when printed wallpaper was perfected in the mid-1700s. There also seems to have been a vogue (which continued into the Federal era) for plain, unpatterned paper, especially in blue with a gilt border.

THE wooden plank floor was still common at this time though it took on a more finished character; plank widths ranged from four to six inches in better homes. Later in the era painted floors came into style in a variety of colors including pumpkin, gray, blue, ochre, dark green, brown, and terra cotta. The paint either covered the whole floor or was confined to a border. Some painted floors were solid, others were patterned to copy carpets or pleasant designs. Mopboards (baseboards), common from late in the period, were developed to keep the wooden floor from rotting away from repeated washings; the mopboard stopped water from leaking underneath the floorboards.

In the Corbit-Sharp House for example, the baseboards were frequently painted a different, darker color than the walls. If one wall, for instance the wall with doors or closets, did not have a baseboard, the painter represented one, painting a strip along the lower wall where the baseboard would have run. This preserved a continuity of design that is obvious when you glance in at the rooms.

Looking out an eighteenth-century window was a much easier matter than trying to see what was going on outside a seventeenth-century window. In the 1690s the sash window was developed, and from then on windows steadily grew larger. Windows two feet wide were common with arrangements of six- to eight-inch panes. After 1720 the magnificent Palladian window appeared, although in America the Palladian influence was strongest during the second half of the century. In 1767 venetian blinds arrived to change windows forever. The early blinds were wooden slats, usually in a natural finish, which hung from the *outer* frame of the window. By the end of the 1700s, they were hung within the frame, as is the case today, and stained or painted to match the woodwork.

Another fixture that developed during this period and sur-

This room was inspired by Mount Pleasant, one of Philadelphia's magnificent colonial homes, once owned by Benedict Arnold. The drawing room is furnished in the mid-eighteenth-century style: a Chippendale lowboy with claw-and-ball feet is at the left next to a Chippendale side chair with the French foot not often found on American-made pieces. A matching chair stands in front of a window (note the venetian blinds) next to a highboy. There are also a high-back settee; a wing chair, a birdcage, tilt-top tea table, and a smaller pedestal table with a tiny candle screen. The built-in cupboards have the broken pediment treatment at the top. Other architectural elements include a molded cornice, paneled dado, a detailed overmantel, and a fancy plasterwork ceiling. The fireplace is faced with marble. The crystal chandelier is an especially beautiful example of miniature craftsmanship. *Courtesy of the Art Institute of Chicago, Gift of Mrs. James Ward Thorne*

vives to this day is the dormer window, an extreme rarity before the 1700s. Shutters also were used. On brick homes paneled shutters hung inside the house, whereas they hung outside on wood homes. Some shutters were constructed to operate much the way modern bi-fold closet doors do.

The overmantel, the space directly above the fireplace, was made increasingly elaborate as the years passed and, like ceilings after 1750, sometimes had ornamental plasterwork applied in raised designs. From the second quarter of the eighteenth century delft tiles were used to frame fireplaces in parlors and bedchambers.

The fireplace itself was smaller in these rooms than the fireplace of the Pilgrim's keeping room. It sometimes had a mantel shelf and often was surrounded by bolection molding, a projecting, rounded molding. In some finer homes marble slabs were used to face the fireplace, or for the hearth. Architectural details like columns and pilasters set off the fireplace, with pilasters flanking the opening.

In Scandinavian homes corner fireplaces were popular and other homebuilders adopted the idea as well. We know of corner fireplaces in both urban and rural homes; some very fine molded corner fireplaces were built in Philadelphia houses. In a two-story house, fireplaces that heated ground-floor rooms were duplicated on the second floor using the same chimney. As in the seventeenth century, the Dutch favored a jambless fireplace with a fabric valance. Made of everything from linen to velvet, the valances were changed frequently for cleaning. You will find this is a very good way to put some variety in a room while experimenting with color because the valances, in solids and checks, were made in many different colors.

By the mid-eighteenth century, the hood of the fireplace, which had been about eighteen inches from the ceiling, was lowered still further and the fireplace sometimes sprouted side walls. Dutch fireplaces were tiled. In Charleston, South Carolina, fireplaces were frequently tiled and the city is known for its white tiles and coal-burning grates which substituted for andirons and logs.

Eighteenth-century firebacks were highly decorative. Ships, people, flowers, historical events, and coats of arms can all be seen molded in the iron.

Heating the colonial home was always a chore and sometimes it was attempted without adding a fireplace for every room. By midcentury the five-plate stove had become an alternative; the five plates refer to the relatively thin metal slabs that formed the top, bottom, and three sides of a box. The open side was butted against a hole in the wall that had been knocked through from the back of the big kitchen fireplace. The five-plate stove helped expose the heat of the fireplace to the adjoining room. In the 1760s the stovepipe was perfected to the degree that the five-plate stove became the self-contained six-plate stove and moved away from the wall far enough to permit it somewhat better heat circulation. The metal plates were decorated with designs and sayings. The Franklin stove, which ultimately became its own metal fireplace, began as an open metal box set inside the fireplace. Benjamin Franklin developed it in the early 1740s.

By midcentury many homes throughout the colonies were turning to brass or iron grates for coal, mostly in parlor fireplaces but in some kitchens too. The trend was especially picked up in the cities.

As noted in Chapter One most Southern chimneys were outside the exterior wall rather than contained in it. The risk of fire was reduced as was the heat produced, but that is of less importance to miniaturists than the fact that this chimney placement leaves more floor space because the hearth does not reach so far into the room.

Fireplaces were regularly repaired, altered and replastered. You can take advantage of this to alter your own miniature fireplaces or perhaps to create a vignette showing a brick fireplace in the process of being plastered or a new hearth being laid.

We'll discuss the kitchen fireplace in Chapter Five. The subject of kitchens (and baths and laundries) seems to deserve separate treatment so we can relate developments over several periods for a more detailed and unified picture.

Some houses did not have inside kitchens at all but rather separate buildings, often with huge hearths and brick floors. This was especially true in the South and among Dutch colonists. An eighteenth-century farm, plantation, or estate might also have several outbuildings besides the kitchen, including an office, a smokehouse, an ice house, a wash house or a laundry (usually an open-sided pavilion), a dairy and a brick hearth for boiling laundry water. In the 1760s it became customary to connect these various dependent buildings with closed or open passageways.

The plantation house was built around a central hall with a staircase. To one side of the hall were the front and back parlors which were connected by double doors. Often plantations provided separate visitors' quarters just as they did separate kitchens.

Even in the first quarter of the eighteenth century Southern homes of quality were known for their elaborate carved woodwork. More attention often went to such detail because there would be more skilled craftsmen associated with the self-sufficient plantation, perhaps slaves or bondsmen. There also was a richer decorative tradition, at least initially. In Maryland, whose first real mansion was built in 1733, a hallmark of such homes was the use of gray-white paint for the interior walls.

To the North, in rural Pennsylvania, houses featured a narrow mantel shelf above a fireplace that was often built with a tall opening over a raised hearth. Pennsylvania homes, especially in Chester County, also had deep windows and built-in wooden cupboards.

Colonial New England home design reached full flower in the 1760s when trade brought prosperity to the region. Craftsmanship, taste, and the new wealth combined to favor a gracious way of life.

Southern plantations of Maryland, Virginia, and the Carolinas were uncomfortable in the summer and wealthy owners often moved into town for the season. Town in the eighteenth century meant Annapolis, Williamsburg, or Charleston. The Charleston townhouse was a temple of refinement, at least insofar as was known during the eighteenth century. Three or four stories high and one room wide for ventilation, these townhouses had verandas and galleries on several floors. The main public rooms (parlors and ballrooms) were usually on the second floor, a common arrangement throughout the South. Creole cottages, for instance, reserved their first floor for storage and the servants' use. The public rooms often opened onto a long veranda, each room with its own door to the outside. There were a number of L-shaped houses in the South containing three rooms and there also were U-shaped houses with two front rooms linked by a hall and two back rooms forming the sides of the U.

FURNITURE

THE William and Mary era introduced or brought to prominence many exciting new furniture forms, one of the most comfortable of which was the wing or easy chair. The protruding wings on the sides of the upholstered wing chair were draft-cutting headrests and sometimes protected the sitter against the intensity of the fireplace. Wing chairs were usually reserved for the sick and elderly and as a consequence were frequently placed in bedchambers. Although the front of the chair might be upholstered in a rich fabric, the back was often covered in cheap cloth.

The colonial home welcomed several other new chairs as well, as the benches and stools of the early seventeenth century yielded to more sophisticated pieces. The banister- or baluster-back chair developed during this period and remained popular through the eighteenth century. It usually had a rush seat and very often was

This William and Mary table and chair were made by Don Buckley. The table has a deeply scalloped skirt, and flat stretchers with a finial and bun feet. The banister-back chair has a rush seat and plainer turnings. Except for the tabletop both pieces are finished in the traditional black of the period.

The Flemish scroll is evident in the legs of this walnut chair by Helen Dorsett. The seat and back are caned. Note the pierced crest and front stretcher. *Photo by Don and Cindy Massie*

painted black. It earned its name because the chairback was designed with a series of vertical baluster-turned spindles, halved lengthwise so that the sitter's back rested against the flat side. There were, however, some banister backs with just the reverse configuration—the bulging side facing front—which must have been uncomfortable for the sitter.

Tall-back chairs also were making their first important appearance here. These chairs were just that: usually narrow side or armchairs with tall backs. They were upholstered with leather, cane, or colorfully patterned wool or velvet cushions. Colonists were taken with cane and we often find it on chairs exported from England. Boston was another exporter of the era, sending many leather tall-back chairs to other colonial areas, so many that the chair itself is sometimes called a Boston chair. Antiques enthusiasts will also encounter the term "Flemish" chair, used to designate a tall-back chair with especially flourishing carved legs, supports, and stretchers. The Flemish scroll, which gives these chairs their name, is a swirling elongated curve.

The corner, or roundabout chair, which is very popular among miniature-craftsmen, came to the fore during the early eighteenth century. Often set at a desk or in a corner, it was basically a round-backed chair with a leg in front. It was executed in whatever was the prevailing style and the form remained popular through the colonial period and well into the nineteenth century in rural areas.

The wainscot chair, described in Chapter One, fell out of fash-

A much-used settle with paneled back that spanned the entire eighteenth century. It was made by David White of White Mountain Woodworking.

Here is a good expression of the William and Mary style in a highboy and mixing table made by Emily Good. The highboy is a Virginia piece in walnut with most of the William and Mary hallmarks: rectilinear lines, flat stretcher, drop pulls, flat top, trumpet-turned legs, and bun feet. The mixing table has the usual marble inset. The delft bowl is modeled after one dated 1765 and the ladle is a copy of a 1790 Philadelphia piece which is in Mrs. Good's family. *Photo by Emily Good*

ion but another seventeenth-century type, the slat-back, remained extremely popular, often moving from the parlor to less formal rooms. The slat-back of the eighteenth century was a gentler looking chair than its earlier counterpart, with curved slats and thinner turnings. Also continuing in use, of course, was the traditional settle.

The development of the spoonback chair signaled a trend toward more comfortable seating. This chair was designed to conform more or less to the shape of the back instead of jutting ramrod-straight from the seat as earlier chairs did. The perfection of the spoonback came with the Queen Anne style.

Among William and Mary case pieces we find several new and soon-to-be-revered items including the secretary and the highboy. The secretary was a large, blocky cabinet with pigeonholes and drawers hidden behind a fall-front facade: Dutch secretaries took this form. There was a heavy Dutch influence on furniture in general, understandable since King William was from Holland. As impressive as the secretary was the highboy which first appeared as a flat-topped chest of drawers raised high on six legs that were joined by turned or flat stretchers.

A companion piece to the highboy was the lowboy although neither term was used then. The lowboy began with only one drawer and eventually grew to hold two side drawers and a center drawer. It also was known and used as a dressing table. The highboy and lowboy, among the most durable colonial furniture, were

Desk-on-frame by Warren Dick. Note how the desk box resembles those of the seventeenth century when it's removed from the frame. The shoes are by Sylvia Rountree of the Dolls' Cobbler.

often made as a matching set and assigned to the bedchamber.

The desk-on-frame developed at the transition of the early seventeenth century to the William and Mary era. It grew more sophisticated and added drawers until it turned into the slant-front desk that graced many elegant colonial homes. One impetus to the development of the desk was the formalization of colonial mail service which made letter writing a much less futile business than it had been.

Case pieces like the highboy were often supported on legs with trumpet turnings and either ball or bun feet. Brass hardware was a sign of good furniture and many William and Mary drawers had drop pulls that looked like pendant earrings. After 1700, the more familiar bail handle was seen and eventually the most common drawer pulls were of the bail type on a batwing escutcheon.

Remember that grand pieces like the secretary were not the stuff of which average homes were made. Much of the furniture of the mid-seventeenth century (see Chapter One) continued to stock colonial homes during and long after the William and Mary era.

One significant difference between the homes of the first settlers and those of the turn-of-the-century colonists was the number of tables. Several delightful new tables became popular during the William and Mary period. While there had been a rudimentary gateleg table earlier, the gateleg as we usually think of it is associated with the William and Mary period, frequently as a dining table. The butterfly table, that quaint American institution, was a charming William and Mary addition. It was characterized by the wing-shaped supports that swung out to hold up a drop leaf. Splayed-leg tavern tables abounded, some with drawers, some with drop leaves, and most with round or oval tops. The splayed or flared leg with stretchers gave the table greater stability, especially important in a small table, as most tavern tables were.

Although they were not very common, tea tables, generally rectangular in shape, first came on the scene during these years. The tea-drinking custom was only in its infancy as a British Empire tradition. Another new table was the serving table. Grandparent to the sideboard, which did not bloom until the Federal period, the serving table might also be a mixing table where food or drinks were prepared. It often had a top of inset slate, tile, or marble and was relatively simple; it was basically a side table that somewhat resembled the lowboy in design.

Candlestands, important during the eighteenth century, were usually tall stands with small tops made to do one thing: hold candles. Because they were stationed for convenience, you would find candlestands in hallways, at staircases, and near work areas and chairs.

Beds in the William and Mary period were not greatly different from the seventeenth-century types but were more plentiful.

This fully open gateleg table by Bill Sevebeck is a reproduction of a c. 1690 gateleg in the Museum of Early Southern Decorative Arts, Winston-Salem, North Carolina. It is believed by some to be the oldest surviving American gateleg. Compare it with the gateleg in the later Queen Anne dining room from Winterthur and you will see that this table has a much heavier, almost medieval look. *Photo by Don and Cindy Massie*

Some bedsteads were very high whereas others crouched low to fit under the eaves of attic bedchambers. The tester bed was very popular and the hangings during the colonial period were made of serge, calico, linen, damask, silk, wool, and various printed cottons although woolens were usually used prior to the Revolution. Some bed curtains hung from brass rings, much like shower curtains.

Modern decorators do all that is possible to avoid putting beds against windows, but in colonial bedrooms which were full of chimneys, doors, and windows, it was not always possible. If you have a small bedroom in your dollhouse that is short on wall

Here is an assortment of tables and stands by Emily Good who also made the accessories. The triangular, splayed-leg stand at left is an early eighteenth-century piece; the tavern table with drawer and interestingly carved skirt is a bit later, c. 1730–50; the table at right is earliest of all, c. 1700. Notice the full set of pewter measures and the wooden mortar and pestle—the last a necessity in colonial homes. *Photo by Emily Good* space, you can stand a bed against a window and know that some colonial homemakers had to do the same. Another way to conserve space is with the press or closet bed. The press bed was either freestanding or sunk into the wall but its virtue was that it folded up during the day.

A bed that made its primary appearance in the William and Mary home is the daybed, really a cross between a bed and a settee. It was found in public rooms and sometimes acted as an extra sleeper. Long and narrow, often with an adjustable back, many daybeds were caned while others were cushioned or upholstered in embroidered work, velvet, wool, leather, or some other fashionable material. One of the patterns available was the flame-stitch design, a staple of ensuing years.

The storage chest endured and took on new forms, for example, the Taunton chest with its Tree of Life and bird design, and the Guilford chest which was famous for all-over painted patterns of flowers and foliage. During the years bridging the seventeenth and eighteenth centuries it became popular for chest builders to inscribe dates and the initials of the people for whom the chest was made; many dower chests bear such markings.

Several other new ways of decorating furniture came to the attention of the colonists. Veneering was introduced and a great deal of burl walnut was used because of its entrancing grain. In fact, so much furniture was made in walnut at this time that the William and Mary era has been called the Age of Walnut. Oak was less important in stylish homes than it had been during the seventeenth century, while maple and fruitwoods were used regularly.

One of the most spectacular decorative techniques was an old Oriental practice called japanning. Often done on highboys, japanning was a way of applying a lacquer finish usually featuring

The adjustable wooden candlestand would have been more common than metal types which were quite expensive. The splayed legs on this tavern table by Warren Dick are turned although the stretchers are plain. From the collection of Jack and Shirley Bloomfield.

This chest from Studio B is a
Guilford-type chest, identified by its
free-flowing floral painting. From a
New York collection.

Donald Dube built this William and
Mary highboy which has been
japanned by Linda Wexler-Dube.

an Oriental motif or scene. The most common colors were red
and gold and sometimes the painting was done over lightly raised
designs fashioned with gesso, a plasterlike material that could be
molded into intricate designs. Black was the most common base
color on which this magic was worked.

The William and Mary style eased into the Queen Anne style
with a multitude of transitional pieces which included splat-back
chairs on Spanish feet. The Queen Anne style did not figure in
this country until the 1720s, quite a while after the 1714 demise
of the English queen for whom it was named. The Queen Anne
style lasted a very long time, particularly in New England, and to
this day it is one of the most popular furniture styles ever developed. It was a tradition of gentle curves and well-built, graceful
furniture. Fortunately for collectors it also is an era that has at-
tracted many miniature-craftsmen.

Regional differences were probably more pronounced during
the Queen Anne and following Chippendale years than at any
other time. However, there was a considerable amount of trade in
furniture among the colonies, so it is perfectly within reason for
an eighteenth-century-style dollhouse to contain pieces that bear
hallmarks of different regions. Three main centers of furniture-
making activity were New England, New York, and Philadelphia.
Philadelphia, the Queen City of the colonies and capital of art and
culture, was known until the Revolution for its curvy, sophisticated furniture. In New England furniture was plainer with less orna-

The Spanish or brush foot appears on both of these pieces by Emily Good. The William and Mary stool (1710–20) well suits the banister-back chair (1700–1725). Notice the pierced carving in the chair chest. *Photo by Emily Good*

ment and slenderer lines. New York mixed elements from both with a dash of the robust Dutch style.

The Queen Anne style relies on the cyma or S-curve which gave us the brilliant cabriole leg. Though some Queen Anne furniture, especially in the country, stayed with the straight leg, the cabriole leg is an emblem of the style. In New York the cabriole leg was somewhat heavier than elsewhere and has a prominent knee. Before the use of the cabriole leg, all chairs had stretchers as extra support, but afterward most chairs dispensed with stretchers except in New England, where furniture makers were loath to surrender them. Frequently New Englanders stayed with a block-and-spindle stretcher where the Philadelphia artisan would not think to include it.

At the bottom of the graceful cabriole leg there usually was a club foot sometimes resting on a small pad. Other popular feet were the Spanish, slipper, snake, and trifid which was most frequently found in Philadelphia, often with a sock. The sock, expressed with thin ribbed lines, also appeared on other types of feet and harked back to Ireland where it was a standard feature.

Ordinarily we think of the claw-and-ball foot as belonging to distinctly Chippendale pieces, but it was seen on some Queen Anne furniture, although certainly not often. Among the strongest decorative motifs were the fan, the sunburst, and the shell, all related and all found on many different kinds of furniture.

An exciting development during the Queen Anne period was the Windsor chair. Depending on which authority you consult,

George Passwaters made this protective candlestand and Queen Anne chair with horseshoe–shaped seat, vase splat, and shell-carved crest. Notice the trifid feet on the chair and the snake feet on the candlestand.

A New England braced bow-back Windsor by Studio B showing the typical saddle seat. Bow backs such as this were very common. *Photo courtesy of Studio B*

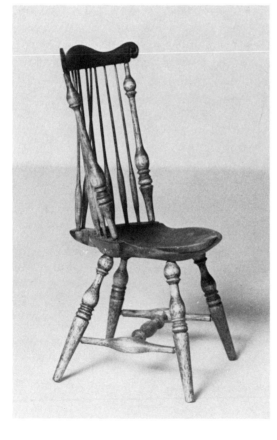

A side view of a Studio B fan-back Windsor illustrates the attachment of the back braces. *Photo courtesy of Studio B*

the introduction of the Windsor chair to the U.S. is assigned to either the early 1720s or the 1740s. Many miniaturists are surprised that the Windsor was so late in coming to America. Once here it traveled from Philadelphia to New York and New England and it is generally acknowledged that by the 1780s Windsors were everywhere. You can be generous with Windsors in a dollhouse, for many homeowners had several at a time; George Washington is said to have had thirty or more at Mount Vernon. Windsors often were used as porch or garden furniture or in halls, although they could be found throughout the house.

Windsor chairs were made from more than one kind of wood; the spindles, legs, stretchers, and seats all required something different from a piece of wood. The eighteenth-century Windsor could have three to five kinds of wood in its frame. Maple, ash, oak, hickory, pine, and tulip were probably the most commonly used. Largely because of this variety Windsors were usually painted to achieve a uniform look. Green was the first and, for a while, nearly exclusive color choice with red, yellow, black, blue, and brown coming later. Experts disagree over whether there ever was a white Windsor.

There were many different kinds of Windsors and there were also marked regional differences in them, particularly between Philadelphia and New England chairs. New England, especially Vermont, New Hampshire, and Maine, was essentially rural whereas Philadelphia was one of the most cosmopolitan urban centers of the British Empire. The Philadelphia Windsor had a

The chair on the left is Jim Ison's copy of a braced comb-back Windsor which was made in Pennsylvania between 1760–90. A New England version of this chair would undoubtedly lack the finished foot you see here. Notice the rakish angle of the turned legs and the volutes on the ears of the top rail, both signs of a fine chair. On the right is another chair from the Middle Atlantic region, specifically the Delaware River Valley. Based on a c. 1725 chair, this piece by Don Buckley has ball-and-ring turning on the stretcher and the arched slat typical of the area. Both chairs are painted a deep green which was perhaps the most common color chosen at a time when many more chairs were painted than you might think. The author made the plain, ageless candlestand.

ball foot, a deep seat cut straight across the front, tapered spindles, and a ball stretcher. In the New England Windsor there was no foot but rather a tapered leg, a shallow seat with a curved front, and spindles and stretchers with a swollen bulb. In general, Windsor seats were shaped for comfort rather than planed flat. American Windsors were made with backs entirely of spindles whereas the English Windsor had a pierced splat in among the spindles.

Other chairs with a Queen Anne background are the slipper chair and the commode chair. The slipper chair was a bedroom chair indistinguishable from other side chairs except that it was built lower to the ground. The commode chair, as its name implies, was a chair fitted with a chamber pot. Commode chairs looked like other side chairs except for a very deep skirt which hid the pot. Some wing chairs and many corner chairs were fitted for chamber pots as well.

Corner or roundabout chairs became tremendously popular and the Queen Anne roundabout, often found at a card table or a desk, had splats that most earlier roundabouts lacked. Slat-backs remained in constant use and the Delaware Valley exhibited a particularly fine arched slat.

The colonists also used an upholstered side chair called a back stool, which was the precursor of the lolling or Martha Washington chair. The Martha Washington chair was a colonial form that was given a more distinctly American attitude during the Federal era. In the 1730s a cockfighting chair appeared, designed so that

A Queen Anne settee with a high back by Virginia Merrill pairs well with a Chippendale bombe-front chest of drawers by Douglas Kirtland. From a New York collection.

Queen Anne settee with a double
chairback by Ivan Lawson.

the sitter sat backwards with the splat in front of him. Cockfighting chairs sometimes had slanted bookrests attached to the back and some had candlesticks as well.

Daybeds continued to furnish colonial homes although not in the number they had during the William and Mary era. The completely upholstered settee or sofa was slow to gain favor. Quite beautiful settees were made that looked like the chairs of the day except of course that they were longer and had two or three chairbacks.

Case pieces took on a new character, which continued with Chippendale and later interpretations. While the chest of drawers went briefly out of style, the highboy and lowboy remained popular and many beautiful pieces were made. They usually had four legs but some had drop pendants of carved wood along the bottom of the skirt, vestiges of the fifth and sixth legs of their William and Mary ancestors. That was most often true in New England while in the Middle Atlantic region the skirts were wavy without the drops.

The outstanding feature of the highboy and the Queen Anne secretary was the scrolled or broken arch top, a sort of divided peak. Philadelphia and New England gave us some exquisite scroll tops and finials while New York favored a flat top. As a rule, highboys were a bit shorter and fancier in Philadelphia than they were to the north. A stair step platform with two or three levels was set on the top of some highboys as a stage for exhibiting china. In Connecticut secretaries rested on short cabriole legs; they had bracket feet elsewhere.

Lowboy with drops (recalling the two
extra legs which were common on
earlier lowboys), stylized sunburst or
shell carving and batwing hardware.
The rather wide overhang of the top
is a particularly American trait. The
lowboy was made by Edward Norton.
The wing chair by Kathy Sevebeck
has a stretcher that echoes a New
England origin. From a New York
collection.

Queen Anne lowboy with a deeply
carved skirt and an inlaid parquet top
by Terry Rogal.

Japanned black-lacquered highboy
with a broken arch bonnet top and
shell carvings by Harry W. Smith.
Photo courtesy of Harry W. Smith

The chair is a special type called a writing-arm Windsor because of its writing surface which opens to reveal a compartment for paper and pen. The writing-arm Windsor was not a common type. This chair is by Edward Norton. The corner cupboard is by Terry Rogal.

We have mentioned built-in corner cupboards but there were also freestanding models. These were popular from 1725 on and had either open shelves or shelves behind glass or paneled doors and an enclosed cupboard below. A wide variety of dresser-type cupboards, often painted, filled eighteenth-century homes as well.

The linen press, still used today in some parts of Europe, was found in Queen Anne homes and a few were around as early as 1700. Homemakers or servants literally pressed the family linen by using the screwlike device atop the cabinet base.

Some of that linen was destined for the dining table, which during the Queen Anne era was most often a drop-leaf, swing-leg type. The swing leg, a refinement of the gateleg, was an elegant table with cabriole legs whose popularity banished the old gateleg to rural areas.

Another drop-leaf table used for eating was the handkerchief

This extremely handsome (c. 1740) Pennsylvania dresser with its rattail hinges was made by Emily Good of Heirloom Replicas, as was the early-eighteenth-century child's highchair. Mrs. Good also made the plates, teapots, and mugs. The ceramics—extremely sophisticated for most of the country—were undoubtedly imports. *Photo by Emily Good*

This dresser by David White is an eighteenth-century pewter cupboard and would have been used well into the nineteenth century. The pewter goblets were made by Emily Good; Lee-Ann Chellis-Wessel made the redware jug and crock. The paint on the dresser is worn at logical places including around the latch on the bottom enclosure.

The Queen Anne drop-leaf table with its plain, delicate legs and club feet, is from Andrews Miniatures. The chair was made by José Rodriguez. It's probably a New England piece; the stretchers generally disappeared from Queen Anne chairs made in Philadelphia. The popular shell motif is seen in the crest. The hurricane shades are from Chrysnbon and the arrangement of pink and white roses in a Chinese-influence vase was made by Joyce Hight. *Photo by Ross Klavan*

table. It featured a triangular-shaped leaf and was usually quite small, often used for breakfast.

Mixing and side tables were used as was a new-style serving table, the dessert server (sometimes called a dumbwaiter), which consisted of circular, often revolving tiers. It held dessert or other food and would be moved close to the table at an appropriate point in the meal. A butler's tray with cut-out handles in the rim of the tray was also used for serving and either rested on a folding frame or was attached to a small tablelike base.

Gaming and card tables developed into a popular form as it became fashionable to play various games of chance and skill. These tables often had folding tops with a green baize covering. In the 1730s tea drinking became something of a mania and the tea table at last achieved prominence. Tea tables were both rectangular and circular, and some had dished tops and tilting mechanisms so that they could be moved out of the way when the tea was over. Although homes had become more comfortable, it was still necessary for many families to conserve space. Tea tables would fit in front of or between chairs.

The spice cabinet developed in the seventeenth century and continued through the eighteenth. It held spices and sugar, which came in cones of various sizes. There is speculation that spice cabinets, especially in rural areas, were also repositories for jewelry or favored trinkets.

In Philadelphia the spice cabinet was a wonderful diminutive piece like a miniature highboy, with tiny drawers hidden behind locked doors. You might find it in the parlor or, if there was one, in the dining room. New England spice cabinets were simpler things with tiers of small drawers that formed a box on the kitchen wall. They usually did not have doors and were not always locked. In the South the spice cabinet was more often the spice or

This highboy and spice cabinet were made by Donald C. Buttfield. Note the relative size. From a New York collection.

Kentucky sugar chest of cherry by T. C. Cottrell, Jr. Although it resembles a blanket chest, it is considerably smaller, perhaps less than half the size. *Photo courtesy of T. C. Cottrell, Jr.*

sugar chest. The sugar chest was a bin mounted on short legs, sometimes with drawers and interior dividers to hold what would have been much larger portions of staples than were stored in Northern cabinets. Some sugar chests looked like ordinary clothes chests except that they were smaller, and a few opened from the front rather than the top. Sugar chests are most often associated with Kentucky.

Throughout this period the bedchamber continued to grow in

All these items were made by Emily Good. The wildly flaring wing chair is based on one in the Peyton Randolph House at Colonial Williamsburg. The stand—for kettle or candle—is dated to 1725–50. The prototype of the chandelier is made of iron and wood. *Photo by Emily Good*

popularity and, as noted earlier, often resembled a sitting room more than a present-day bedroom. The eighteenth-century bed-chamber might have several different kinds of tables—tea, break-fast, even gaming—as well as a wing chair, a side chair, a highboy, a lowboy, a daybed, and a bed. Canopied beds were the favorites of the affluent and Queen Anne beds often featured short cabri-ole legs. Cradles were both hooded and open.

DURING the Queen Anne period, furniture makers favored such woods as walnut, maple, cherry and, especially in the country, pine. These woods continued to be used during the Chippendale era although the signature wood of good Chippendale craftsmen was mahogany, a wood that had been in use since 1708 in America but which was not fashionable until the midcentury. Those who could not afford mahogany often tried to imitate its rich red with an oxblood stain.

The Chippendale era was responsible for some truly remark-able furniture and it also signaled a change in the way we desig-nate periods in the history of the decorative arts. Prior to the emergence of Thomas Chippendale, the premier figure in British cabinetmaking, we generally call a period after the reigning mon-arch, but beginning with Chippendale, the names of furniture makers and/or designers identify the styles.

While furniture was changing, the world outside the home was changing, too. More people had more money and it was *de rigueur* for wealthy colonists to tour the Continent where they supposedly absorbed culture. America still looked to Europe for inspiration, and *American* Chippendale—a particularly satisfying version of the style—derived from English, Irish, and Scottish sources.

Chippendale beds developed out of what had gone before. There were low-post beds on cabriole legs and more of the tester beds with cabriole or straight legs. A new form was the pencil post, so called because of its six-sided posts. Posts in general were tapered and reached seven or eight feet in height. The bed itself was high, too, as high as eighteen to thirty inches off the ground which made the bedside stepladder a decided convenience.

The field bed with its curved canopy frame was a fully devel-oped form by the Chippendale era. It derived from the tradition of campaign furniture taken by military commanders into the field, furniture marked by its plain lines and relative portability (which often meant collapsibility). However, the field bed in its residential form is usually associated with the Federal era.

Daybeds also faded from popularity; the larger houses built during the Queen Anne period cut down the need for convertible furniture. We shall see the daybed revived in the form of a distant relative—the *récamier*—during the Federal era.

In the 1760s the Windsor settee came out and chairback set-tees were also made, but a new and significant form—the camel-

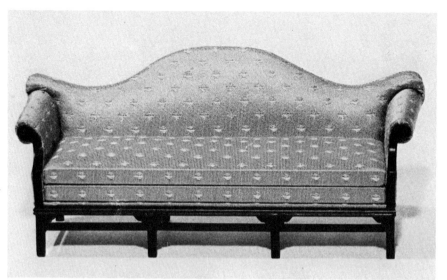

Typical camel-back sofa with straight legs and stretcher by Terry Rogal.

Betty Valentine made this white upholstered Chippendale settee, lovely for its clean lines—straight at the base and curved in the back and arms—which suit their parts so well. From the collection of Jack and Shirley Bloomfield.

We might call this a sophisticated version of an unsophisticated country piece. It is a wagon-seat settee (c. 1780) from the Hoffman Collection.

back sofa—was the prize. With its serpentine back, scroll arms, and cabriole or straight legs, it was a major advance in gracious living. There were several versions of the sofa including some high-back styles and some smaller love seats.

Also new to the colonial home was the window seat, an upholstered bench with two arms but no back. From about 1750 the wagon seat—a primitive settee—brought convenience indoors for less affluent families. It was a wagon seat that lifted out of the family chariot and moved to wherever it was needed inside, including church.

Chippendale chairs are a marvelous expression of Chippendale style with their pierced splats and claw-and-ball feet. Interestingly enough, the claw-and-ball foot was of Oriental derivation—represented a dragon clutching a pearl—an association that makes the claw-and-ball foot at once more romantic and mysterious. It should be noted that in the most famous of the Chippendale design books, not one claw-and-ball foot appears. Chippendale favored the French foot, a dainty appendage with a turned-up swirl at its base. It appeared on a few Philadelphia pieces.

Another Oriental feature of Chippendale era chairs was the pagoda-shaped crest which, rather than curve down into the stiles or rear uprights, flared out at either side like the upswing of a Chinese pagoda roof. There were other Oriental influences during the Chippendale era which we shall examine later.

This photograph illustrates the transition from seventeenth- to eighteenth-century chairs. In the chair on the left, by Betty Valentine, the crest rests between the stiles, the back is straight and tall with its bottom rail above the seat, and the legs are turned but straight. The middle chair, made by George Passwaters, is a transitional step between William and Mary and Queen Anne periods. The crest tops the stiles and melts into them; the curved spoon-back has an urn-shaped splat; the bottom rail of the back is still above the seat but the turned legs terminate in the Spanish or brush foot. The full Queen Anne armchair at the right is by John Hodgson. The shorter back and cabriole legs are further developments and the chair has early claw-and-ball feet, not unusual in English imports like this. Most, but not all, American Queen Anne chairs had club feet.

A comparison of typical William and Mary, Queen Anne, and Chippendale chairs reveals some major points of design divergence.

	seat	leg	crest	splat	foot
William and Mary	square	turned carved	carved straight	solid	blunt
Queen Anne	curved	cabriole	curved	solid	club
Chippendale	square flared	cabriole straight	pagoda	pierced	claw-and-ball

There was also a transitional Chippendale chair that led into the Federal era, where it thrived. Commonly called a pretzel-back, it was the best Chippendale slat-back with straight legs and an open back of thin slats that bore pretzel-twist knots in the middle.

CHAIRS show us some of the most distinct regional differences. For instance, the diamond shape in a pierced splat is almost always associated with New York although it did appear elsewhere. Another New York favorite was the tassel design. In New Hampshire the work of John Dunlop gave us cut-out S-shapes in the splats with scalloped seat-rails. Probably the most intricate chair-backs were found in Philadelphia shops where the Irish sock foot was popular and probably the best carving was accomplished. In Philadelphia chairs tended to be a bit squatter with shorter legs and lower aprons.

One point of difference between New York and Philadelphia

This strong chair is a fine interpretation of the Chippendale style by Ibes Gonzalez of Miniatures by Ibes. Examine the shell carving, pagoda crest, claw-and-ball feet, slip seat, and masterful carving on the back splat and legs. The needlepoint seat was worked by C. J. Originals.

Richard L. Mann crafted this pretzel-back armchair. It is a transitional piece that takes us from the late colonial Chippendale era into the following Federal period. *Photo by Ross Klavan*

Chippendale block-front secretary on ogee-curved feet with corkscrew finials and scroll top with rosette carving. There are two slides that pull out to hold candles just above the desk area. The artisan is Ernie Levy. *Photograph courtesy of Ernie Levy* .

wing chairs was the position of the arm. In Philadelphia the rolled arm of the wing chair pointed out at an angle from the chairback whereas in New York the arm pointed up as though it were growing out of the seat. Remember that this is a generalization and not a hard and fast rule.

Chippendale case pieces were innovative, the most significant new treatment being the block front which had a Dutch heritage. It was brought to its artistic height in Newport, Rhode Island, a seaport with luxurious homes. Local cabinetmakers Job Townshend and John Goddard are credited with carrying the block front to its ultimate aesthetic conclusion. The block front appeared on case pieces throughout New England but was not produced elsewhere. In Rhode Island and Connecticut the blocks were topped by carved shells, a juxtaposition original to America. Another special New England highlight was the bombe front, a swollen front with a particularly rich look.

Highboys and secretaries were somewhat fancier than their Queen Anne counterparts with more carved detail. Massachusetts used corkscrew finials while Philadelphia had flame-shaped ones plus small wooden busts used as finials or centerpieces for broken-pediment tops. The highboy was never a factor in Charleston but elsewhere it appeared in bedchambers and parlors. Its companion lowboy frequently had a mirror hung over it.

Of simpler design was the chest-on-chest, a tall and somewhat inconvenient piece that was exactly what its name indicated: a large chest of drawers supporting a smaller chest of drawers. The single chest of drawers itself returned to popularity during the Chippendale years.

The kneehole desk spread throughout the colonies from England where it had emerged late in the Queen Anne period. De-

Look at the details that lift this Philadelphia Chippendale highboy into a special realm both as a miniature by Harry W. Smith and in its full-size version which is in the Museum of Fine Arts in Boston. The swan's neck pediment, flame-and-urn finials, reeded treatment on the chamfered corners, deep rococo carving, fretwork brasses, and spectacular open-carved cartouche center finial combine to designate a most worthy piece. From the collection of Mrs. Katherine Jennings. *Photo courtesy of Harry W. Smith*

A setting with furniture and accessories by Emily Good. The late-eighteenth-century New England chest-on-frame with its scalloped top is an interesting form. The chair (c. 1778) resembles one owned by John Quincy Adams. Mrs. Good painted the portrait of her ancestor Daniel Harris. *Photo by Emily Good*

spite its name the kneehole desk was often the kneehole dressing table and some were fitted with convertible tops complete with compartments for toilet articles and a mirror. In New England the kneehole desk was more popular than the lowboy dressing table. Supporting these heavy pieces of furniture was a bracket foot with a gentle ogee curve. Highboys and lowboys of course were mounted on cabriole legs.

With regard to personal grooming, the Chippendale era saw the development of the basin stand, also known as the wig or powder stand. The basin stand had a hole in the top into which a basin was fitted. It was used as a little washstand and, judging from the size, very little washing was done. Basin stands had small drawers for toiletries and there was a space near the bottom of the stand to hold a bottle of water. It appears that handleless ew-

Two desks by Edward Norton. The one on the left is a sophisticated Queen Anne desk-on-frame; the other is a reverse serpentine-front Chippendale slant-top. From a New York collection.

A c. 1720 wing chair that has retained its stretcher; a lowboy (c. 1720–40) used as a dressing table; and a late Chippendale era mirror (or, more colloquially, looking glass) with fancy crest and bottom. Emily Good made these pieces as well as the accessories except for the wig, which was made by Cheryl Vilbert. *Photo by Emily Good*

ers were used for this purpose most frequently. Although many people now use basin stands for planters, that is a distinctly modern adaptation. The shaving stand developed at midcentury; it was a table or stand with a basin, mirror, compartments for toilet articles, and a cupboard or drawers for the storage of shaving paraphernalia.

One outstanding development of the period was the breakfront or library bookcase. Its name comes from the fact that rather than having a flat front, the straight line was broken by a protruding middle section. The shelved breakfront top had glass doors, usually set with small panes, and a cupboard base. Before the Chippendale era, such large freestanding bookcases were practically unknown in this country.

A Southern storage piece elegant enough for the dining room was the cellarette which held the family liquor or wine supply. It often had a drawer or two with a slide-out mixing surface and was compartmented with eight, ten, or twelve sections for bottles. Wine coolers, which were wooden or metal tubs on a stand, sometimes accompanied the cellarette.

We can judge the popularity of tea drinking during the Chippendale era by the amount of furniture devoted to it. It was then that the pie crust-top tea table with a birdcage tilting mechanism

This lowboy from Miniatures by Ibes has features emblematic of the Chippendale style: the claw-and-ball feet, shell motif, carved center drawer, batwing hardware, and hardy attitude. The candlesticks are from Roger L. Gutheil, Inc., and the exquisite painted bowl is from Theresa Welch-Stalbaum.

Breakfront with broken pediment, flame-and-urn finial and Chinese-pattern glass doors from Roger L. Gutheil, Inc. In many homes there would have been a fabric panel or curtain fastened to the inside of the glass doors. *Photo by Roger L. Gutheil, Jr.*

(Below left)
Richard L. Mann made the tea table with claw-and-ball feet, a tripod pedestal base and tilt-top. It's obvious why these tabletops are known as piecrust tops. The candlestick is from Roger L. Gutheil, Inc. while the tea caddy was made by William Robertson; the lovely China-trade teapot came from Deborah McKnight.

(Below right)
This view of Richard Mann's tilt-top tea table shows the tilting mechanism which also permitted the top to rotate. Tables with such boxy galleried mechanisms were called "birdcage" tilt-tops.

appeared. Like the highboy, the birdcage tilt-top did not attract a following in Charleston. The kettle stand was added to the tea service to hold the fancy silver teakettle. It was a tall, narrow stand with either a fixed protrusion or a tiny slide that pulled out to hold the teacup. The top often was surrounded by an open-work rim or gallery. Teapoys were closely related pieces: tall narrow stands topped by tea caddies from which the hostess spooned loose tea.

In addition to the tea table, the teapoy, and the kettle stand, there also was the china table. This was essentially a tea table with a gallery to prevent the china from accidentally crashing to the floor.

More side tables appeared during the second half of the eighteenth century, some with marble tops. The most common dining table was the rectangular drop leaf.

The drum table was new with its round thick top and pedestal base. Many drum tables had leather tops while cloth tops were common on gaming tables. Gaming tables often had indentations for playing pieces and candles; the porringer table had a rounded extension at each corner to fit the candlestick. Some tables had a gameboard design on their surfaces and some, especially in the South, had a fifth leg that supported the folding top when it was open.

The wiry spider table found its place in the home during this era. Like so much other furniture the spider table took its name from its appearance, the flat thin drop-leaf top resting on many thin straight legs. The Pembroke table also joined the colonial household at this time. It was a small table, often used for breakfast, with narrow leaves on the sides.

Emily Good made this Chippendale China table and accessories. The silver is based on eighteenth-century originals. The wooden tea caddy has Oriental painted decoration and the table brackets add another Oriental touch. *Photo by Emily Good*

This selection from the Thorne Rooms Collection represents a drawing room from the Jeremiah Lee Mansion built in 1768 in Marblehead, Massachusetts. The furnishings blend Queen Anne with Chippendale and include a Chippendale settee and wing chairs with Queen Anne side and armchairs. The gaming table is a porringer type. Two candlestands help distribute the light as do a marvelous chandelier and three-armed sconces. The bombe-base clock and the Queen Anne secretary are outstanding as are the room paneling, the marble-faced fireplace, and the carved overmantel. *Courtesy of the Art Institute of Chicago, Gift of Mrs. James Ward Thorne*

These matching Chippendale chairs with straight legs and a pierced splat were made by Betsy Zorn of the Ginger Jar. The chairback reflects a Chinese influence. From a New York collection.

We already have alluded to Oriental influence in the pagoda-shaped chair crest and the claw-and-ball foot, but the straight legs and fretwork on many Chippendale pieces also were grounded in Oriental tradition. Another manifestation of the Eastern appeal was the craze for bamboo tables and chairs, many of which were imported and many of which were faked by furniture makers who imitated bamboo with turned wood.

Another appropriate addition to a miniature colonial setting is the fire screen, designed to protect those sitting near the fire from too much direct heat. Fire screens came in several sizes, some mounted on adjustable poles, some sturdy enough to contain a drop-down writing surface. Candle screens, smaller versions of the fire screen, acted as draft protectors for candles and sometimes, when made of metal, also as reflectors. Miniature fire screens provide a colorful accent for dollhouses and scale rooms because they often have needlework panels.

In the country and in the homes of less affluent colonists, the Chippendale influence came late, and then in a decidedly country guise. For instance, the legs of Chippendale country chairs were invariably straight and often the splat was not pierced. There was a great tendency to paint furniture, and some of the more common colors were red, yellow, brown, black, green, blue, and gray. Country furniture had a certain charm about it that has—along with the high prices of the urban versions—made it extremely popular today. Part of that charm comes from the fact that the

Both of these chairs are from the Hoffman Collection and seem suited to the country, especially the chair on the right which is obviously a country interpretation of Chippendale. The pagoda crest is an up-to-date Chippendale feature but older habits survive as seen in the raised bottom rail on the chairback. The solid splat, straight legs, and rush seat are other country notes. The corner chair lacks the city's splats altogether. The dark brown earthenware is from Carolyn Nygren Curran and the cattails come from Roberta Partridge of the Bird House. Cattails were frequently coated with fat and burned in rushlight holders.

Don Buckley made these two chairs, both of which are painted. The chair on the left has a yoke-shaped crest of a type often seen on chairs of the Hudson River Valley and lower New England. Such chairs were made from the early 1700s into the nineteenth century and were usually painted black or reddish brown. On the right is a banister-back chair with a heart-and-crown crest traced especially to Milford, Connecticut. Chairs like this were made beginning about 1700. Notice the paint has been partly rubbed off the stretchers and legs—signs of wear, more than of age-related decline; despite the rubbed paint, the chairs are sturdy, complete, and even.

On the other hand, this sawbuck table (c. 1750) by Jim Ison shows definite deterioration from wear *and* age, especially in the rounded ends of the bottom rails and the ends of the top.

furniture makers were more influenced by the folkstyles of their homelands than the latest London style. Although England was the homeland for many, there were other rich and diverse traditions. In New York, for example, the Dutch influence prevailed in the country even when New York City and Albany were going wholeheartedly Chippendale. The Germans and Scandinavians also lent an especially colorful country style, particularly in the Middle Atlantic region.

IT appears that the colonists stationed most of their furniture along the walls of a room, ready to be moved into action when necessary. There was no static "arrangement" as we know it today, largely due to shifting sources of light and heat. Furniture was placed as needed and as suited. When you are arranging dollhouse rooms, reminding yourself of the *use* of a piece of furniture, rather than its aesthetics, will lead to logical positioning. In a classic example, considerations of use, and the conditions of eighteenth-century illumination will direct you to put a desk under a window.

In addition to sensible furniture placement, you'll want to be sure there's some life to your rooms even without people. Con-

Jim Ison built this Pennsylvania Dutch dresser based on a mid-eighteenth-century original. Note the rat-tail hinges, the notched middle shelf which served as a spoon rack, and the effective distressing most evident in the cupboard bottom.

sider changing your rooms for summer, which is fairly simple to do. When summer set in during the eighteenth century curtains came down except for the valance, and rugs were taken up in favor of bare floors or straw matting. Careful housekeepers put gauze coverings on gilt work, mirrors, chandeliers, and even pictures. Furniture got a covering, too, with muslin, chintz, or linen slipcovers. These slipcovers were often ill-fitting affairs, rather loose and secured by ties. Favorite colors included red-and-white and blue-and-white checks. In servants' quarters or taverns slipcovers could be used all year round. To further enhance your summer preparations you might gather some objects—a mirror, figurines—for wrapping and storage, leaving your packing material strewn about and slipcovers only half in place.

ACCESSORIES

FOR those with money like the merchants of the North and the planters of the South times were growing kinder, and this prosperity was reflected in the accessories that decorated their homes. Essentially all the accessories discussed in the seventeenth century can be carried over into the eighteenth century, often with some refinement. This trend toward richer decorative themes is no better exemplified than in the mirrors found in colonial homes.

During the seventeenth century mirrors were relatively rare. They remained expensive in the later colonial period and although they were usually imported rather than produced locally there were many more of them nonetheless. Eighteenth-century mirrors tended to be taller and narrower than earlier examples. During the William and Mary period many mirrors had plain molded frames, sometimes with a carved crest. That crest grew more ornate with the passing years and the carving was extended down the sides of the frame until by the Chippendale era, carved pieces were added to the bottom, balancing the crest.

Dressing glasses, some set on a base of one or two tiny drawers, topped chests of drawers and lowboys. From the fourth quarter of the eighteenth century the cheval glass was used in a few colonial homes. The cheval glass was a full-length dressing mirror that stood in a frame. It was mounted on swivels that allowed it to swing so that it could be adjusted conveniently.

The major development in dressing glasses came at midcentury with a manufacturing improvement that made it possible to make larger mirrors from one sheet of glass. Previously most mirrors had been made by putting two or more pieces of glass together. This advance did not bring an end to such mirrors, certainly, but the variety and size of mirrors were greatly increased.

In the 1740s gilded frames added a touch of opulence that led naturally into an even heavier use of gilt with the later curvilinear rococo mirrors. Gilt frames were made more imposing by appliqués of gesso built up and molded into intricate designs. Similar to the gilt frames were girandole mirrors with richly carved gilt or metal frames. They were usually circular and surrounded a convex mirror; candleholders were attached to them on either side. Girandole mirrors reached the height of their popularity during the succeeding Federal period. Mirrors were not exempt from the

Deborah McKnight made the delft shaving bowl dated 1706 and identified as to use by the curved cutout in the rim. It also has holes in the rim so it can be hung on the wall. The other items pictured come from Studio B including the tavern table which has a drawer and finely turned legs and stretcher. The tinware covers a range of utilitarian pieces: a hanging tin candle box, a set of measuring pitchers, a candle mold, and a betty lamp. The candleholder is really a tinderbox—the thick bottom is hollow and contains flint and kindling. The candleholder is the lid.

Oriental influence and some Chippendale mirrors had Oriental motifs with fretwork frames.

The tall, decorative pier glass—also a fixture of the Federal period—was initially made to hang on a narrow wall space, for instance between two windows. The pier glass might reach to the floor or it might be short enough to hang above a table.

Mirrors are especially useful in designing or furnishing miniature rooms or vignettes because they give you an added dimension. Although seeing part of a room or piece of furniture in a mirror removes you a step from the real thing, often that distance gives miniature furniture and accessories a more realistic look. In addition, just as interior decorators suggest mirrors to open up rooms that suffer from too little space or too few windows, so, too, miniaturists can use mirrors to make their rooms appear less confined.

Pictures also lend a note of realism to a miniature setting. Decorating an eighteenth-century home gives you more leeway in regard to pictures than furnishing an earlier house; as the colonists had more time and money to devote to their homes, they added more and more pictures. Itinerant painters traveled the settlements of the colonists and while their work ordinarily was crude it is attractive to miniature collectors because its roughness carries a pioneer spirit.

Primitives that could have been painted in city or country are pleasing in a colonial room and there are many available in the inch-to-the-foot scale. People, townscapes, and landscapes were favorite subjects. Landscapes of all kinds were especially popular during the second half of the eighteenth century, including romantic pastorals executed with refined technique. There appear also to have been a great many portraits of military men. Well-to-do colonists had their own portraits painted (and often those of family, friends, or figures they admired) either by American artists or by Europeans who sometimes worked on commission across the ocean.

Around midcentury artists began painting on glass and some also turned to tinsel painting for colorful effect. Engraving appeared at the end of the first quarter of the century and many of the earliest engravings were maps. Black and gold frames were often used and some had their own decorative design.

LIKE pictures, clocks are fairly easy to find in one-twelfth scale. The bracket clock, which we discussed as a seventeenth-century fixture, continued to be popular and was joined by the masterful tall case or grandfather clock. During the last two decades of the seventeenth century the grandfather clock generally had a flat top and a case that touched the floor as opposed to being mounted on footed supports. Grandfather clocks sometimes had paneled doors enclosing the works. The bell-shaped top appeared at the beginning of the eighteenth century when the William and Mary bun foot was added. The arched top with paneled doors and ogee bracket feet was popular during the first quarter of the century. Queen Anne clock case tops were more complicated with the broken arch appearing as it had on secretaries and highboys. There was carving on the doors which was still more elaborate during the Chippendale era when there also were scroll-top tall case clocks. Chippendale clocks had bracket, claw-and-ball, and French feet. From the early 1700s tall case clocks were made in the colonies so the colonists did not have to rely solely on imports. There was, however, very little clockmaking during the Revolutionary War when manufacturing attention was diverted to war production.

The Revolution affected tableware, too. The earliest settlers had depended to a great extent on woodenware dishes as did their descendants again during the war, when metal, which had replaced much of the woodenware, was devoted to weaponry. During most of the eighteenth century there was a variety of dishware with some very fine utilitarian and decorative imported pieces. Earthenware and stoneware were the common ceramics. Decorative techniques which lasted through the eighteenth century (and much of the nineteenth) are evident in the colorful slipware and *sgrafitto* pottery of the day. Slipware is heavy pottery onto which a design was applied with a creamy clay of almost paintlike consistency (the slip). The designs usually consisted of wavy lines or script spelling out people's names and mottoes. In *sgrafitto* the designer cut through a coating of (usually lighter) color to expose the undercoating.

Delft, an enameled earthenware, was the most popular ceramic tableware during the first half of the eighteenth century. It was known as majolica in Spain and Italy, and as faience in France. It was favored until the 1760s when creamware and pearlware emerged; by the end of the period they would become favorites. Creamware was the first truly mass-produced ceramic and, as a result, was relatively cheap and plentiful.

At first porcelain was imported; it was eventually manufactured here as well but was not produced successfully until the nineteenth century. The variety of colonial dishware increased substantially at midcentury, for instance with the familiar Wedgwood, which appeared in England in 1759 and quickly traveled to the colonies. Japanese imari ware with its delicate Oriental motifs on plates and bowls was popular even earlier, along with a great deal of fancy bisque in the form of knickknacks or famous pieces such as those produced as Staffordshire or Meissen. The Toby jug, available to miniaturists in a number of styles, is a good addition to an eighteenth-century dollhouse and its colorful face brightens any setting. Color was especially a keynote of Dutch homes and Dutch homemakers hung multicolored plates on the walls by stringing a ribbon through a hole in the plate rim. Sets of dishes for the table in the affluent colonial house included plates, tureens, covered and uncovered vegetable dishes, bowls, and platters.

Colonial hostesses used coal-heated braziers on marble-top tables to keep serving dishes warm. Plate warmers were kept by the hearth. They consisted of vertical metal rods that stuck up from a base on which the plates rested. Other plate warmers looked like buckets with an open side. Such plate pails were used to carry dishes from the kitchen to the table.

Hanging shelves for displaying china were used during the Chippendale years as were a number of other hanging accessories, including paired wall-mounted cornucopia vases. Another authentic flower holder was a brick made of delft with holes in the top for flowers. A somewhat similar idea was a fan-shaped vase consisting of five hornlike protrusions on a small base. The flowers were stuck into the "horns" and the vases—perhaps two or three at a time—set on the mantel. During the winter dried flower arrangements substituted for fresh.

As ceramics grew in diversity so did the silver. The eighteenth century marked a high point in American silver design and production. There was an especially large amount of silver in Pennsylvania and not just in Philadelphia. As early as 1740, Lancaster was a prosperous town producing beautiful work.

Forks with two or three tines were much more numerous than they had been during the seventeenth century and the care with which silver flatware was treated is expressed in the beautiful knife boxes that were made to hold it. Knife boxes were made of wood or metal, usually with a slanted top; they had slots in the interior of the box in which to store the silver. Knives themselves often had rounded tips.

Among the more exciting silver pieces available to miniaturists is the monteith bowl, a large punchbowl with a deeply scalloped rim. Another is the epergne which sat on the richest colonial tables from about midcentury. It was a branched centerpiece bearing tiny dishes to hold fruit and sweetmeats for dessert. The epergne sometimes rested on a long, low silver or gilded platform known as a plateau. Plateaux were most common in Boston, New York, and Philadelphia, the premier American cities.

Eighteenth-century tea sets consisted of a coffeepot, teapot, sugar bowl, creamer, waste bowl, and teakettle on a stand, although properly speaking they were not sets at all. The colonial tea service was made up of unmatched pieces, and sets as we think of them—everything of a pattern—were a development of the Federal era. From the 1760s the larger tea urn for hot water was popular and usually stood on its own tall wooden stand. Although there is not a great deal of differentiation in most miniature silver and pewter with regard to region, you might be able to follow some evidence of differing regional styles, for instance, by collecting taller beakers for a New York home than for a New England

Knife boxes by Simms Miniatures. The slant-top form was common during the colonial period. From a New York collection.

home and by remembering that the cities would have more silver and more elaborate pieces. In general the styles were rounded with curving lines.

During the eighteenth century pewter was being replaced by china and pottery in fine homes but most colonists did not have fine homes and even the most sophisticated would have had some pewter pieces. Among other metal accessories was the Battersea box made from the 1740s. It was a small copper box covered with colorful enamel. There was also some painted tinware or toleware here during the Queen Anne and Chippendale periods although its heyday came later—as did Britannia, a silver-finish alloy used in England from the middle of the eighteenth century but most popular in the nineteenth century.

An early-eighteenth-century chandelier modeled on one at Marlpit Hall in Middletown, New Jersey, shines over this collection of chairs by Emily Good. Two slat-back children's chairs flank a black-painted vase-back chair (c. 1720–50) with ball-and-ring turning and a yoke-top rail. The child's chair on the left has a restraining bar while the one on the right has mushroom finials on the front stiles. *Photo by Emily Good*

GLASS accessories add sparkle to the shine of silver. Much glassware was imported in the 1700s, including the famous Waterford crystal, but glass was also made in the colonies through the eighteenth century. The most famous of the decorative glass manufacturing centers were located in southern New Jersey. The first major New Jersey glassworks was established in 1739 in Salem County. In addition to goblets, glass decanters were popular in the homes of the wealthy. Colored glassware was introduced into colonial homes about 1720 and engraved glass followed a decade later. Then there was Bohemia ware, a colored glass from which the colored layer was cut away to reveal a design in plain glass underneath.

Graceful glass shades for candles, which we know as hurricane shades, appeared in the mid-1700s. Originally an English export, they protected the candle flame from drafts. There were also some glass candlesticks. Other lighting accessories were of the same basic type as those of the seventeenth century but as with most other things they grew in number and ornamental value. Ordinary rushlights and betty lamps fit well in the eighteenth-century home, while candlesticks can be fancier. Some wealthy homes had elaborate sconces and impressive chandeliers dripping with delicate glass pendants. A number of chandeliers are made for miniature rooms including some accurate copies in glass, brass, pewter, and tin. Obviously a resplendent chandelier would have been beyond the reach of most colonists but that does not mean a plain chandelier, perhaps with only two or three candles, could not hang appropriately in a country- or farmhouse.

Along with the candles went the candle snuffer and wick trimmer. In one form it looked like a pair of scissors with a tiny box attached. The scissors blades trimmed the wick, which would fall into the box. We know candle snuffers were made in iron, tin, silver, and even gold. After 1750 improvements in the construction of the wick itself made trimming candles less of a necessity as the flame consumed the wick.

In the summertime, parlor and bedchamber fireplaces were not needed for heat so the openings were often boarded up with snug-fitting panels. These were painted with many different designs including *trompe l'oeil* images of the inside of the fireplace which was concealed. Other subjects were flowers and scenics.

While you are dressing your fireplace, give a thought to adding a dummy board or two. A dummy board is a one-dimensional wooden figure, a wooden cut-out in the shape of a person or animal, the front of which is painted in some detail. European forms are known from the seventeenth century while they seem to have become popular in the colonies during the eighteenth century. They often are associated with fireplace decoration although they could fill any empty space in the room—or perhaps sit in a window to fool potential intruders. No one is quite sure what purpose they served—perhaps they were just a happy manifestation of colonial whimsy. Most probably were between thirty and forty inches high although there are examples of dummy boards that are somewhat shorter and a good deal taller.

Often dollhouse owners and builders give a great deal of attention to lighting their rooms but only with the idea of illuminating them as brightly as possible. Yet remember how dark colonial rooms would have been in the early morning, evening, and night—the darkness pierced only by flickering candles and the ever-moving flames of the fireplaces. Think of the wonderful dusky shadows. Even in the daytime, light would be concentrated at windows and doors. Look at your own home (with your electric lamps off) and follow the pattern of light. Try to translate what you see into your dollhouse. It could mean a radical reworking of your lighting and it could also mean you won't see as much as *easily* as you can now. Make sure you think not only about what you want to see but *how* you want to see. Whether you opt for lots of light or light created to recall the way colonial rooms really looked, try to arrange your light *sources* in a natural way. It will give your rooms a good deal more drama and reality. Of course our quest for authenticity shouldn't overcome common sense. After all, you do have to be able to *see* the rooms and for some that means a strong, uniform light.

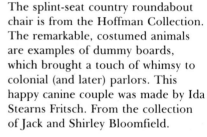

The splint-seat country roundabout chair is from the Hoffman Collection. The remarkable, costumed animals are examples of dummy boards, which brought a touch of whimsy to colonial (and later) parlors. This happy canine couple was made by Ida Stearns Fritsch. From the collection of Jack and Shirley Bloomfield.

This country scene rests on a canvas floorcloth by Thomas C. T. Brokaw. The chair is an Old Sturbridge Village relic from the Hoffman Collection with sausage-turned stretcher. The arms are repeated often in Delaware River Valley chairs but the chair itself could just as easily have come from New England. The cupboard is a very early-eighteenth-century kitchen dresser also from the Hoffman Collection and also copied from a piece at Old Sturbridge Village. The elongated C-curved sides are plain but effective. The *sgraffito* ware plates and dish (inscribed "John") were made by Deborah McKnight and the other pottery comes from Lee-Ann Chellis-Wessel of Demi-Tasse Miniatures.

FLOOR rugs first became customary during the eighteenth century but they were not so common as most people assume. Carpeting was not the rule until the mid-nineteenth century although some elegant colonial homes did have exquisite carpets. The sanded floors of the seventeenth century carried over through the eighteenth century and on into the next in rural areas. There were more canvas floorcloths and stair runners. It was not unusual for a colonial homemaker to lay a small rug over a floorcloth. The opposite was also practiced: a floorcloth of linen or baize was laid over a carpet as a protective device. Oilcloth—floorcloth treated with oil for waterproofing—was used in many colors and patterns. Straw mats were laid during the summer in many midcentury homes and braided rugs appeared, the product of home labor and the economic necessity of stretching everything—even scraps of cloth—to get the most use. Turkey-work carpets came off the tables where they lay during the seventeenth century and onto the floors. They were popular partly because they looked something like that most desired object, the Oriental carpet. Wealthy colonists coveted fine Orientals and there are many made for dollhouses both by hand and by machine.

There were three major kinds of good carpet imported to this country: Axminister, a low-cut pile closely woven and colorful in imitation of Turkish carpets; Kidderminster, a reversible flatweave ingrain (which became a middle-class favorite during the nineteenth century); and luxurious Wilton and Brussels, with a long pile of uncut or cut loops in a variety of colors and designs. During the last half of the eighteenth century, needlework rugs, some in cross stitch, were very popular, particularly for bedrooms. Bed rugs or coverlets with wool yarn designs in gay patterns are other good accents for eighteenth-century dollhouses and miniature rooms.

The quilt is another popular miniature accessory for the colonial bed. The patchwork quilt developed in this country in the late seventeenth century and remained a staple homecraft for 200 years. The quilting process, like the candlemaking procedure described in Chapter One, gives you a chance to do something special with a room.

A quilt was put together using a frame which could be as simple as four strips of wood laid in a rectangle and supported on the backs of chairs. Cloth was bound around the wooden frame and the quilt was basted to that. Quilt-making went on in all the colonies. Building a simple frame for a miniature room, moving the

Flax wheel, stool, and churn by Jim Ison. *Photo by Rich La Mar and Associates*

Allen Martin crafted this vertical spinning wheel which he identifies as a Castle wheel (or parlor, cottage, or traveling wheel): notable for its compactness which made it easy to transport—for instance to a neighbor's where the tedium of spinning might be relieved by visiting. The small diameter of the wheel made it necessary to work the treadle quite fast so it was a wheel that required a lot of pumping on the part of the spinner and because of that may have lacked universal popularity.

chairs around to support it, and basting a half-finished patchwork to the frame are easy steps to take to show activity in a room.

Many miniaturists do not people their dollhouses and rooms but want nonetheless to give them the feeling of human presence. Showing an activity like quilt- or candlemaking—or even dressing, with a few pieces of clothing strewn on a bed or a shoe lying underneath—is a good way to inject a human element.

Another way to suggest family life without a family is to include a pet dog or cat. Birdcages, besides being attractive in and of themselves, accomplish the same thing. During the eighteenth century there were some very fancy ones of wood, wicker, and wire.

Samplers and needlework pictures give a room a homespun touch. Design emphasis changed during the eighteenth century and an interesting cycle evolved. Early in the century biblical scenes and texts were popular including the Lord's Prayer and the Ten Commandments, the latter especially well known in Pennsylvania. At midcentury, nature scenes took precedence and during the last third of the century religious themes were again common.

All kinds of needlework devices can be used to decorate colonial houses. In addition to the spinning wheel there were large looms on which colonial seamstresses wove the cloth to make almost everything they needed. There also were tape looms, which consisted of pieces of slatted wood small enough to use comfortably on the lap or tabletop. These were used to make trimmings and the tapes that held the slats of the venetian blinds in place, among other things. Lace-making pillows also fall into the category of hand-held accessories. A design was drawn on the pillow and the thread worked to fit the pattern. Some pillows were mounted in the stand much like needlepoint frames.

Colonists did use tablecloths (with or without napkins), but if you are setting a miniature table remember that custom called for the removal of the tablecloth for the dessert course.

Fabrics were more important for windows now too, with a greater variety of curtains and draperies. While most common houses still depended on simple cloth panels, usually hanging within the window frame and reaching from the top of the window to the sill, there also were extraordinarily beautiful draperies for finer homes. Draperies often had matching valances and the tiebacks were of metal or glass.

The 1700s also saw venetian shades of heavy fabric or lighter silk and cotton. This type of shade bunches at the top when raised. Formal curtains hung extending to the outer corners of the architrave or molding around the window. Some windows were dressed with elaborate curtains and draperies including jabots, swags, and festoons. Others simply had a short swag hanging at the top with no long side curtain. Lambrequins (stiff fabric pieces) or cornices (wooden projections) often covered the top of

Harry Halter made the gateleg table from the late seventeenth or early eighteenth century. Notice the trestle-type base complicated by the gatelegs. The pipe box comes from Barbara Davis of Country Cottage.

the window. A window might have very plain dressing—perhaps a single wide panel hanging from the top, pulled to one side with a tieback in the daytime. Curtains also hung from French rods that were mounted above the window and protruded at either side.

SEVERAL kinds of boxes were used in eighteenth-century homes. Deep triangular boxes were made for the celebrated tricorn hat, and oval and round bandboxes of varying size held neckwear and ordinary, round hats. Wall-mounted boxes for candles and long pipes continued to be used into the eighteenth century as the need for them remained.

MOST musical instruments were imported from Europe with some domestic manufacture beginning in Massachusetts in 1720. Spinets and harpsichords, two of the most impressive instruments, and harps, violins, and brass instruments all found their way into the eighteenth-century music room. Pianos as we know them began to appear in colonial homes in the third quarter of the century.

The era introduced some nautical instruments, too, which you should consider for a New England sea captain's home. The sextant, invented in 1764, and the dial barometer also fit well into homes of the second half of the century.

A harpsichord by Edward Norton.
From a New York collection.

HAND tools as mentioned in Chapter One were still important to colonists, as were lanterns. They were made of wood, tin, or iron and were kept by the door. Instead of glass the openings might be punched tin or thin, shaved horn. Another practical addition to the frontier home was the gun. Long rifles and muskets were used, as was the famous blunderbuss with its trumpet-shaped muzzle. You are best advised to hang guns over doors or windows or even from ceiling hooks rather than over the fireplace, regardless of the many pictures that show a gun mounted over the hot and dangerous fire.

You can add dignity to your dollhouse by mounting the family coat of arms on the wall. Colonists hung framed coats of arms called hatchments and upon the death of a family member put the hatchment outside the front door.

Near the door in the front hall would be a table or desk on which a silver salver was placed to receive the calling cards of visitors. Doorstops made of iron and brass, with or without handles, complete a hallway scene of the late eighteenth century. A similar appointment is the bootjack and it is reasonable to put one in each bedchamber.

A distinctly Southern touch, perhaps for a Natchez plantation, is a large fan suspended over the dining table. A string running from the fan to an inconspicuous corner of the room was pulled by a slave to keep diners comfortable in the heat of the summer. It also stirred up (and, one hoped, out) the insects.

THE important thing to remember when putting accessories in a home, just as when choosing furniture for it, is the type of home you are creating and the kind of people who would have lived in it. If you think in terms of people using the rooms, perhaps even inventing a family to fill it, you will be saved from inconvenient placements of furniture and accessories. Walk around the rooms mentally as though you had to live in them. Bear in mind also the economic station of the family. The eighteenth century, particularly in the second half, can be called an age of "silk and silver,"

Lighting devices from Studio B. From left to right: a punched-tin lantern of a type known popularly as a "Paul Revere" lantern; a double candlestick; and a square lantern with glass windows. The latter is thought by modern historians to be closer to the kind of lantern that Paul Revere might really have been watching for (for one thing, it would throw a lot more light than the tin one!). All have rings which made it possible to hang them conveniently. *Photo courtesy of Studio B*

These three lovely pieces would grace the best of colonial tables. The china bowl was made by Theresa Welch-Stalbaum while the silver is from the Acquisto Silver Co. The jug came across the ocean in a shipment of goods to a wealthy colonist who probably had an agent working for him and spotting just such prizes in London. It was made by a Dubliner, however, Thomas Walker, in about 1718. The salver is a home-grown product. It was made c. 1761 by Paul Revere II and can be found in full size in the Museum of Fine Arts in Boston.

but those who could afford such luxuries were still in the minority. Some observers have pointed out that we may have a slightly distorted view of how well the colonists lived because of the things that have survived and been preserved; that we may get the idea from the beautifully detailed restorations of old homes that the average farmer or craftsman lived in a style which was really beyond the grasp of any but the affluent. Do not be misled by the fact that crystal chandeliers and Oriental rugs and sumptuously carved highboys were found in some homes. Most people did not own them. Homes as plain as the meanest early dwellings of the seventeenth century were still common during the eighteenth and nineteenth centuries. But neither should you be tied to convention when furnishing your dollhouse. As I have said before, often the best test of whether something fits in a room is whether it *looks* right to you. If you have an odd piece of exquisite silver in an otherwise obviously poor rural home, there is no reason why you cannot justify its use, maybe even giving it a place of special honor in the home. All you need is a reason that satisfies you, perhaps devising a fictional history of a once-glamorous family fallen on hard times who managed to retain a lone heirloom. All your imaginings need not be so melodramatic (and the fictional family idea need not be carried to overly cute lengths to fulfill its purpose), but the point is that before all else you should enjoy your miniatures and learn to *adapt* these notes on the history of the decorative arts rather than become a slave to them. What you do want to avoid is using an item in a 1750s home that was not invented until 1800.

Ivan Lawson made this Dutch-inspired dollhouse with a storage drawer in its base and handy side handles. This house is a copy of the Van Cortlandt Baby House which is believed to be one of possibly only two extant, documented colonial dollhouses. The original is believed to have been built in 1744 and belongs to the Van Cortlandt Museum of New York.

THREE

THE REPUBLIC

1780-1840

THE Federal era, which dates from the Revolutionary War to the beginning of the machine age, encompassed two major styles. The first, usually referred to simply as the Federal style, drew its inspiration from the work of English architects and furniture designers. Chief among them were brothers Robert and James Adams who changed the way British homes looked during the last half of the eighteenth century. Their influence was transferred to the United States late in the century, filtered through the designs of English furniture makers George Hepplewhite and Thomas Sheraton. The second important style, that of the American Empire, began around 1815 and relied on French initiatives. The United States' attention to things French was encouraged by our wartime alliance with France and grew with our continuing friendship. Joining the English and French styles was the ancient heritage of Greece and Rome, recalled for postcolonial Americans—as for all the world—by eighteenth-century excavations at Herculaneum and Pompeii. The artifacts unearthed sparked interest in the decorative themes of classical antiquity and a neo-classical thread runs through all the elements of interior design from doorways to china. At the turn of the nineteenth century, similar expeditions to Egypt resulted in the inclusion of Egyptian motifs in furniture and interior design.

As we have seen, the Orient was another world that influenced American decorative arts. A very lucrative direct trade with the East developed during the late eighteenth century and continued during the 1800s. In fact many decidedly Occidental-style pieces were produced in China specifically for the Western markets. In cities like Salem and Portsmouth substantial fortunes depended on the China trade, while in the South the economy rested strongly on the plantation system.

As Paris became the international style center New York emerged as the premier American city. New York naturally assumed a position of political primacy as our first national capital; it was New York that saw the first full flower of the American Empire style.

Federal homes were sometimes three or four stories high and might be perfectly square (especially in New England) or T- or L-shaped with wings on the side of the central core. Charleston homes were three stories high, three rooms deep, and one room wide, which was not an uncommon pattern elsewhere.

Despite the concentration of fine homes in the urban or Eastern areas which had some claim to wealth, lovely houses were built in the hinterlands, too. This was frequently the result of the military taking civilization with it to the territories. As early as the 1820s, for instance, there were some very refined homes built for senior officers in the Northwest Territory.

The growth of American cities in general put the brick townhouse in a position of importance and gave us the now familiar row house. Row houses took a fairly standard form, especially those built for moderate budgets. On the first floor there was a hall, two rooms to the side of the hall and perhaps a back room. There were some double parlors with connecting doors. On the second and/or third floors were the bedrooms, the front one designated usually as the "best" one. This pattern also prevailed during the Victorian period. The fireplaces in these homes were built into the side wall next to the neighboring house because this was more economical. Generally, Federal builders chose to put the fireplace in an outside wall rather than between rooms.

Townhouses commonly featured a doorway atop a flight of exterior stairs rather than set flush with the ground. For the dollhouse owner this is an important note because this construction often meant that some rooms were in the basement, usually the kitchen and other workrooms. The lower-level kitchen led to the installation of dumbwaiters in homes. Servants would load a tray with food or dishes and, using a pulley contraption, raise the tray to the dining room or upper-floor pantry through the dumbwaiter shaft. Dumbwaiters were enclosed in walls or, as at Thomas Jefferson's country estate Monticello, concealed in the side of a fireplace. In the South the basement kitchen was very common in both urban and rural homes. The kitchen fireplace of the Federal era was much the same as that of the colonial home.

Despite the invention of the steam radiator in 1784, most homes still depended on the fireplace for heat. Coal fires built on grates for parlor and kitchen became increasingly popular early in the nineteenth century with the beginning of domestic coal production.

The Franklin stove, usually positioned inside or in front of the fireplace, was also gaining prominence although it did not eclipse the fireplace until later years. By that time, what might have been called the Franklin stove was far removed in style from Franklin's design. Federal stoves were enclosed and frequently had ornamental feet and finials. Along with cast-iron stoves there were some in ceramic tile.

Mantel shelves became common for the first time and many fireplaces had candleholders that swung out from either end. The mantel might rest on supportive columns or sculptured figures. Those who could afford it had mantelpieces of white, black, or colored marble. Wooden mantelpieces were frequently painted black and polished or marbleized to achieve the richer effect. There also were soapstone mantelpieces and in some cases the back or frame for the mantelpiece was made of cast iron. Many fireplaces were lined with iron plates. Iron coal grates were in use everywhere by 1830. Intricate carving often surrounded the fireplace and sometimes the entire fireplace wall, although the elaborate overmantel of the colonial home was giving way. Mirrors and painted panels appeared more and more over the mantelpieces.

Paneling as a wall treatment faded in popularity and plaster

This is a miniature version of the dining room in the Harrison Gray Otis House in Boston, c. 1795, and is among the Thorne Rooms in the Art Institute of Chicago. Although it is of the same time as the Kenmore dining room, the feeling is different as is the style of most of the furniture. With its fancier marble fireplace and taller pedimented doorways, this room is less intimate than the Kenmore room. The furniture is Hepplewhite and the inlaid table and shield-back chairs are true examples of the style. The secretary has the new squarer lines, different from its colonial predecessor. The most spectacular furniture is the sideboard, really three pieces—a sideboard with two pedestals. The pedestals support large urn-shaped knife boxes which contrast with the rectangular, slant-topped knife boxes of the earlier eighteenth century. This room is a study in symmetry from the position of the doors and windows to the placement of chairs and the appointment of vases and wall sconces. *Courtesy of the Art Institute of Chicago; Gift of Mrs. James Ward Thorne*

This room mixes colonial and Federal elements in just about equal doses and therefore might serve as a model for joining furnishings from different eras. The Chippendale chairs have "owl's-eye" backs; other definitely colonial pieces include the daybed, the highboy, and the mirror over the lowboy dressing table. The corner washstand (with its over-sized basin and pitcher reversed) and Martha Washington chair by the fireplace are of course Federal era developments. There appears to be a good deal of Staffordshire, especially on the shelves. The symmetrical, plain paneling could be colonial and the satiny smooth floorboards are exceptionally nice. The wallpaper echoes the copperplate print textiles of the Federal era. A jarring note is the inclusion of two lamps—one near the daybed, the other on the dressing table—which would be remarkable indeed in so early a room (and which probably should be reserved for a Victorian setting). *Courtesy of the Phoenix Art Museum; Gift of Mrs. James Ward Thorne and Mr. Niblack Thorne in Memory of Marie G. Thorne*

walls became fashionable. The plaster walls retained the dado and sometimes were decorated with fancy appliqués. The walls were papered, painted, or even upholstered. Recent studies, for instance at Mount Vernon, show that the early Americans used much brighter interior colors than previously thought. Restorers now are covering over time-honored creamy pastels with such shockers as electric blue.

Both silk- and leather-covered walls were known in grand homes and wallpaper turned up in many more homes during the Federal era because improvements in production made it cheaper. Endless rolls as we know them came in 1799.

Besides solid-colored paper with gilt borders, wallpapers came in many designs. Vertical stripes, florals, toiles, and other scenics were among the most fashionable designs. The best scenics were

PLATE 1: A mahogany highboy (*left*) (c. 1765–75) from Philadelphia made by Harry Cooke. This remarkable Chippendale piece has carved vases of flowers for finials, heavily carved legs, and claw and ball feet; more flowers in the garlands run the length of the chamfered corners. The brasses are extremely intricate and there is open lattice carving in the scroll top. The carved panel in the bottom (which is a drawer) illustrates the fox and grapes from Aesop's *Fables.* Courtesy of Dearring-Tracy, Ltd.

PLATE 2: A John Hodgson chair and a Richard L. Mann table (*below*). The candlestick is from Roger L. Gutheil, Inc., the tea caddy is by William Robertson, and the China trade teapot is by Deborah McKnight.

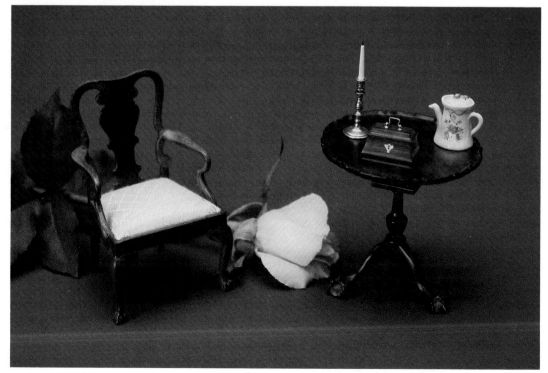

PLATE 3: Mary Grady O'Brien made small chests and chest of drawers. The lining and wallpaper come from Millie August Miniatures.

PLATE 4: Ibes Gonzalez of Miniatures by Ibes made the Chippendale lowboy and the chair, which has a seat worked by C & J Originals. The bowl was made by Theresa Welch-Stalbaum and the candlesticks are from Roger L. Gutheil, Inc.

PLATE 5: The Windsor chair is from Studio B, the hooked rug from Shuttle Hill Herb Shop, and the yarn winder, known as a squirrel cage swift, is from Bill and Donna Gibbons. Allen Martin made the spinning accessories, including a niddy noddy and a drop spindle.

PLATE 6: Jim Holmes made the painted settle. The rug is by Marj Crueger, and the stool is by Barbara Davis of Country Cottage Miniatures. The cattails are from Roberta Partridge of The Bird House.

PLATE 7: Beatrice Thomas painted this rather stern young child, and Sylvia Rountree, of the Doll's Cobbler, made the rosette-decorated shoes (*left*). *Photo by Ross Klavan*

PLATE 8: This room (*below*) is based on George Washington's office at his Valley Forge headquarters. It features a gateleg table; a late eighteenth-century ladder-back (also called a pretzel-back); a much earlier paneled chair of the wainscot type; and a Chippendale secretary. Among other noteworthy items are the marble facing on the fireplace, the large hatbox and the small lap desk resting atop the table at right. Kupjack Studios of Park Ridge, Illinois, made the room. *Photo by Jay Kupjack*

PLATE 9: Lafayette was welcomed in this stair hall as were dozens of other luminaries of post-Revolutionary America. This is the Montmorenci Stair Hall now at Winterthur Museum, reproduced in miniature by Kupjack Studios of Park Ridge, Illinois. The hallway was the glory of Montmorenci, a fabulous home built about 1822 at Shocco Springs, North Carolina. The table under the round mirror at left is a copy of one made by the renowned Charles Honoré Lannuier, a Frenchman who set up a workshop in New York. The chairs, settee, and sewing tables came from another famous workshop, that of John and Thomas Seymour of Boston. The porcelain is Chinese Export. *Courtesy Henry Francis DuPont Winterthur Museum*

PLATE 10: Marie Friedman made these federal era pieces. Jean Verona painted the blue and white plate on the left.

PLATE 11: This bedroom (*above*) is copied from a late eighteenth-century room in Salem, Massachusetts, and is in the Thorne Miniature Rooms collection of the Dulin Gallery of Art. It is full of Chippendale and later pieces copied from originals in the Metropolitan Museum of Art. *Photo courtesy of the Dulin Gallery of Art, Knoxville*

PLATE 13: Thomas Jefferson's study and bedroom (*above*) demonstrate the innovative spirit that runs rampant at Monticello, the third president's home in Virginia. A few items illustrate his penchant for efficiency: the revolving barrel-back chair with attached candlesticks; the *chaise longue* extension and table, both on wheels; the pantograph on the table, which made copies of letters automatically as they were being written; and the bed positioned handily (and space-savingly) in the open alcove between the rooms (contrary to fable, the bed was not made to be raised out of sight when not in use). Jefferson even designed the draperies and bedspread. The washstand has a shaving mirror and pitcher and basin plus drawers to store toiletries. The octagonal table at the far left serves as a file and was known as a rent table. There is a violin resting on it along with an Argand lamp. Jefferson is said to have been among the first Americans to buy an Argand lamp, in 1784. In the background, the telescope and globe show Jefferson's wide-ranging curiosity about the world, in those days a sign of a true gentleman. The stairway at the left does not go to another floor but to a clothes closet above the bed. This suite, made by Kupjack Studios of Park Ridge, Illinois, represents Jefferson's very private world—largely unvisited by others—until his death there July 4, 1826. *Photo by Jay Kupjack*

PLATE 12: We look "over the shoulder" of a Chinese Chippendale chair by Hermania Anslinger and into a marble-faced fireplace of the Morris House parlor (*left*). The mantel holds a fashionable (and typical) five-piece garniture by Deborah McKnight. The flame-stitch chair was made by Bob Bernard of Dolphin Originals; the impressive secretary with closed bonnet top is by Paul Runyon, who also made the Hepplewhite inlaid side table and candlestand. Don Buttfield made the andirons, and the portrait was painted by E. W. Allen, Jr. The tilt-top table comes from the Hoffman Collection. This parlor is on the second floor of a miniature replica of Philadelphia's famous Morris House, a 1787 triumph which still stands in the Society Hill section. Howard Hartman made the house for Mrs. Jean Stuart, who herself made the rug and faced the mantelpiece with "marble."

PLATE 14: Sunlight playing through the window into a Federal-era dining room seems to bring the room (and the bird) to delicate life. Emily Good made the furniture and setting. *Photo by Emily Good*

PLATE 15: A pert geranium from Rosemary Dyke tops Franklyn J. Morley's typical pie safe. The chair was made by Jim Ison; the apples are from Wise Miniatures. Jean Tag made the transfer-ware pitcher. Transfer patterns adorned ceramics in England from the mid-1700s, and such ware peaked in popularity here about 1820–40.

French imports. Sometimes only two walls were papered, a reminder of earlier days when it was not unusual for the four walls of a room to share two or more decorative treatments.

Sometimes walls were stenciled to imitate wallpaper. Florals, geometric designs, Oriental motifs, and stars were favorite patterns. The stencil could cover the wall or be confined to a border near the ceiling or around the doorway. Both the affluent and the less well-off employed stenciling, the middle class using it primarily for bedrooms and "good" rooms.

Columns and pilasters were placed on the walls, often framing

This room takes us away from the slender, straight lines of Sheraton and Hepplewhite to the luxurious Empire season of the later Federal period. On either side of the fireplace with its marble sculptured supports are Greek-inspired lyre-back *klismos* chairs. Pedestal tables against the back wall also carry the lyre motif. The two chairs in the middle of the room are in the *curule* style drawn from ancient Rome. The sofa is a Sheraton piece and the breakfront bookcase has concealing drapery tacked behind its glass doors. The round girandole mirrors with candlesticks and triumphant eagles are excellent examples of a common feature in homes of the wealthy. Notice that over the fireplace the mirror takes up what would be the entire overmantel area, a signal of a style that becomes more popular as the Federal era turns toward the Victorian. The room copies the drawing room at Andalusia in Bensalem Township, Pennsylvania, as remodeled 1834–36. *Courtesy of the Art Institute of Chicago; Gift of Mrs. James Ward Thorne*

This serene entrance hall taken from the Pierce Mansion in Portsmouth, New Hampshire, is another of the Thorne Rooms. The fanlights over the doorways and sidelights at the front door were familiar elements in many Federal homes. Note the pilaster treatment in several places. The hanging lamp with candles is usual for the time. Its eagle decoration speaks to the patriotic fervor of the era as the glass smoke bell on which it rests speaks to the less romantic need to protect the ceiling from the smudges from the burning candles. Smoke bells were used until electric light bulbs lit homes. The dominant furniture in the hall is the curved Hepplewhite chairback settee. The plain, plastered walls with modest classical trim are keynotes of fine Federal interiors. Notice that the only paneling here is in the doors. *Courtesy of the Art Institute of Chicago; Gift of Mrs. James Ward Thorne*

doorways, windows, and mantelpieces. The addition of a pediment to windows and doors completed the classical picture. The columns were plain, fluted, or reeded. Fluting indicates a pattern of concave grooves whereas reeding describes convex or rounded lines. We shall see later that both were important to Federal furniture. Molding tended to be more delicate than during the earlier eighteenth century and master carvers like Salem's Samuel McIntire created some of the most exquisite interiors of American history. One of Salem's special motifs was the snowflake and we see nature themes throughout the country with fruit and flowers and wheat sheaves included in many mantel carvings. Principal rooms often had niches in the walls.

Federal ceilings were higher than those of previous eras and in addition to carrying fine cornices, were decorated with relief carvings. They often were tinted green, pink, or blue.

Windows grew steadily bigger and a six-over-six configuration was now standard for sash windows; that is, six panes above and six below. The panes were bigger and the muntins thinner than during earlier times. Window screens were used from the 1780s and were fairly common within a hundred years. Some Federal windows reached from ceiling to floor and some were narrower than their colonial predecessors. Windows were part of doorways, too, and semicircular glass transoms topped the principal doors, which were flanked by narrow strips of side windows.

Another lavish touch was the double door of which there are many examples in Federal homes. Interior doors had long panels with scored or beaded quarter-round moldings. Rooms were also joined by doorless arches. Cast-iron and brass butt hinges spread to replace many earlier wrought-iron hinges.

Painted floors were popular with board construction still the

There's a cleanness in the severity of this room with its quiet decorative woodwork and almost plain ceiling. Notice the marble frame around the fireplace. The two side tables at the left are colonial holdovers as are the Chinese Chippendale shelves. The table is typical of Federal pieces as are the shield-back chairs and the two Martha Washington chairs, the latter rather unusually pulled up to the table. The sideboard and side tables hold Oriental china. The most overwhelming items in the room are the sparkling chandelier and sconces which so dominate the décor that at first you don't notice how plain the room itself is. (We would argue with what appear to be basin stands used as plant holders although basin stands have been found in rooms other than bedrooms and conceivably could have been used as other than basin stands.) *Courtesy of the Phoenix Art Museum; Gift of Mrs. James Ward Thorne and Mr. Niblack Thorne in Memory of Marie G. Thorne*

most common. You can also experiment with imaginative floor treatments like parquet which are not hard to duplicate in miniature. Proof of how varied American lifestyles were is the fact that, along with the highly polished wooden floors, we know of rural areas where homemakers still sanded their floors as their seventeenth-century ancestors did. This should remind us that, although a new classical fashion was abroad in the land, the vestiges of the eighteenth and seventeenth centuries did not disappear. In rural sections particularly there really was little change from the eighteenth century in home design and decoration. While the rich gathered new things around them, their poorer contemporaries

This dining room from the Thorne Rooms Collection of the Art Institute of Chicago recalls Kenmore in Fredericksburg, Virginia, and although the museum dates it c. 1750, the furnishings are of the later Federal period. At the left wall there is a Sheraton side chair showing the characteristic square back. The inlaid sideboard has a metal rim or gallery along the back and side of the top and over it hangs a typical Federal mirror with columns topped by a fine swag. Toward the back of the room is a window seat or backless bench popular during the period. Martha Washington chairs flank the marble fireplace and the table is one of the extension type that came into prominence in the late Federal period. Two particularly fine bow-front chests, sometimes called commodes, sit on either side of the door. The chests have the French foot (not to be confused with the upturned French foot we've seen on some Chippendale chairs and will see again in Louis XV styles in the next chapter). The commodes are handsomely inlaid. Note the hurricane shades on each one. *Courtesy of the Art Institute of Chicago; Gift of Mrs. James Ward Thorne*

held fast to the old ways out of economic necessity. The Federal era is indeed a time of great choices for the miniaturists.

In fact, there are a number of choices with regard to the rooms themselves. If you are interested in a home with a lot of rooms, this is your opportunity to indulge yourself. For the first time, dining rooms were standard in better homes, some with shallow alcoves cut out for sideboards. There were new anterooms serving the main drawing room. There were conservatories, family parlors, and company parlors. Affluent families had nurseries, maids' rooms, and rooms for such specialized purposes as storing cleaning equipment, dancing, and even flower arranging. An especially useful room for miniaturists is the pantry which, when lined with shelves, makes an excellent place to display a scale china collection. The late-eighteenth-century trend toward upstairs bedrooms continued, although in the country many parents still slept on the first floor and there were still beds in the kitchen and the hall.

An exciting development in room construction during the Federal era can be, but seldom is, copied by dollhouse builders. Inspired by James Hoban's plans for the White House, oval rooms became fashionable after 1792 as did octagonal and circular rooms. Such rooms are ambitious for the dollhouse builder but are certainly worth considering.

Spiral staircases, of which there are some prefabricated examples in miniature, were also in Federal homes and there were a number of impressive double staircases, too. Often the home's main staircase was interrupted by a landing with a Palladian window. Portsmouth, New Hampshire, was famous for a stairway with three different kinds of balusters to each step, one turned, one spiral, the other fluted.

The Greek Revival in this country deserves special treatment here, in part because it was such an American tradition and also because it was found especially in the *new* towns, founded after the first wave of settlement and often after the Revolution itself as people pushed west. There are, for instance, many magnificent examples of Greek Revival architecture in Ohio. Greek Revival was most popular between 1820 and 1850 and was a relatively simple style based on the Greek temple. Americans were interested in the Greek war for independence then being fought and there was an undercurrent of feeling that our new democracy was closely related to the ancient Greek ideals of government.

Greek Revival houses featured tall columned porticos that ran the height of the house. Front doors were placed to the side of the facade or at the corner rather than centered. The transom windows on the top of the doors were more rectangular and windows often extended to the floor. Sometimes eyebrow windows, small windows with bottom hinges that opened inward, ran along the top of the house, near the roof line. Columns were built between major rooms and interior doorways became wider. Walls were made of plain painted plaster without colonial-style paneling or dado. Sometimes, however, they had large rectangular panels topped by a frieze of Greek ornament. Among the favored colors were pale blue, lavender, yellow, and green with buff, cream, or gilded trim. Naturally the Greek Revival interior shared many of the details of earlier Federal era homes and there were some ornate cornices and fancy plaster appliqués on the ceilings. Rooms were tall, often taller than colonial or earlier Federal predecessors, with carved marble mantels and many mirrors.

FURNITURE

FEDERAL era furniture was startlingly different from colonial furniture and within the period itself there were major differences between the early pieces and those of the later Empire style. Colonial furniture had been forthright in its strong curves and sturdy posture but after the Revolutionary War furniture took on a much lighter, almost airy aspect. Straight, tapered legs replaced cabriole legs and decorative treatments emphasized delicate inlays and veneers. Inlay was not as important in Salem or Portsmouth as elsewhere, however, perhaps because master carvers like Samuel McIntire were a local staple. There was a great deal of painted, formal furniture, and japanning was still used to decorate special pieces.

We have said earlier that many colonial rooms did not have much furniture. Federal era homes were similarly, if not even more severely, furnished and, relatively speaking, Federal interiors were generally pretty bare. If you look over a collection of drawings of Federal interiors done contemporarily, you'll probably be surprised at how empty some of the rooms look.

As during the colonial period, furniture commonly rimmed a room, the pieces placed neatly against the walls until they were needed, when they were brought out to serve specific functions. This means that a room would look different on a Monday when the mistress was sewing than it would for Tuesday evening guests or Wednesday afternoon tea. We'll see how changes in lighting were to alter this pattern.

Federal era cabinetmakers used much the same woods as they had during the preceding half-century, with mahogany by far the most popular for good furniture. Cherry was still a favorite wood of Connecticut furniture makers and there was also a good deal of tulip, maple, pine, and birch, often stained to imitate mahogany. Inlays generally were of light woods like holly or satinwood, and there were many pieces made wholly of the light-colored woods. Walnut and locally plentiful woods were used in areas isolated from the Eastern coast.

Isolation, however, was less a factor than it had been and the new land and waterways were critical in taking Eastern style inland. In 1807 the steamboat changed the Hudson River Valley and its arrival on the Mississippi in 1811 committed New Orleans with its French and Spanish traditions to national eminence forever. Other pathways opened during the early Federal years too: the Cumberland Road linked Cumberland, Maryland, and Wheeling, West Virginia, and the Erie Canal ran from Buffalo to Albany.

You can better grasp the importance of these developments when you remember that for these early Americans the West was Ohio, Illinois, Indiana, and Iowa. Those western lands were not untrod by any but Indians. Illinois, for instance, was not organized as a territory until 1809, but because it had been reached by the French through Canada, there were some fine French homes already there even as it became our frontier.

Everywhere, the most popular upholstery was the strong haircloth, a material with horsehair woven in the cotton, linen, or wool upon which it was based. Leather was very common, the colors usually being red, blue, green, or black. Just as in the eighteenth century, silk and satin were the prize fabrics of wealthy families, used in the best drawing rooms and occasionally in a regal bedroom. Chintz, calico, linen, cotton, and woolens were available to a broader range of people than before. Fabrics were checked, striped, and printed, and the free-flowing florals of the earlier eighteenth century turned somewhat more restrained and stylized. Federal era upholsterers were known to add piping, ruffles, and some fringes. The not-always-practical fashion was for all the furniture in a room to be upholstered in the same material, harmonizing with or matching the curtains. This matching fervor

This pianoforte with its lyre-shaped pedal support and upholstered bench are typical of the painted furniture popular in Baltimore from around 1820 to 1840. The pieces were made by Mary Frances Cochran who copied the pianoforte from a piece by Joseph Hiskey in Hampton Mansion, Towson, Maryland. *Photo by Russel Werneth*

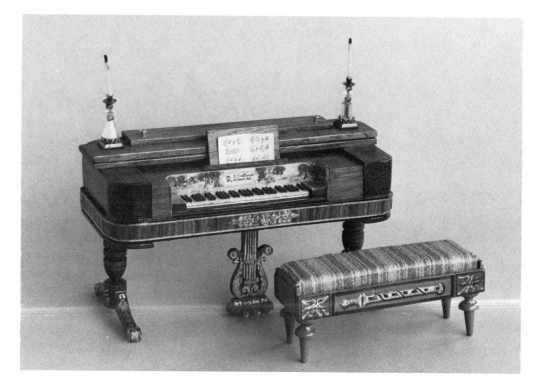

decreased with the Empire style when more variety was allowed.

Regional differences diminished but did not disappear during the post-Revolutionary years. Many pieces were exported from New York, Philadelphia, and New England to the Southern tier which stretched from Baltimore to Georgia. Of the regionalism that did develop during the period, perhaps the most celebrated is Baltimore painted furniture. Baltimore clung to English styles longer than other cities and distinguished its seating and case pieces with paint and gilding, often over a black base. Skilled Baltimore painters simulated woodgrain (as did many less artful country furniture finishers) and the city's cabinetmakers contributed to American furniture history a technique called *eglomisé*. Used particularly in embellishing tables and secretaries, *eglomisé* refers to small, painted glass panels, usually oval, inset on furniture. The paintings usually were of classical subjects and flowers.

With the emergence of the new nation, patriotism was running high and it was best exemplified in what might fairly be called the most popular design of the era, the eagle. Made our national emblem in 1782, the eagle appeared on everything from doorways to china to chairs. Some truly majestic eagles were inlaid, painted, and carved on American furniture. Other common decorative designs included the pineapple (symbol of hospitality), lyres, wreaths, wheat sheaves, urns, and swags of fabric and carved woods. Masonic emblems were popular during the era and throughout the nineteenth century.

While Sheraton and Hepplewhite influenced furniture style

Ibes and Annabell Gonzalez collaborated on building and finishing these pieces from Miniatures by Ibes. The Hepplewhite table features a satinwood inlay and mahogany veneer. The sabre-leg Duncan Phyfe chair has a magnificent gilded and carved eagle center splat. Just visible are the gilded rosettes at the sides of the top and front rails. The ubiquitous Federal eagle shows up again in the bowl by Deborah McKnight, painted by Priscilla Lance.

A Hepplewhite sideboard with exquisitely executed inlay that circles the handles, outlines the drawers, decorates the legs, and bands the feet. The curved front is appropriately delicate. Linda La Roche is the artisan. From the collection of Jack and Shirley Bloomfield.

This table has Sheraton legs, heavily reeded and carved, and a gently curving front typical of New England. It could act as a side table or a vanity in the bedroom. The table is by Hermania Anslinger and is from the collection of Constance Simone. *Photo by Ross Klavan*

the most, some historians give the lesser-known Thomas Shearer equal importance, claiming that he really was responsible for one of the significant developments of the era, the sideboard. There is little difference between Sheraton and Hepplewhite furniture, at least to the casual observer, but in very general terms we can say that Hepplewhite tended to emphasize curved chairbacks and Sheraton squarer backs. Sheraton added slender columns to the corners of chests and case pieces and Sheraton legs were more rounded than Hepplewhite legs.

Another furniture-maker who influenced the American scene was Duncan Phyfe, the Scottish immigrant who made his name in New York as the proprietor of what was the early-nineteenth-cen-

These are late Federal pieces of the Empire style by Ibes Gonzalez of Miniatures by Ibes. The chair is a Duncan Phyfe side chair with sabre legs and cross-lattice back. The center table takes a marble top and has legs gilded by Annabell Gonzalez. This nicely proportioned table is a simple but distinctive shadow of much heavier Empire and Victorian tables to come. It is a transitional table in that respect, based on classical antecedents. In form it is greatly similar to a table made in Massachusetts about 1820 and owned by the painter Henry Sargent.

Pay special attention to the delicate carved detail in the shield-back chair. The style of the splat was especially favored in New England. Also notice the change from the colonial slip seat to the more fully upholstered Federal seat. The Sheraton side table has mahogany and cherry veneer with turned knobs. The small dressing box is from a Hepplewhite design with satinwood inlay. All three pieces are from Miniatures by Ibes.

Linda La Roche made these spade-foot chairs, part of a set of dining chairs in the collection of Jack and Shirley Bloomfield. They are very like originals believed to have been made in New York City c. 1800–1810 by Slaver and Taylor and noteworthy for, among other things, their thin colonettes which terminate in flared caps, forming a series of Gothic arches.

tury equivalent of a furniture factory. Many people think there is a Duncan Phyfe style as there is a Chippendale or Hepplewhite style, but Phyfe depended on other men for his inspiration, for instance Sheraton, to whose designs he gave special expression. The furniture we usually associate with Duncan Phyfe was made late in the era, during the Empire period, but even then Phyfe was a follower of style, not a creator of it. In the last decade of the period his sure touch faltered and he turned the corner into early Victorian with a very heavy hand.

Miniature-collectors who enjoy delicate workmanship are especially drawn to Federal furniture and perhaps the best examples of this new lightness are the chairs. The year 1790 was the dawn of the American shield-back, one of the most famous chairs of American history. Other chairbacks were heart-shaped, oval, or rectangular. The slip seat of the colonial furniture craftsman gave way to seats that were upholstered over the front chair rail, the material often attached with brass studs set in thin rows or in scallops. Chairs were commonly sold in sets which ranged from a few side chairs and an armchair to ten side chairs and two armchairs.

The Windsor style expanded to embrace several new variations, among them chairs, settees, and cradles with the bamboo-turned spindles that became popular during the last decade of the eighteenth century and remained in fashion into the Victorian era. Rod-backs with simple straight spindles and arrow-backs with spindles flattened to an arrow shape at the top rail were standards that developed during the first two decades of the nineteenth century. The arrow-back was especially well known in western New England and New York State. Windsors were the workhorse chair of the period, frequently taking their place in hallways where their strength and painted surface helped them stand up to rough wear. Kept in the hallway, they were handy for removal to the porch for summertime sitting.

A stylistic relative of the Windsor was the Boston rocker, a high-back rocking chair with rodlike spindles slightly bent to fit the sitter's back, and a comfortable rolled front seat. Rockers in general first became popular during the Federal era, which undermines the notion that rocking chairs were common appointments in early colonial American homes; there were some colonial rocking chairs, but not many. The first rocking chairs were conversions, usually slat-back chairs to which short, stubby rockers had been attached. These earliest rockers were even front and back but as time passed the back of the rockers grew longer and the chair turned into the rocking chair we recognize today. The first true rocking chairs, not converted side- or armchairs, appeared about 1790. Fortunately rocking chairs are available to miniaturists in great variety.

Another chair that is identified with the Federal period and that remained popular well beyond it is the fancy chair. That rather all-embracing term describes a small, light, usually painted or stenciled chair, the epitome of which was the Hitchcock chair named for Lambert Hitchcock who ran a successful chair business from 1826 to 1843. Fancy chairs had rush or cane seats and were frequently accompanied by a matching settee. Decorations usually were gilded or colored designs on black backgrounds and after 1820 the designs were most often stenciled. There were also some japanned fancy chairs. They were found in many Federal bedrooms, following the fashion for placing lighter chairs there. Dining rooms required somewhat stronger side chairs with leather or horsehair upholstery while the very best, most decorative chairs were reserved for the drawing room.

In about 1805 a new kind of chair appeared that took its cue from the ancient Greek *klismos.* Sabre legs and a rolled top rail were the earmarks of the *klismos* which hit its height in popularity with the Empire style. These chairs had open backs, featuring plain or carved crosspieces. As the style developed the top rail became wider and slightly concave. Some were gilded or painted in bright colors.

This Boston rocker is like one in the Brooklyn Museum. Note the curved seat and rolled front as well as the high, spindle back. It was made by Emily Good. *Photo by Bob Sigmon*

This water bench holds a collection of early pewter and a wooden saltbox. The chair is an example of a bamboo Windsor, the original of which is in the collection of Dr. and Mrs. John R. Ledbetter. All the pieces were made by Emily Good. *Photo by Emily Good*

(Above)
This Hitchcock chair and bench along with the portrait and other accessories were made by Emily Good. *Photo by Emily Good*

(Below left)
A fancy chair with cane seat made by Betsy Zorn of the Ginger Jar. The Wellington boots with copper toes were made by Sylvia Rountree of the Dolls' Cobbler. The chair is from the collection of Marie Friedman. *Photo by Ross Klavan*

(Below right)
This elaborate Sheraton fancy armchair features the tiny balls that were a common Federal touch. The chair was made by Bill Sevebeck and the seat was rushed with split strands of yucca leaves by Kathy Sevebeck. *Photo by Don and Cindy Massie*

Hitchcock chairs with pillow-style top rails and caned seats. The legs have ring turnings and the stretchers are done with ring-and-ball turning. The chairs were made by Bill Sevebeck and painted to represent stenciling by Kathy Sevebeck. *Photo by Don and Cindy Massie*

Here are two sabre-leg Duncan Phyfe *klismos* side chairs from Miniatures by Ibes. The most outstanding features of these chairs are their center splats—one gilded foliage, the other the popular carved eagle.

The base is by W. Foster Tracy. Terry Rogal made the gilded sabre-leg chair with its appropriate lyre back echoing a popular motif of the day. From the collection of Jack and Shirley Bloomfield.

Along with *klismos* came another seat shape out of antiquity, the *curule.* This style, distinguished by crossed legs, was applied to chairs, settees, backless benches, and stools. It was most popular in New York.

Other chairs were remembered and modified from earlier days: the lolling or Martha Washington chair, the pretzel-back, which was the Federal era's finest slat-back, the easy or wing chair.

Many Federal wing chairs showed a change in construction from the colonial easy chair which gave them a slightly different silhouette. The wings of colonial wing chairs seemed to grow out of the back and, while that style continued, the wings on many Federal easy chairs were separate, sometimes enormously wavy pieces attached to the back and arms. This enclosed the chair more and gave it a deeper profile. Most such chairs had horizontal rolled arms and the vertical arm, most closely associated during the eighteenth century with New York, lost favor. Makers frequently paired the easy chair with a small footstool which was called a gout stool, for obvious reasons. There were also several other upholstered easy chairs, such as the comfortable tub or barrel-back chair.

Even more comfortable, and much rarer, was the recliner. The

A late-eighteenth-century Martha Washington chair goes well with a late Sheraton (c. 1815) worktable with the standard corner decorative posts, pull-out candle slide and metal tips on the feet. The pole screen (c. 1800–1810) has a lovely painted shield-shaped screen. Emily Good made all the items in the photograph and painted the portrait of her ancestor Eliza Gay Bentley. *Photo by Emily Good*

early nineteenth-century version had a back that tilted and either a wide front skirt that lifted up or a pull-out slide leg rest.

Interestingly, the Federal era saw a new use for the word cabriole, which was no longer reserved to describe the bandy leg on eighteenth-century furniture. The nineteenth-century cabriole chair was a side or armchair with a partially upholstered back. Sometimes the upholstery was nothing more than a dainty tuft set in the middle of an otherwise openwork back.

Sofas stood on straight legs that were tapered, rounded, or turned. Often the legs of sofas, like those of case pieces, were reeded or fluted. In most of New England stretchers still were the rule and chair legs reached straight to the floor. Elsewhere, particularly in the cities, legs terminated in a spade foot. In Philadelphia and the South the spade foot was less a block than a rounded cylinder.

The square shape of Federal couches with the boxlike formation of arms and back was a change from the rolled arms of the Chippendale sofas. Chairback settees were made in all the popular chair styles.

After about 1810, as the Empire style gained influence, another new look in sofas appeared: the richly carved swirling Empire sofa with rolled arms and curved legs. These Greek-inspired pieces often wore separate summer and winter looks: in the summer version the caned back was left uncovered; in colder weather

This chair combines two Empire motifs—dolphin supports and hairy paw feet—into an imaginative fancy by Susanne Russo. Sharon Garmize created and worked the intricate needlepoint seat. This chair is much like one made in Philadelphia c. 1840 and considered to be unique. It will be just as "at home" in a Victorian parlor as a Federal one. From the collection of Jack and Shirley Bloomfield.

This pretzel-back chair by Paul Runyon sits next to a typical lady's sewing table; its fabric bag gently holds work in progress. The sewing table is from the Ginger Jar. From a New York collection.

The epitome of the quiet Sheraton sofa by Paul Runyon. Note the fluted, rounded legs, the open space in the arm and the curved front. From a New York collection.

This Sheraton sofa was made by Ibes Gonzalez of Miniatures by Ibes. Note especially its dignified but delicate bearing and the fine but restrained carving on the top rail.

pillows covered it. Two celebrated Empire settees made for the yacht *Cleopatra's Barge* were eleven feet long, but that was extreme and most sofas had much cozier dimensions. The name Cleopatra probably came out of the Egyptian influence also prevalent during this period. Winged feet, hairy paw feet, animal-leg chair legs, and carvings of the sphinx appeared on many pieces.

You can add still another new kind of seating piece to your scale rooms in the form of a couch called a récamier. It took its

name from Madame Juliette Récamier, a famous French beauty painted by Jacques Louis David while she reclined on a Greek-style couch. Although it was not the case with Madame Récamier's couch, usually one arm was higher than the other or was missing altogether, much like the modern chaise longue.

Two considerably less grand seating pieces of the era were the wagon seat settee—borrowed from a wagon and brought inside home or church when needed—and the mammy bench, a Windsor-like settee or rocker one end of which was protected like a crib so that a baby could rest safely while Mother sat nearby, her hands free for work.

In fine homes sofas often had their own long narrow tables with drop leaves at the end. You should put the table in front of the sofa or otherwise conveniently near it, but do not place it across the back, which is a modern placement. In the middle of some rooms there was a table that resembled a big Pembroke of colonial days, often with the legs sweeping out from a heavy central baluster support. The Pembroke table itself was still popular and various small tables frequently turned up beside beds.

(Above)
This snake-foot table is labeled appropriately for filing. Note the round drop-drawer pulls that became popular during the Federal period. Dr. Milton Silver made this table.

(Top right)
This magnificent center table with hairy paw legs could go from its Empire home into the Victorian period with ease. The table is the work of Hermania Anslinger and the astral lamps were made by Ellen Krucker Blauer of The Miniature Mart®. From the collection of Constance Simone. *Photo by Ross Klavan*

(Bottom right)
A classic Pembroke table by Edward Norton has the legs and drawer pull of the Federal era. The Pembroke was sometimes used as a breakfast table which brings us to the silver breakfast service from Miniature Silver by Eugene Kupjack. From a New York collection.

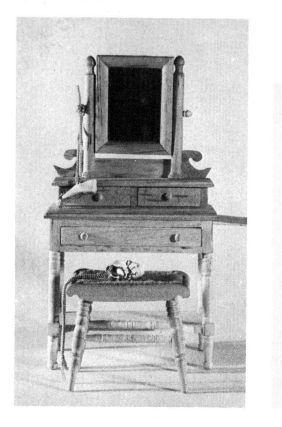

The Federal era dressing table was more true to its function
than the earlier lowboy; its attached mirror definitely established
its use. A special Sheraton desk or dressing table called a harle-
quin table hid compartments under a lid that was opened when a
leaf was raised.

Federal dollhouses need at least one pier table. The pier table
got its name because it was designed to stand against the pierlike
wall space between windows or next to doors. Often these tables
were set under mirrors.

Ladies of gentility kept their worktables near them in the parlor and the table was light enough to be easily portable. The typical worktable had a fabric bag hanging underneath a drawer or
two to hold the sewing. Other worktables consisted of two or
three levels of trays with gallery rims. Also in the parlor were teapoys, small utility tables for use at tea time. They were really
bases for the tea caddy. Sometimes the caddy was one piece with a
tripod-legged base. The kettle stand was very popular too.

In the bedroom or dressing room stood the washstand. It was
an expansion on the Chippendale basin stand, much bigger and
more serviceable. Quite often it was triangular to fit in the corner
and it frequently had a marble top as did many kinds of tables,
especially during the Empire period. There also are examples of
more elaborate washing tables outfitted with their own water
tank, spigot, basin, and mirror.

In the dining room, tables were getting bigger with extra
leaves now fitted into extension tables or semicircular tables add-

Here are two diminutive lady's worktables by Emily Good. Both date from about 1800: on the left a Sheraton worktable; at right, a satinwood sewing table with delicate painted decoration. *Photo by Emily Good*

From Heirloom Replicas by Emily Good comes this collection of candle, kettle, and game tables and stands. Most of these follow originals from the early 1800s. The tea urn is somewhat later. *Photo by Emily Good*

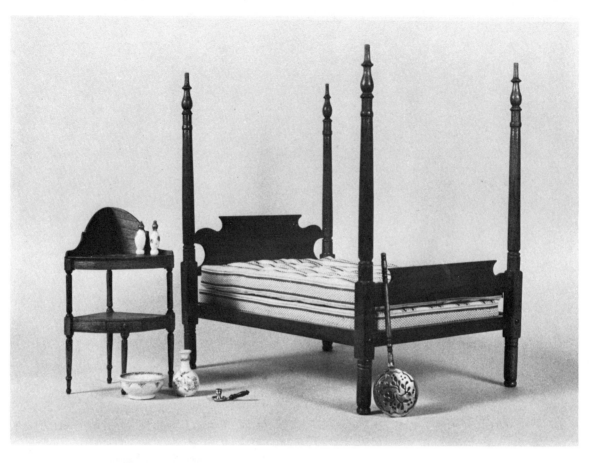

Emily Good made these pieces. The typical corner washstand (c. 1790–1800) has a Chinese export bowl and water bottle (notice the handleless bottle which, for the era, was more common than the pitcher). The bedwarmer is like many of the period with its long handle and cut-out lid. The c. 1815 high-post bed is a replica of one in the family collection of Mr. and Mrs. Howard C. Jones. *Photo by Emily Good*

Arrayed around this Hepplewhite washstand by Roger L. Gutheil, Inc., is a Worcester chamber set, c. 1780–1800, by Jean Yingling of Wee Treasures. It includes a chamber pot, candleholder, shaving mug, pitcher, and washbowl, and a slop jar to handle water waste. *Photo courtesy of Jean E. Yingling*

This dining table is extended to its full length, the middle leaves supported on tiny legs. The metal tips and casters on the legs are typical of the period. Notice the carving on the legs. Linda La Roche made the table. From the collection of Jack and Shirley Bloomfield.

ed to the raised leaves of a banquet table. In the Empire period dining tables were massive and often round.

Mixing tables were popular still, some with built-up backs and a rolltop covering compartments for decanters. The most outstanding addition to the dining room was the full-fledged sideboard. Sideboards developed from plain side tables to tables with pedestals and knife boxes at their ends to the self-contained sideboard, consolidating storage, serving, and display functions in one convenient piece. Sideboards are dated from 1788 and as designed by Hepplewhite usually had tapered legs on spade feet; Sheraton sideboards had rounded reeded legs and corner columns. Some had metal rims or galleries to which candleholders were attached and against which fine china was propped for dis-

The c. 1815 table in two parts is remarkable for its spiral carved legs. Emily Good modeled it after a family heirloom. Notice the same spiral motif on the legs of the (c. 1810) serving table. The dumbwaiter holds a rich selection of accessories including a sugar caster, tea caddy, servants' bell and teapots. The unusual boatlike tray on the serving table is a cheese server, a replica of one in the collection of Mrs. Lee Clements. Emily Good made all the furniture and accessories including the rug. *Photo by Emily Good*

Hepplewhite cellaret by Terry Rogal is a study in straight lines of the early Federal period. The glassware is by Francis Whittemore.

At the left is a kidney-shaped hunt table designed also to serve wine. The pedestal bases on the hunt table and on the small dining table are common on Federal tables.

play. Some dining rooms kept the pedestals at either end of the sideboard. One might be lined with tin as a plate warmer while the other could hide a basin of water for clean-up. There even are reports of chamber pots being kept behind the cupboard doors of some sideboards!

Empire sideboards seemed to grow downward and carved wooden backs replaced the frailer metal galleries. By the end of the Empire period, in its most debased form, the sideboard was a massive cabinet, reaching to the floor and often with a marble top. During the first third of the nineteenth century there developed a sideboard called a butler's secretary. It was a heavy piece with a false drawer front that hid a drop lid.

A related and distinctly Southern piece was the huntboard. It was taller than the sideboard and high enough to be comfortable for leaning because it was originally used as a serving piece around which hunters gathered for a buffet. Huntboards appeared in the homes of people of all classes and when first made were kept in the back hall, sometimes to be hauled outside for the meal. The first huntboards really were nothing more than boards laid on legs without the drawers that appeared later when the huntboard became one piece.

A curved hunt table, something like the King Arthur's round-table in Colleen Moore's dollhouse, was also pressed into action when gentlemen gathered for an evening together. Placed before the fire, the hunt table was used to serve wine. And, as in the previous era, the Federal dining room of the South featured sugar chests and cellarets.

Another furniture convenience that grew in popularity and variety was the bookshelf. Like the Chippendale breakfront and secretaries, many bookshelves had glass doors and wooden

Harry W. Smith of Barnstable Originals copied this piece from a desk in the White House collection. It has many outstanding features, perhaps the most remarkable of which are the tambour doors. Some tambour enclosures work from top to bottom (like a rolltop) rather than side to side. Other wonderful things about this desk are the string and floral inlay; the drop-down leaf (notice the hinges and pull-out slides); the urn finial; and modified bell-shaped top. *Photo courtesy of Coe-Kerr Gallery*

cupboard bottoms. If you have a glass-doored bookshelf or secretary and wish to do something a little different with it, try following one Federal fashion and carefully tack pleated silk panels to the inside of the doors.

China cabinets similar to bookshelves were very popular at the turn of the century and there were more large breakfronts for storing china, some as wide as twelve feet and as tall as the ceiling. Small movable bookshelves much as we know them today were also popular and during the Empire period small revolving bookcases were used. Sheraton believed a small bookshelf was a good bedroom appointment.

Secretaries remained stylish although in a somewhat different form than before, many losing their scroll and bonnet tops and taking on a squarer look. The secretary, which was essentially a desk, hid the desk portion behind a drop leaf or a tambour cover. Tambour fronts were sliding enclosures made by attaching many slender strips of wood to a canvas backing, forming a flexible sheet.

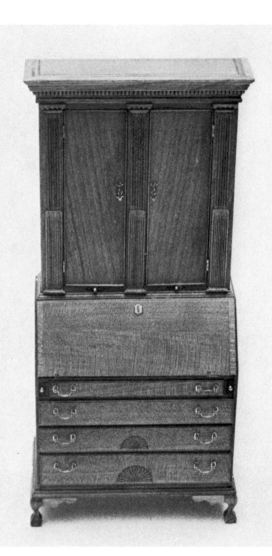

This Federal secretary by Donald C. Buttfield has the pilasters and pediment associated with the era and the cherry and short claw-and-ball feet associated with Connecticut. From a New York collection.

This desk on casters is by Donald Dube. It resembles but is not identical to a desk used by George Washington. From a New York collection.

The bow-front chest was a frequent addition to fine homes; some were used in bedrooms, others in drawing rooms or dining rooms. Chests of drawers took over from highboys and lowboys as bedroom storage and complementing them were large wardrobes with shelves and trays. Some outstanding wardrobes or armoires were made to suit the Empire style and are readily available in miniature.

Hardware on Federal case pieces changed from the typically eighteenth-century brass batwing escutcheon to round, oval, and octagonal plates with bail or ring handles. Brass and glass knobs were important new features on furniture as were metal casters and metal tips on table, sofa, and chair legs. Craftsmen who make scale furniture should bear in mind that it was not just the shape of furniture that changed but the decorative accents as well.

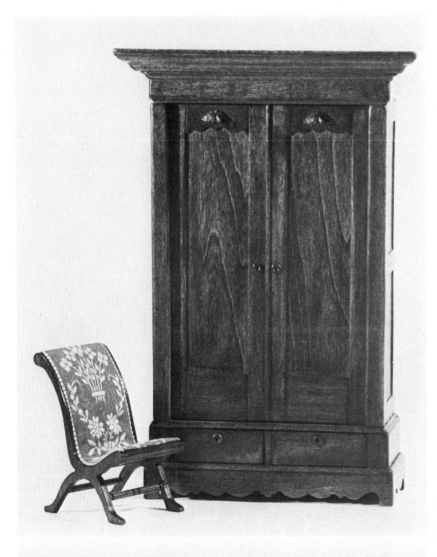

An Empire "sloop" chair with typically elaborate upholstery and an armoire by Terry Rogal. Both pieces have a French feeling and would look good in a New Orleans townhouse.

A small Hepplewhite lady's desk with its straight legs and delicate proportions is by William Robertson. The small Sheraton table with inlay, knob pulls, and fluted legs is by Donald C. Buttfield. From a New York collection.

A four-poster bed from Chestnut Hill Studio. The spread and hangings are a typical copperplate print of the kind that became fashionable during the Federal era. From a New York collection.

This handsome field bed is from Studio B as is Wendy Birkemeier's naive portrait after a famous one of Harriet Leavens by Ammi Phillips (c. 1816). As in many such portraits of young people and children, the subject's demeanor and dress show a curious blend of innocence and sophistication.

Beds changed as the early Federal style passed into the Empire style. In the last decade of the eighteenth century and the first years of the nineteenth, the most popular beds were the high and low posts. High posts with testers wore hangings like those of the colonial period. The material ran the gamut, anything from cotton, wool, silk, chintz, or damask to calico in prints and checks. Copperplate prints were very popular on curtains and bedhangings. There were prints of patriotic motifs, people, animals, buildings, and pastoral scenes. Wealthy families tried to match the hangings with the curtains and the upholstery of other bedroom furniture but obviously that was not possible in all circumstances.

Mahogany was favored for sophisticated high-post beds and the posts were carved, turned, stained, or painted. A special four-poster that gained popularity during the Federal era was the field bed, known for its curved canopy. These beds had slightly shorter posts than the typical tester bed and were better suited for low-ceilinged rooms. They therefore often wound up serving in children's and family servants' rooms. Low-post beds frequently were made of maple or local woods and are known to have been painted, usually in red or green. In a miniature Southern mansion you can add filmy netting to any bed as did the homemaker anxious to keep out mosquitoes and other flying insects.

A crib by David Usher. This is only the frame that supports a mattress and a canopy. From a New York collection.

The Empire style brought with it the sleigh bed. Appearing around 1810, the bed was first made of wood and shaped like a sleigh. Eventually some were made of cast iron. They were meant to have their sides to the wall unlike previous styles which stood with their heads to the wall. A number of homes, including Monticello, were built with recesses in the walls which fit a bed neatly.

Another innovation was the twin bed which began under Sheraton as "summer beds," so called because they were designed for comfort in hot weather. Twin beds were not very common here during the Federal era although they gained in popularity steadily through the nineteenth century. In Sheraton's design they were positioned about two feet apart and joined by an arch.

With its penchant for light furniture, the Federal period also brought us *papier-mâché* furniture, usually small tables or chairs. Although there was a patent for *papier-mâché* as early as 1772, it was not until the first quarter of the nineteenth century that it became popular. *Papier-mâché* furniture was painted, gold-leafed, and decorated with mother-of-pearl.

When deciding what pieces to put in specific rooms, you might learn from Sheraton's attitudes toward the appropriateness of

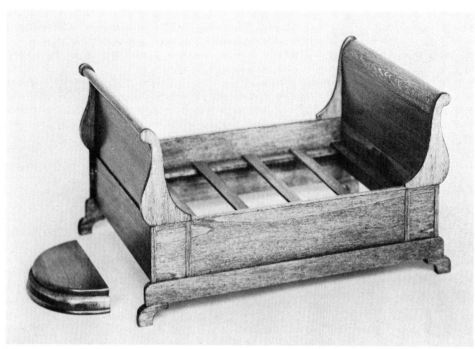

(Above)
This Empire sleigh bed (c. 1820–30) by Franklyn J. Morley is a copy of a Southern antique. The half-round piece at the foot of the bed is a drapery crown. It was fixed to the wall above the bed so that mosquito netting could be suspended from it (or any other fabric the mistress of the house might choose). *Photo courtesy of Franklyn J. Morley*

(Below)
The colorful dower chest from the Hoffman Collection appears here in a late-eighteenth-century incarnation. The dueling pistols are by Jim Holmes. From a New York collection.

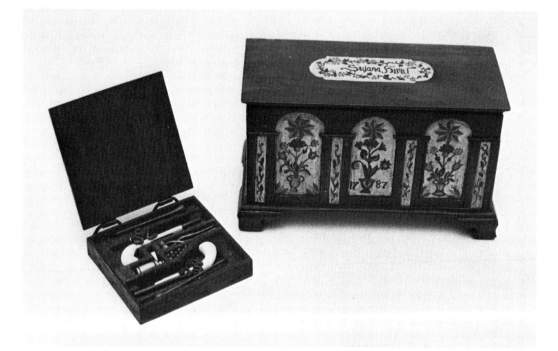

David White of White Mountain Woodworking crafted these two painted chests. On the left is a William and Mary style chest (c. 1720–60) but with decoration dating to c. 1825—making it an example of an old piece which has gone through several transitions (including the addition of mid- to late-eighteenth-century hardware). The low chest on the right is a Hudson River Valley piece dating to c. 1820–35.

"Uncle" Jim Hastrich of The Tin Feather made these painted chests. At left is a red chest with interesting flared feet (a reminder of a formal French-inspired foot on some of the finest Federal case pieces) and heart and flower design. It is dated c. 1825. Compare the chest on the right with the one made by David White in the preceding illustration. Both were copied from the same original but there are some subtle differences including the use here of earlier hardware. *Photo courtesy of The Tin Feather*

furniture to its setting and how rooms were used. Sheraton felt that drawing rooms should hold the richest of the household furniture but should not be cluttered even with pictures and books; they might be too distracting to good conversation. An anteroom off the drawing room where guests might assemble before going into the main parlor was to be furnished with sofas and perhaps a piano for light entertainment. He did think that distractions were good for children and suggested putting pictures, flowerpot stands, and painted furniture into breakfast rooms or other places where youngsters would gather. He describes the elegant dining room as one equipped with sideboard, table and chairs, mirrors, and portraits.

However, something else to keep in mind is that furniture suit-

Marj Crueger made the stripped rug. Barbara Davis of Country Cottage Miniatures made the prim country table with its heavily scrubbed top, and the cupboard (c. 1825) with prominent L hinges and a common, wavy, combed pattern in the paint. The slipware plate by Deborah McKnight repeats the wavy pattern. Lee-Ann Chellis-Wessel made the mid-1800s pitcher from one at Old Sturbridge Village as well as the c. 1850 cake dish with the remarkable funnel in the center. The basket of peaches came from Wise Miniatures.

These pieces are typical of late Empire–early Victorian furniture. They are essentially in the Grecian style—especially the (c. 1830–50) chairs. These pieces are quite like the models developed by cabinetmaker John Hall. This furniture was made by Roger L. Gutheil, Inc., in cooperation with the Margaret Woodbury Strong Museum in Rochester, New York, which has a substantial collection of both full-size Victoriana and antique dollhouses. *Photo courtesy of Roger L. Gutheil, Inc.*

ed to one room might, for reasons we don't fully understand, wind up in another. A sofa might be found in a dining room, for instance, or a washstand in the hall. Such haphazardness will remind some people of the seemingly careless furniture placements they remember from visits to Grandmother or bachelor uncles living in old-fashioned houses. There might be no better explanation than that happens to be the only place the odd piece of furniture fit. Maybe whoever lives there doesn't care—or maybe whoever lives there likes to relax in the dining room. Take your pick—it's your dollhouse.

ACCESSORIES

ACCESSORIES of the Federal period are perhaps the most elegant of any period in American history, but it is also important to remember that thousands of homes throughout rural areas and in small towns were not much changed from the late seventeenth and early eighteenth centuries. This is fortunate for miniaturists because we can carry over accessories from previous eras.

One trend that continued from the colonial era was the reliance on mirrors for decoration. Federal mirrors had a more architectural look than their colonial predecessors and a great many of them were rectangular in shape. That did not, however, make them austere. On the contrary, many of them are draped with golden swags and other fine detail. One of the most famous Federal mirrors was the tabernacle or constitution mirror. This mirror was rectangular with a cornice top and a painted glass or

Federal mirror by Constance Simone has identifying balls and the architectural lines of the period. The decoration is reverse painting on glass. The Martha Washington chair is by Terry Rogal.

Two sets of matched portraits in the primitive style by Beatrice Thomas. The window with an outdoor scene was a typical device and might or might not be taken from life. In fact the bodies of the sitters might or might not be real since traveling painters frequently stuck a sitter's head on a stock body. *Photo by Ross Klavan*

wood panel in the upper section. These mirrors were sixteen to thirty-six inches tall and often had tiny balls hanging from the cornice. Sheraton mirrors had columns on the sides just as Sheraton furniture did.

Many more mirrors were gilded during the Federal period and large mirrors were placed over many mantels. Vying with the rectangle for popularity was the circular bull's-eye mirror with its convex glass. These girandole mirrors with candleholders graced elegant Federal homes. Frames on mirrors tended to be black or gilded rather than natural wood and a number of frames were stenciled. Some mirrors were in elaborate gilded frames that carried them as high as the ceiling.

On the walls with the mirrors were pictures of course, many of them portraits. There was a growing American fascination with silhouettes which had been popular in Europe. There also were mourning pictures that might be painted or worked by needle. They bore cemetery scenes or other mournful reminders of the deceased. The romantic Hudson River School landscapes were popular and have been called realistic but reverent. Lithographs were perfected in 1798 which puts them solidly in the Federal era. Many of what we now call primitives were also painted during the period. Pictures were not always hung and it wasn't unusual to find one resting on a mantel leaning against the wall.

Wall clocks were extremely popular during the period and one of the best known was the banjo clock, patented in 1802. Mass

A pillar-and-scroll clock by Paul
Runyon. The clock and the early-
nineteenth-century bonnet are from a
New York collection

production made clocks more accessible to common people than
before and Connecticut was particularly noted for its production.
In the early nineteenth century there were at least two dozen well-
known Connecticut clockmakers working and countless less famous craftsmen. There was a boom in grandfather clocks with
painted dials and cases were made in the prevailing furniture
styles. In about 1785 the grandfather clock was joined by the
grandmother clock. It was about half the size of the tall case clock
and appropriate on the floor or shelf. During the early nineteenth
century many shelf clocks had painted panels like the constitution
mirror and the most elegant of them went on mantels. The pillar-
and-scroll clock (perfected about 1816) belongs to the period as
does the lighthouse clock with its pedestal surmounted by a glass
dome.

Federal mantels also held sets of china vases or flowerpots, as
many as five pieces to a set. The fanlike flower horn was popular
and cachepots with flowers and potted plants often stood in front
of unused fireplaces. Other china ornaments for the home included Staffordshire figures with patriotic themes as well as cheaper,
imitation Staffordshire in plaster known as chalkware. There were
ceramic toilet sets and even cuspidors.

There was more porcelain here as the first lots brought in
American ships from China rather than via the English trade arrived. Much of the Chinese product bore patriotic motifs or land-
scape designs as did a large amount of the European china sent to
these shores. There were the years of Canton, with its blue river
scenes, and Rose Medallion, the multicolored gilded pattern of
flowers and mandarins. The famous willowware came here about
1780 and in general blue and white china and other ceramics
were extremely popular. Many families could not afford good
dishes, however, and we still find an abundance of earthenware

and stoneware. All homes had their share of earthenware and stoneware crocks and pots.

Domestic porcelain was successfully manufactured in this country during the second decade of the nineteenth century. Ironstone is dated from the same time and was usually white with ornamental detail in a blue pattern or as relief. Rockingham ware arrived during the Federal era and frequently had a mottled brown or yellow glaze. The first production was at Bennington (from which we get the other name, Benningtonware) in 1793. Rockingham was made elsewhere and was popular through the mid-nineteenth century.

A new fad for decorated plates developed, bringing us the plates with painted alphabets and maxims. George Washington's face also graced many china plates and bowls.

There was more flatware than before and forks now had four tines. Flatware had metal, wood, bone, and ivory handles. You are not likely to find its counterpart in miniature but it's interesting to note that during the post-Revolutionary era, silversmiths inscribed a dove of peace with an olive branch in its beak on the backs of spoons.

Although pewter was a mainstay in some homes, in general it

Lee-Ann Chellis-Wessel of Demi-Tasse Miniatures made all four *sgraffito* ware plates. Though such plates date to at least the 1760s in this country, they were most popular between about 1810 and 1840. They were found all over the country and frequently were showpieces not in everyday use. Their themes came from Europe and the tulip, birds, and flowers seen here are usually associated with the Pennsylvania Dutch.

This tea caddy, tray, and document box from Studio B are examples of popular painted toleware. *Photo courtesy of Studio B*

was losing popularity and by 1825 had been shunted aside. There was a large amount of tinware, much of it the very colorful toleware that miniaturists like to copy. Toleware is considered the highest order of decorated or painted tin.

Silver now had softer curves and was less rococo than during the colonial era. There were many straight-sided tea sets with reeded, fluted, or beaded decoration on relatively plain surfaces. Designs were symmetrical and classical, at least until the introduction of the Empire style which was rounded and squat. In the 1820s the highly ornate repoussé-work emerged. The period also gave us many presentation pieces in the form of bowls and urns and the first matching tea sets graced delicate tea tables.

There was also greater variety in glassware that now came in etched, cut, and plain styles. Pressed glass came in the 1820s and by 1825 many kinds of glassware, from tumblers to salts, had found their way into the average home. Colored glass was very popular too.

Tables were not set as ours are today. The main meal was served in the afternoon on a table covered with a half-dozen to a dozen dishes of food and enough places and silverware for each person. Glasses were set on the sideboard and during the first part of the period napkins weren't used. Instead diners used the tablecloth until napkins returned in the 1820s.

Knife boxes were still popular despite the fact the sideboard had become one-piece. Knife boxes were often urn-shaped instead of rectangular as they were during the Chippendale period. They did go out of favor as the period closed.

A lavabo hung on the walls of many dining rooms. It consisted of a tank, spigot, and bowl in which servants of the day washed flatware during the meal so that it could be recycled. We shall also see the lavabo in the bedroom in the discussion of bathing in Chapter Five. The colonial era wine cooler or cistern advanced

The tinware displayed on this country dresser is by Constance Simone. The document box on top and the book lying on the bottom shelf were designed to hold important papers or perhaps a few valued trinkets. The coffeepots have both crooked and straight spouts. The smaller pitcher is a syrup pitcher. The colors are black, red, and green predominantly, although the tray on the second shelf is white with pretty flowers for presentation to a bride. The cupboard was made by Tony Botelho of Donna's Dollhouse.

The knife box is by Ernie Levy in a colonial style brought into the Federal era by its fine border inlay. The silver service from Acquisto Silver Company is modeled after an original that dates to 1797–1810. The galleried plateau and centerpiece come from Eugene Kupjack. From the collection of Jack and Shirley Bloomfield.

into Federal homes. The tublike wine cooler was zinc-lined so that it could keep bottles cold in ice.

The hot candle flame still lit most homes and brass chandeliers were popular among the wealthy as were some made of glass or silver. One lovely quasi-chandelier was a simple hanging glass globe in which candles burned.

Candleholders were made of china, pottery, glass, and the usual metals. On tables, mantels, and sideboards candleholders were protected from drafts by hurricane shades and in the 1800s there were metal shades as well. But lighting was to change during the Federal period as fuel-burning lamps grew more sophisticated. They burned whale and other types of oil and consisted essentially of a stand, a fuel reservoir, and one or two wicks. Some had globes or shades.

The major development was the Argand lamp which was invented in 1783. It took its name from Aimé Argand, the Swiss scientist who perfected it. The Argand lamp had a round wick and its new way of feeding more oxygen to the flame made it burn more brightly than any previous lamp. It came to America in the 1780s or 90s. Among the types of Argand lamps was one called the astral lamp—a lamp designed not to throw a shadow. It was well-established in the 1820s. There were several forms of astral lamp including glass-shaded types on columnar bases, and one- and two-armed varieties. Some were very fancy with elaborate reservoirs for fuel and cut-glass prisms.

The introduction of Argand and other sophisticated fuel lamps affected the way furniture was arranged. During the colonial and Federal eras furniture lined the walls. As light became more reliable much of that furniture came out from the walls into more permanent arrangements. These arrangements were fairly static—grouped around a table on which stood an astral lamp, or

These two wooden chests were made by "Uncle" Jim Hastrich of The Tin Feather. Both are Maine designs, the small one c. 1825–40; the large one c. 1830–40. The painted canvas floorcloth was made by Mary Grady O'Brien. The double-wick camphene lamp was made by Studio B and befits the scene in time and mood.

centered around the increasingly more effective heating stoves. In winter, there might be a long cover on the center table which warmed the legs of the family members circled around it. Almost one at a time the pieces moved from wall to center arrangement with the table going first.

Argand lamps were used until kerosene lamps were perfected in the Victorian era. In most homes during the Federal period, however, candles and cheap tin lamps outnumbered the Argand. One very popular lamp was a small blown-glass lamp with a reservoir on a stem. It was called a sparking lamp. Another small lamp, a peg lamp, was made with a peg on the bottom by which it could be fitted into candlesticks that the family wanted to update. Although there was a gaslight experiment in Newport in 1806 (and, in fact, a Philadelphia demonstration even earlier, in 1796) and limited service in Baltimore in 1816, in most areas gaslight was still a curiosity at the end of the period. (It might be useful to re-read the discussion of lighting as it relates to colonial dollhouses on page 80.) You might, as a result, consider *darkening* your dollhouse or at least directing your light more realistically.

Federal floors wore a variety of coverings and here again we find ample evidence of the unevenness of American life in terms of amenities. Imported Aubusson, Turkish, and Oriental-style carpets adorned the homes of the wealthy, but might even in a fine home be mixed with painted canvas floorcloths. Some floorcloths and oilcloths, painted in colorful geometrics, florals and in imitation of "Turkey" carpets, covered other better carpeting.

Often floors were painted directly following a design stenciled on the walls. Needlework carpets were made but were not abundant partly because of their fragility. Straw matting was a summertime favorite just as it had been in previous years. (See p. 69 for suggestions about summerwear for furniture.) Even wallpaper was known to substitute for carpeting!

Still, it was not until the nineteenth century was well on its way that many towns got carpeting of any substance, including the Axminsters, Wiltons, and ingrains introduced in the previous period. Homemade striped carpets brightened many parlors. These rugs consisted of half- to a full-yard-wide striped panels sewn together. They were colorful, first appearing in soft browns, pinks, greens, and blues produced by the old vegetable dyes. As manufacturing developed, so did the dye process and colors turned brighter and in many cases harsher.

Rag rugs were another homemade covering made by braiding oddments together and sewing the processed rags into whatever size rug was needed. Woven, embroidered, and appliquéd throw rugs were popular. Chenillelike shirred rugs were found in later Federal homes, about the same time hooked rugs came into fashion.

It is surprising to many people that hooked rugs developed so late, especially as they are frequently and incorrectly found in miniature colonial reconstructions. There is no certainty about when they were first made here, but those we can date come after 1830. They became ubiquitous in the second half of the century. Hooked rugs came in a variety of colors and designs often exhibiting a lack of sophistication in graphics. At the same time, the patterns with horses as big as barns and flowers as tall as people display a naive flair on the part of American homemakers that is more appealing to many eyes than any design a trained artist could devise.

The familiar jacquard spread came into being during the period with the development in France of M. Jacquard's loom and its translation here, first to New York, in the 1820s.

The late Sally Smith made these two hooked rugs celebrating bonneted little girls and a sturdy pet dog. *Photo by Ross Klavan*

Three pieces still being worked on by a talented early-nineteenth-century hand. The needlework frames hold unfinished work while the portrait by Joan Vaber (after Thomas Sully's *Boy with the Torn Hat*) is just on its way to being framed. The needlework frames are from the Ginger Jar. From a New York collection.

The colorful patchwork quilt was very popular as were whitework bedcovers. There were three primary types: Marseilles quilting, which was like the modern stuffed trapunto, candlewicking, which relied on French knots and other stitches, and embroidery, which used white thread on white linen or cotton.

Other needlework included the ever-popular sampler, now frequently a very elaborate piece of work that was framed and hung in the best parlors. After 1800 many samplers bore family records and genealogies and there were some embroidered maps. Many of the samplers were made by young girls who took school training in needlework and produced an especially noteworthy body of work. It is no surprise that women and girls also paid attention to the way they stored their sewing implements, painting fancy designs on their sewing boxes.

As hats became taller, so did hatboxes. There was a variety of decorated wooden and pasteboard hatboxes for both gentlemen and ladies. Bandboxes were the most popular from about 1825 to 1850. Men's wigs were going out of fashion while women were donning wigs of considerable intricacy.

Globe stands, short and tall, made their way into better Federal homes. A well-equipped library would do well with such an appointment. Also in the library we can now place a Webster's dictionary of which there are several miniature versions. The small Webster's came out in 1806 and the large volume was published in 1828.

Other small details that lend life to a Federal room are toe-dancing shoes; in 1827 toe dancing came to New York. The

The China trade echoes through these items from the Federal era home of a merchant or sea captain. With the telescope is an orrery, a device that demonstrates the position of the planets. The clipper ship bowl is from Chestnut Hill Studio and the pagoda-decorated bowl is by Deborah McKnight. From a New York collection.

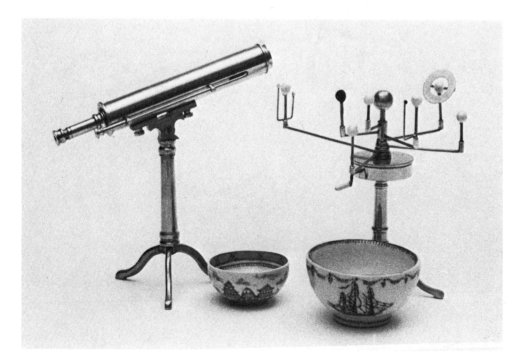

Sussex Crafts made this mantelpiece with pilaster supports and carved frieze. The leather firebucket was a common Federal household accessory kept near the doorway for emergencies. Sylvia Rountree made this one and, like its historical antecedent, it carries the homeowner's name and a design: in this case a burning building in "Bridgeville," Delaware (one of the author's childhood homes).

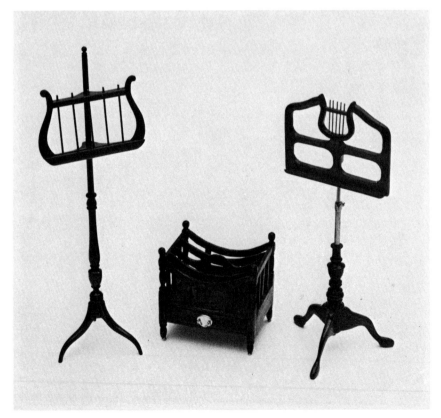

These two music stands were made by Paul Runyon (left) and William Robertson. The canterbury for music was made by Rose Barell. From a New York collection.

marching Hessian soldier andirons were also popular during this period and, as during colonial days, fireplaces were covered by decorative fireboards during the summer. Fenders and tools of brass completed the best fireplaces and you might bring forward the enchanting dummy boards of earlier times described in Chapter Two. A finishing touch for the Federal music room is the canterbury. It was a small rack used to file music sheets. The canterbury looked like a magazine rack and was sometimes used to hold plates and trays.

You can draw a great many different kinds of curtains and draperies on your Federal scene. The lambrequin, which often topped important windows, was elaborate, with scalloped edging. Valances and cornices were also intricate, dominating draperies that hung straight or in flouncelike jabots. Materials ranged from copperplate print cotton to silk and there were some braided and fringed trims. Accommodations to summer were similar to those outlined for colonial window dressing.

POLITICALLY, the Federal period brought forth an exuberant new nation, diverse yet whole. Much the same phenomenon was reflected in the decorative arts as strong new furniture styles emerged. The end of the Federal era signaled the beginning of a new period of growth for the United States, years when the East rushed headlong into the machine age, and many Americans rushed West.

VICTORIAN PERIODS

1830-1900

THE Victorian interior is a reflection of Victorian life: sentimental, heavy-handed, eclectic often to the point of jumble, and periodically bursting with contradiction. The
Victorian style is not one style at all but a confusion of styles,
most of them borrowed, settling over the century as though a pic-
nic supper of fashions was shaken out of a tablecloth. This makes
the Victorian era attractive to many miniaturists because they
think they can join the elements of a disparate collection into
some sort of whole. But disparate too often means undisciplined;
be advised that you cannot simply organize the odds and ends of
your collection into a happy mix and call it Victorian. It takes a bit
more concentration than that. Nevertheless the Victorian setting
can indeed be a wonderful repository for pieces that just don't
seem to belong anywhere else.

American Victorians were a curious bunch in many ways, their
styles an expression of individualism combined with imitation.
They relied on themes from the past and judgments from abroad,
particularly from England and France. But they put a very special
stamp on this procession of outside influences that was sometimes vulgar, sometimes pious, but always proud and new and distinctly American.

Also coming into this country was an infusion of immigrant
stock that strengthened American society and put an end to its
absolute stratification, although society retained its layered structure through most of the century. The middle class was growing
and for the first time had quite a bit of money to spend. In fact the
country was turning from a nation of producers to a nation of
consumers. Although what people bought was not always in good
taste, it is as wrong to dismiss the era as a blight on the history of
the decorative arts as it is to relish every curlicue as quaint.

Stepping into the Victorian home, we start a trip that may take us through two dozen rooms, many of them highly specialized. It is often impractical to have so many rooms in a dollhouse but within the limits of reason it is good to add to the basic "living room/dining room/kitchen/bedroom" configuration of most dollhouses; of course those miniaturists who are working with separate room settings rather than the limited number in a doll-house can have the proverbial field day.

Working from the outside in, you will want to consider a piazza, veranda, or the more prosaic porch. Good Victorian houses greeted guests with a large reception hall, often opening beyond a smaller vestibule. Even in small houses a large hallway was often eked out to give an immediate impression of immense space within, whatever the reality beyond the front hall. Some hallways had one or more doors that led nowhere and were meant only to impress visitors with the hint that a much larger house lay hidden from view. Adding a false doorway is one of the easier alterations you can make.

As for rooms, you can include such prizes as a ballroom, an after dinner smoking room for gentlemen, separate parlors for everyday and Sunday entertaining, a library, a sewing room, a conservatory and/or greenhouse with fountains, a music room, a billiards room, a chapel, a picture gallery, family and formal dining rooms, a breakfast room, a kitchen (see Chapter Five) with pantry, a laundry, and that haven of drudgery, the scullery. In the servant-heavy nineteenth century, homes frequently had servants' halls, dining rooms, and sleeping quarters in an *Upstairs/Downstairs* motif. A dumbwaiter will help carry that theme and you can run such a mini-lift from the basement to the top floor. Closets were at last standard in better homes, often deep and roomy and oddly shaped, and some houses had bathrooms (again see Chapter Five).

For some collectors, trying to inject this diversity into a house will require some rearrangement and even sacrifice in available space. But miniaturists who are confined to a house with a limited number of rooms need not feel thwarted. Decide where your interest and resources lie. For instance, if your collection is devoted primarily to parlor furniture you may decide to tear out a wall and make the dining room smaller, or give up a bedroom for use as a second parlor. If you are taken with kitchen furnishings and like the thought of a back kitchen and pantry you might build a kitchen suite. You could trim the existing kitchen to build a new wall and create a pantry and perhaps wall up a back porch to become a scullery.

The reception hall, which many dollhouses lack, can be borrowed by reducing the size of the parlor and dining room which frequently are adjacent. There's no law that every dollhouse has to have two bedrooms, and if you are not as fond of beds as you are of stoves or couches then you may want to eliminate a bedroom in favor of providing room to display pieces of your collection that give you more pleasure. Authenticity is a guiding principle in this book, and of course one bedroom in a grand Victorian house certainly violates that principle, but sometimes it makes more sense—and certainly more enjoyment for a collector—to take some liberties. More important than reproducing an exact replica of a Victorian house is finding a pleasing, personal way to house a collection and to have fun doing it.

Don't forget that you can borrow vertically as well as horizontally. Inside balconies were not uncommon and can, if the dollhouse has a high enough ceiling, be built large enough to accommodate a gallery or sitting room. The stairway and railing of the balcony level might be made of lacy metal—a fad for ornamental ironwork began in the 1850s.

It is a good idea to make several copies of the floor plan of your dollhouse on graph paper and experiment with alterations, remembering to note electrical work which will be a limiting factor in some prewired homes.

Remember, too, that not all Victorian homes were built on a grand scale. There were many tiny cottages with only a parlor, a kitchen, and a bedroom or two. They are just as charming in miniature as the expensive custom-built house.

Here in the midst of all this renovation I want to remind you that my suggestions for building and cutting and adding-to refer to new and *not* antique dollhouses. I hope that any of you fortunate enough to own nineteenth- or early-twentieth-century houses will recognize their integrity and consult an expert before attempting *any* alteration which should of course be in the nature of restoration. The rule of thumb when handling an antique dollhouse is "When in doubt, *don't!*"

Because of our exposure to doll- and full-size nineteenth-century houses, almost everybody has an idea of what Victorian looks like and in most cases the idea is fairly accurate. But it has become stereotyped and, as a result, is very limiting. I hope this chapter will clear up a few misconceptions, acquaint you with some important turning points in the century, and demonstrate that there were separate and distinct styles within the era. The thing to remember is that these styles overlapped and several were fashionable simultaneously. Perhaps this chapter will give Victorian enthusiasts some new insights and a few new ideas on how to decorate their rooms.

The Victorian era signaled the end of the Greek Revival with its clean, even, spare lines. The Greek Revival was about played out by 1845, a decade after the first signs of what we call Victorian style started to change American interiors. In general we can describe Victorian interiors as being more cumbersome than their colonial and Federal antecedents. Gone was the plain paneling of the eighteenth century, although some walls did show large, rectangular panels outlined in composition moldings. Victorian walls

This New Orleans bedroom from the Thorne Rooms Collection of the Art Institute of Chicago introduces Victorian touches to a late Empire stage. The room contains elements from several grand homes in the New Orleans area and its architectural features are mostly of the Federal era classicism. The chairs are the latest pieces stylistically, and notice also the balloon-back fancy chair partially hidden by the lyre-based table at the right. The Aubusson rug and gilded dressing table are just two of the French notes in the room. *Courtesy of the Art Institute of Chicago; Gift of Mrs. James Ward Thorne*

were frequently made of plaster with paint or paper covering. The dado began the period at the familiar height and grew so that in some houses it reached up three-quarters of the wall. Often it and other woodwork were of softwood with painted graining in imitation of finer stock. Dadoes might be covered with straw matting and fabric (from burlap to silk) as well as paper, paint, and in some instances, paneling. During approximately the last third of the century a taste developed for tile borders along the lower wall. The chair rail to run atop the dado was much wider in Victorian homes, sometimes carrying its own special design.

A useful piece of trim is the plate rail which you can easily attach at eye level or above in the dining room and the kitchen. This is a good place to display the unmatched collection of china plates you have accumulated. In some houses the plate rail was built directly above the chair rail although this seems dangerously low. In addition, there frequently was a picture molding running

This room by Tom and Guy Roberts successfully combines several wallpaper designs including an Arab desert scene. Among the different lamps are hanging gaslight globes with matching wall sconces; a student lamp on the secretary at left; and a number of table lamps on the end tables. The chandelier is by Ellen Krucker Blauer. *Photo by Phillip F. McPherson*

around the room just below the ceiling from which pictures hung on fairly long and obvious wires or cords.

A great amount of wallpaper was used even in plain houses. Building on Federal wallpaper, the early Victorian papers often featured small to medium-size patterns in somewhat controlled, all-over repeats and geometric arrangements. There were florals and pictorials as well as stripes and other designs. The designs grew more daring—if we can equate larger, and more overspreading figures with daring—as the years passed and mid-Victorian papers often exhibit what we might call florid florals as well as stripes, patterns, and such specialties as embossed leather looks and flocked designs. In one room there could be several displays of the same motif in different sizes, for instance on borders and friezes. There might even be a combination of different papers. In paneled rooms the large panels were sometimes papered, the outlining moldings painted. During the 1850s Gothic arches appeared on wallpaper. Elaborate stenciled friezes were popular and there might also be a stenciled border above the chair rail, often varnished for protection. The cove—a concave section joining ceiling and wall—is a good place for paper and stenciling, too.

You can easily add a cove to existing dollhouse rooms using the stock wooden coves sold in many shops.

After the Federal era, white was not a popular interior color even though early Victorian walls are often light in color. Mid- and later Victorian interior colors were deep and often quite rich—red, blue, green, purple, brown, and, after 1859, magenta. There were spatter-painted walls with tiny dots of color splashed on a solid, usually darker, background.

There was another wall treatment which is rare in scale reproduction, but which could be exciting in a Victorian dollhouse if you can manage it, called Lincrusta Walton. It was a linoleumlike wall covering with a raised design. It usually had a finish similar to a brown varnish and was particularly suited for halls and parlors.

A Georgian planter sits under the coved ceiling of this antebellum double parlor (c. 1850) from the Thorne Rooms Collection of the Art Institute of Chicago. This room is the very definition of luxury from its Wilton carpet to its servants' bell pull hanging on the wall near the fireplace. The two chairs near the arch leading to the music room (one of which is partially obscured) are Elizabethan Revival whereas most of the other furniture is rococo. Note the lamps on the pier table at the right and the portrait hanging by its long cord. *Courtesy of the Art Institute of Chicago; Gift of Mrs. James Ward Thorne*

If you want to abide by one dictum of the day, follow the theory that furniture does well against a dark background and pictures against a light surface: design your house with dark wainscoting and pale walls. Even black dadoes were not unknown and could be very daring and effective.

Plank and parquet floors were common, and the better homes exhibited many different kinds of parquet design and wood inlay from simple strips to the intricate inlaid wood map of the United States that was centered in one gentleman's library. There also were some tile floors, especially in anterooms, like vestibules, and in bathrooms. The tiles might be of the square, unglazed type or the tiny white and black kind found in so many bathrooms as late as the mid-twentieth century. Some floors were painted in solid colors or free-hand designs; others were stenciled and spatter-painted. Many decorators felt that doors and trim should be darker than the wall color. This same logic demanded a darker border around the floor. But anyone with money rushed to cover the floor (at least most of it) with carpeting (discussed in Accessories).

Victorian woodwork had a look of pride about it, varnished to a fare-thee-well and hand-rubbed to shine. In oak, mahogany, black walnut, cherry, and birch, the woodwork frequently was woodgrained or marbleized to look like something more than it really was. "Heavy" is a word we often use in describing things Victorian—from chairs to morality—and the woodwork in Victorian houses fits that description too. Although frequently carved or molded with considerable skill, the woodwork was elaborate and substantial. Imposing newel posts and variegated cornices are emblems of the Victorian builder's rather strong decorative statement.

High ceilings were the rule. Some were very fancy, made of wood, plaster appliqué, or tin pressed into extravagant patterns. A tin ceiling in a miniature house would be a striking, unusual, and not necessarily difficult addition. Generally ceilings were lighter in color than the walls. Many times, especially in the 1870s and 80s, they were painted with a design and frequently there was a border framing whatever decorative display was on the ceiling itself. Medallions and molded plaster works were popular, particularly after 1860. Especially in homes with Gothic influence, you might find a vaulted ceiling, perhaps with tracerylike ribs and buttresses.

Steady progress in the manufacture of window glass went with advances in color technique to produce some of the most interesting windows of any era in American history. Tall, rectangular sash windows were standard, with two panes of glass above and two below; two-over-one and one-over-one were the usual configurations. As if unwilling to surrender a part of the past with its tiny paned windows, some Victorians tried for the best of both with convenient plate glass expanses in the lower portion of the window and small-paned glass above.

There was a variety of more daring types as well: latticed windows; stained-glass windows in plain and fancy designs; and windows and doors with etched or cut-glass insets and transoms. Miniaturists can add an authentic note by putting an etched-glass transom over the front door carrying the street number of the house. Sometimes the etched glass was colored, the design outlined in the natural clear color of the glass.

The Victorians also loved French doors, bay windows, and oriels, the latter essentially a bay window that started above the first floor and might be several stories high. Oriels can give plain dollhouses a Victorian flavor because they can be fairly easily assembled from stock parts and attached by anyone willing to cut a hole in an upstairs wall.

While it was not so much the rule as during the colonial period when shutters on brick homes invariably were inside, there were some shutters in Victorian homes, too, including louvered or blind types.

Rooms, particularly parlors, were often separated by sliding doors. Another option was to build an arch. Many times the arches were laden with curtains or portières of glass beads, shells, and bamboo. Ordinary fabric simply hanging from poles also divided rooms. At the end of the period colorful glass screens, both movable and permanent, were used in room partitions.

Stairways were designed in great variety. Circular staircases graced many elegant homes and most houses of substance had several stairways. This gives you a chance to have a circular staircase and a plainer, straight one as well. With the straight staircase you can add a landing with table and chair because Victorian landings were bigger than the plant stands that serve as landings these days. This also is a good place to install a stained-glass window.

One way to construct a Victorian-spirited staircase would be to arrange one staircase to do two things: carry the family and guests from the front of the house and the servants from the back. Start your stairway at the entry hall, building it to a landing and continue it conveniently. Bring a second stairway from the pantry or back hall to the landing but keep that stairway enclosed and put a door from it to the landing. You have a nearly hidden but useful and, in dollhouse terms, picturesque enclosed servants' staircase without having to disturb the upstairs arrangement by cutting another hole in the floor. You might think of installing an elevator in your Victorian home. The first passenger elevator was running in 1857 and self-service residential elevators were advertised for New York homes in the 1880s.

Victorian fireplaces have a much different look than do those of earlier times, although obviously we can expect that some of the bolection molding, McIntire-carved fireplaces survived to live in otherwise Victorian houses. However, many Victorians framed their fireplaces with an arched opening. Mantel shelves were stan-

(Left)
This mantel, c. 1875, was made by
Franklyn J. Morley as a replica of the
fireplace facing in the Russian
consulate in San Francisco. The back
is mirrored, including the area
behind the six shelves each of which
is outlined in delicate turnings. The
galleried effect is often associated
with Eastlake design. The fireplace
opening is tiled and the hearth is
onyx. *Photo courtesy of Franklyn J.
Morley*

(Below)
A Victorian fireplace. The delicate
glassware on the top shelf is from
Francis Whittemore. From the
collection of Jack and Shirley
Bloomfield.

(Left)
A Braxton Payne fireplace with a
built-in metal heating element typical
of Victorian arrangement.

dard, of course, and later Victorians sometimes built whole shelved sections as part of their mantelpieces.

Mantelpieces were made in a great variety of materials including wood, marble (often imitated in wood), onyx, cast iron, stone, brick, and slate. Fireplace interiors were often made of cast iron with cast-iron backs and sides housing an iron coal basket or grate. Cast-iron fireplace surrounds increased steadily as years passed. Spandrels of arched fireplaces were paneled or heavily carved. Some variations included an extension of the Grecian style with flat slablike facings; and the use of heavy mantel shelves supported by full-figured caryatids or other carved, consolelike supports. Decorative "art tiles" were used to adorn fireplaces during the last third of the nineteenth century.

An interesting thing happened to fireplaces during the Victorian era: they started to disappear.

A massive black "marble" fireplace by Braxton Payne, suited for a house of some wealth and refinement. *Courtesy of Wexler-Dube Miniatures*

Two imitation-marble mantelpieces with arched openings and carved decoration including panels and scrolled brackets on the left mantelpiece and acanthus leaves down the side of the mantelpiece on the right. The mantelpiece at left is from Lawbre Company; the one at right from Grandmother Stover's.

The pedestal with its bust is a touch repeated in many Victorian parlors. The fireplace has an arched opening with typical treatment of the spandrels (the triangular areas between arch and the edge).

It's true that many families clung to parlor and kitchen fireplaces but the Franklin stove and its progeny were slowly nudging the fireplace into obsolescence. By the 1880s fireplaces were pretty old-fashioned and in the kitchen had been replaced decisively by cookstoves, as we shall see in Chapter Five. Beginning in the 1840s, the kitchen fireplace had first hosted the stove and then bowed to it altogether. If you wish to take a Victorian dollhouse through its growing pains, you can build fireplaces in all major rooms and brick in a few to show the house had aged and the family adapted to new conveniences including better parlor stoves or even central heat.

Parlor stoves of the era were elaborations of the Franklin stove with doors enclosing the fire. They often were highly decorative with finials on the top. In general they echoed prevailing furniture styles. Parlor stoves sat on zinc pads, tiles, or bricks which protected the floor. The famous potbelly stove was primarily used in public buildings or farmhouses.

Steam and hot-water heat came to America in the mid-1840s and their use spread quite a bit in the 1850s. Radiators were large, often highly decorated and, as seems dictated by some natural law, ugly. Hot-air heat with its furnace, pipes, and registers was installed in some homes by the end of the 1830s. Hot air was cheaper than hot water and therefore more common but two things should be remembered about all artificial heating systems: they were mainly city phenomena for most of the century; and a great many people—including some influential writers on home and social order—distrusted them and believed that for health of

A Franklin stove with all-over molded designs with a Victorian flair. The stove was made by Al Atkins, the Village Smithy. *Photo by Ross Klavan*

the body and the maintenance of the soul the beloved open fire was infinitely preferable. Obviously the advocates of central heat eventually prevailed and if you are going to make your dollhouse conform to the "modern" trend, remember to make way for the pipes. With a hot-air system you'll want to include registers; simply cut holes in the floors and cover them with metal grilles. Gas heating stoves were in use at least by the 1860s.

That brings us to another way to show your Victorian house change with the times; you can install either gas or electricity. There was gas service by the second decade in Baltimore and quite limited service elsewhere even in the 1820s. But it is fair to say that gaslight didn't really move *indoors* till about 1840 and it certainly wasn't universal. Residential gas service is usually associated with houses after the Civil War and might be considered to be in general use by about 1870. The electric incandescent light bulb appeared on the scene in 1878 and was in fairly wide use by the mid-1880s although it wasn't until 1891 that the new sophisticated lighting system went to the White House. It was still relatively unusual to find electricity in average private homes until the twentieth century.

The Victorian parlor stove is from Handcraft Design. Many stoves were very fancy and imitated prevailing furniture styles.

For those of you who are going to install gas, figuratively speaking, it means having a network of exposed interior pipes, an exceedingly awkward note in full scale, but interesting, rare, and imaginative in miniature. If you want a truly authentic look, you'll want to string gas-carrying pipes or hoses from ceiling fixtures to gas lamps on the table.

If your family has electric lights, you may want to string some wires from various electrified appliances in the room—iron, lamp, etc.—to ceiling sockets as was often done. Again, it's not picturesque, but it's certainly comment-provoking in scale.

The Victorian era also gives you some new options as to the kinds of houses you can have. For example, during the last quarter of the nineteenth century the concept of apartment houses changed the look of the city forever. You can build several different kinds of city dwellings, from mansions like those that dotted lower Fifth Avenue in New York City to full-blown apartment houses to fashionable single-family brownstones with their basement kitchens. Midcentury and later city houses were generally narrow and perhaps three or four rooms deep. Quite another kind of housing was built in the South; along with its magnificent plantation homes, there were galleried smaller homes like those in Louisiana, described in the previous chapter. The nineteenth century also took America out West to log cabins, dugouts, and finally frame homes on dusty streets and rural muddy roads (see Chapter Six, "Special Cases").

You can add important extra touches and help establish your dollhouse in a particular time during the nineteenth century if, on the inside, you follow some of the architectural features that marked the outside of various Victorian homes. The Victorian furniture maker did, and some of the stops along the way produced intriguing elements for dollhouse interiors. For instance, the Gothic Revival which began in the 1830s and ran with diminishing intensity through the period, brought latticed diamond-paned windows, some with pointed arched tops, and a great many bay windows. The same pointed arch also adorned the openings of some Gothic fireplaces. The library and the hall were considered especially well suited to Gothic outfitting.

Also getting an early Victorian start was the Tuscan or Italianate style, which borrowed from the villas of Italy a tall square tower complete with cupolas and balconies. Tall windows, some with arched tops arranged in twos and threes, and, again, the ubiquitous bay window fit well in Italianate homes. In addition to laying out an interior that includes a square tower, the use of single-story wings and even octagonal appendages can give you some interesting and atypical (for miniaturists) room arrangements. Use interior arches and scalloped decorations and include a loggia for good measure. This also is a good choice if you are trying to avoid the gloomy look and prefer a lighter, more airy atmosphere—not unachievable despite the Victorian reputation for dungeonlike rooms.

If you are starting from scratch with a Victorian house you might consider the octagon house which was billed as a house of light. The octagon house was promoted by a man named Orson Fowler who preached its benefits—real and imagined—with a missionary zeal that inspired a fad. By the late 1850s there were at least a thousand such homes ranging from small one-story affairs

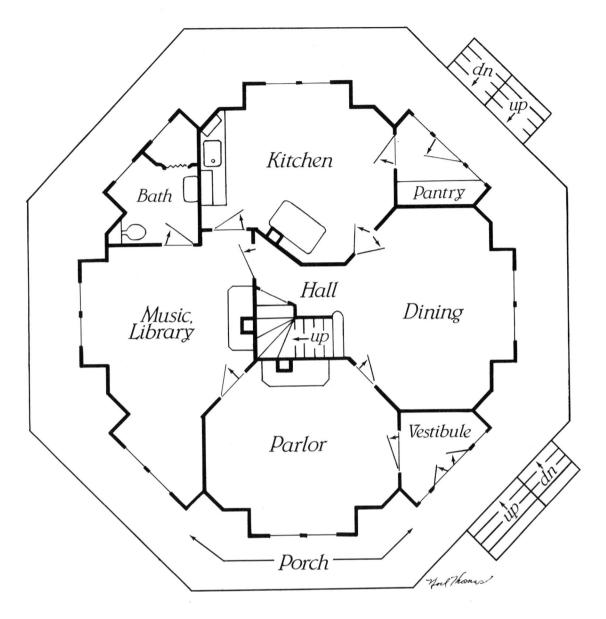

(despite Fowler's belief one story wasn't healthy) to massive temples with sixty rooms. Fowler's favorite octagon houses had tiny triangular entryways which directed visitors first to front rooms through which they eventually reached the much larger central hall with its stairway. Capping all this would be a cupola that amounted to a giant skylight opening up the house from the center. An octagon house with its odd-shaped rooms can be a happy challenge to a miniaturist. Fowler himself built a magnificent octagon near Fishkill, New York, which he lost over debts and which had to be demolished ten years after his death in 1887.

After the Civil War American enchantment with the French châteaux of the Loire Valley brought us mansard styles with their multiple dormers. An advantage to miniaturists in the mansard style is the fact that building a dollhouse with a mansard roof pro-

Here is the first-floor plan for the octagon house made by Noel and Pat Thomas. Its nooks and crannies represent a whole new challenge to furniture arrangement. It could be said that the logic of four walls (not to mention form following function) has been surrendered to the desired shape of the house. The reward for all this is an interesting interplay of shapes, a unique layout, and a great deal of fun. *Plan courtesy of Noel and Pat Thomas of Open House*

This is the late-nineteenth-century furnace in the octagon house by Noel and Pat Thomas of Open House. *Photo by Noel and Pat Thomas*

You can feel the damp in the basement of the octagon house built by Noel and Pat Thomas. This is a true study in representing the atmosphere as well as the physical aspects of a place. *Photo by Noel and Pat Thomas*

vides more attic room with a really livable upper story. If your dollhouse isn't roomy enough, you can remove the existing roof and add an entire floor, enclosing it in a new mansard roof with dormers. This will keep the house integrated on the outside, despite the fact that you can't match the house siding; the roof saves your having to make a match. Windows were often paired in such houses and interiors were elaborate.

In the 1880s and the 1890s Romanesque, a solid substantial style seen in many city townhouses, came into vogue. Arched windows and almost Moorish conceits make this the perfect late-century style to house furniture in the swollen Turkish style (discussed below).

Other post-Civil War architectural styles included the stick style, which is well adapted to seaside cottages. Many stick-style resort homes had as much space outside with their balconies, porches, and galleries as they did inside. We don't often see effective miniature seashore homes and yet a look at Cape May, New

An ingrain carpet sets off this large parlor from a late Victorian home. The eye darts from feature to feature—the Gothic windows, the telephone, the wall pocket next to the fireplace, the fringed center table, the patent platform rocker, the still-popular pillar-and-scroll clock, the Gone-with-the-Wind lamp, and the unusual chandelier mounted on what appear to be three metal cattails (to match the real cattails in the room next door). The carving on the secretary is incised as befits a machine-made piece. The doors with their white doorknobs are very plain. Barely detectable on the table is a photograph album. This room is a bastion of middle-class town life. *Courtesy of the Art Institute of Chicago; Gift of Mrs. James Ward Thorne*

This New York parlor is taken from a room in the Theodore Roosevelt birthplace. Immediately outstanding is the fine Belter furniture including the two marble console pier tables resting under mirrors on the left wall. The carpeting looks like an ingrain and the wallpaper, which adds a competing if not conflicting pattern, is an excellent example of mid- to late-nineteenth-century taste. Notice the lace curtains hanging behind the heavy draperies, the sliding door into the parlor, and the arch on the front paneled door and marble fireplace. *Courtesy of the Art Institute of Chicago; Gift of Mrs. James Ward Thorne*

Jersey, gives us dozens of really fine Victorian models which would translate well in scale. Having so much porch space may not appeal to everyone, but imagine a wide porch wrapped around three sides of a house with an assemblage of wicker settees and plant stands at one end, perhaps some cast-iron furniture or rustic outdoor items in another section, and you can see that unusual yet welcoming miniature homes can be built to suit the style.

Late Victorian exteriors were phased through the half-timber Elizabethan, a lower, more horizontal shingle style, and the potpourri Queen Anne with its festival of turrets and gables. Each allows you flexibility in dealing with the interior as do most Victorian architectural forms, and the generally conglomerate interior that we've discussed so far will work well.

Along with the intricacies of Queen Anne and other late Victorian apparitions there was in the 1880s a swing away from architectural confusion in some circles, led by the proponents of the Arts and Crafts movement. We shall examine the radically changed interiors inspired by this design shift in Chapter Six's section on the "Turn of the Century."

VICTORIAN FURNITURE

THE Victorian dollhouse gives miniature-enthusiasts an opportunity to use not only a variety of furniture pieces but also a variety

Here is a good example of the integration of styles in a room designed and built by Fran and Don Meehan. The Chippendale chairs seem right at home with the fireplace and overmantel which recall the Federal era. The corner cupboard, wallpaper, and carpet give us the Victorian flair. The fireplace is by Derek Perkins and the furniture by the Master Craftsmen of Fantastic Merchandise. *Photo courtesy of Fran and Don Meehan*

of furniture styles. It was not uncommon during much of the nineteenth century to find nearly every room in the house featuring a different style. In fact one of the cries of followers of Charles Eastlake, the influential English designer-critic of the last third of the century, was for consistency within the house itself as opposed to the prevailing eclectic atmosphere.

It is this not-always-smooth blend of styles that gives the miniature-collector so much freedom when furnishing nineteenth-century rooms and houses. It bears repeating, however, that the nineteenth century does not offer a license to throw together everything that looks vaguely as if it was made in the 1800s and call the jumble Victorian.

The most important influence on furniture during the period was the machine. In the 1830s machines began to replace humans in manufacturing. Machine-made furniture was coarser than handmade; the machine could not carve like the craftsman and we often find incised rather than delicately carved work, especially after the Civil War. The fretwork machinery of the 1850s gave a lot of mass-produced furniture an ornate turn. Machine-made furniture borrowed from previous styles and manufacturers made loose adaptations of everything from Elizabethan tables to fancy French side chairs.

Couple this new machine technology with a growing middle class and its lack of aesthetic background and you get what one historian called "untutored indulgence." For the first time large numbers of people who never had money now did. With the exuberance of youth a whole new class of people gorged on whatever the machinery could turn out. The traditionally wealthy families also became infatuated with the clumsy and falsely ornate in furniture and nearly everyone wanted the newest "look," at least until the Centennial when Victorians rediscovered their past.

There were definite styles, though, each contributing different touches to chairs, tables, beds, and case pieces. The period opens with the dénouement of the neoclassical revival, the last strains of which were played out by the mid-1840s.

In the 1830s there developed a kind of furniture called pillar-and-scroll, the first clear transition from the late Empire to the full Victorian, solidified with John Hall's 1840 design book, *The Cabinet Maker's Assistant.* In one form or another, pillar-and-scroll furniture lasted on into the twentieth century. The scrolls replaced carving as the machine replaced craftsman's hands. Pillar-and-scroll furniture was massive, often had marble tops for its tables and—lacking richly decorated surfaces—depended on mahogany and walnut veneers.

High-style rococo furniture was popular in America from the 1850s to the 1870s, although it carried through the post-Civil War period, too, in a modified form. High-style rococo was a fairly light, curvy style with cabriole legs and French feet; it was adorned with carved fruits and flowers, and seating pieces had

A typical pillar-and-scroll table from Robert Carlisle with Bohemia ware lustres from Chestnut Hill Studio. The lustres are from the collection of Constance Simone. *Photo by Ross Klavan*

This Louis XV chair was made by Donald Dube and upholstered by Linda Wexler-Dube. Note the French foot with its saucy upturned roll—also a feature of many English Chippendale designs. This chair is decidedly French in style but might have been made in the United States and would have been found in some especially fashionable American salons. Such chairs were frequently gilded as this one is.

rounded backs. Based on Louis XV furniture, rococo was possibly best exemplified in America in the furniture of John Henry Belter, whom we will discuss later.

There was also Louis XVI, which achieved popularity in the 1860s. Its gilded and ormolu-decorated style delighted wealthy Easterners, the only ones who could afford it. The style called for straight legs and lines and was elegant, and somewhat restrained by comparison with some of the more florid Victorian pieces.

Another upright style was that of the Renaissance Revival. Renaissance Revival furniture began to appear in the 1850s, although it was the 1860s before there was significant production. It was stylish until around 1875. Renaissance Revival was a decidedly vertical style given to massive pieces with rather elaborate decoration including touches of gilt and veneer. Early pieces were

Emily Good made these Renaissance Revival lady's and gentleman's chairs after chairs in her own collection. The small étagère or whatnot was also made by Mrs. Good, who crafted the collection of china and silver knickknacks. *Photo by Emily Good*

marked by heavy rich carving which was replaced later by flatter incised carving. Its rectilinear lines were accented in dressers with tall mirrors, beds with high headboards, shelved high-backed sideboards, and square or oblong seats and backs on seating furniture. Pieces bore heavy finials, columns, molding, and rounded crests and pediments. The legs on Renaissance Revival furniture were for the most part straight and slightly turned. Frequently pieces had bronze ornament and carved-leaf drawer pulls, a fairly common feature on furniture in general during the Victorian period.

The architectural manner of the Renaissance Revival was something of an echo of the earlier Gothic Revival which began in the late 1830s and persisted more or less into the 1860s. In most homes the Gothic touch was limited to a hall stand or servants' chair designed like a Gothic church with spires and pointed arches. But homes that embraced the style completely turned rooms into feasts of trefoils, pointed arches, paneled ceilings, and tracery windows. It was especially suited to libraries. As a style it never dominated the way other styles did, but its traces lingered through the century, with its motifs occasionally adapted for mass-produced furniture.

Mahagony, rosewood, and walnut were the most popular woods of the Victorian period. Black walnut and rosewood were particularly used in making chairs, the shape of which changed with the Victorian era. By the 1840s deep button-tufted upholstery was used on many pieces and chairs grew more comfortable still as the coil spring became common a decade later.

The delicate fancy chairs, increasingly popular in the West, remained in style although by the 1840s they were somewhat less finely stenciled. Boston rockers were especially common in the country and lasted into the 1890s. An armless "little Boston" sat in many bedrooms and nurseries and the famous Lincoln rocker, with its high back, curved frame, and open arms, also was found in many Victorian homes until well after Abraham Lincoln was shot sitting in one.

The proliferation of gaslight furthered the progress made by the Argand lamp, discussed in the section on Federal accessories. Largely because of the more stable lighting of the Federal era, furniture had moved from a traditional placement lining the walls to fairly fluid settings in the room. The center of this movement was usually a stove or a center table with a lamp on it. With gaslight and its better illumination these furniture arrangements became even more fixed. The result, about the middle of the nineteenth century, was the evolution of "sets" of furniture in-

Nic Nichols made the Lincoln rocker with typical Victorian antimacassar. The knitting bag was made by Franklyn J. Morley. From the collection of Jack and Shirley Bloomfield.

Here are three pieces by Emily Good, each a reproduction of a Good family heirloom. Both of the chairs are of the Lincoln rocker type of mid-nineteenth-century vintage. The original of the rocker at left is now in the collection of Mrs. Ethel Hartman. The table in the middle holds accessories by Mrs. Good including a tray of petit fours on a large white doily. *Photo by Emily Good*

Allen Martin made these caned seat pieces from Victorian era models. The rockers—for child and adult—are especially reminiscent of the mid-nineteenth century. *Courtesy of Martin's Miniatures*

cluding matching chairs, tables, and sofas. The placement of the pieces in these sets went from an initial symmetrical arrangement to the asymmetrical which became fashionable in the 1870s. By the late nineteenth century a typical large Victorian parlor might have several groupings, believed to be artistic and appearing almost like little scenes within the room. One of the things that broke up these vignettes and more fully integrated furniture in the whole room was the emergence of another new lighting development—electricity.

The most important chairs in the parlor sets were the lady's and gentleman's chairs. Immensely popular during the midcentury period, the lady's chair was an armless, upholstered chair, usually on short cabriole legs, and often with a matching tabouret, a seat-high stool that when pushed close to the chair formed a chaise longue. The gentleman's chair was a slightly larger, armed version of the lady's chair. The easy chair of the previous century, the wing chair, faded from prominence, although there were other deep, comfortable easy chairs, among them a gondola-seated armchair with leather or fabric upholstery over a curved back, seat, and arms. Other gondolas were of the less massive side-chair type.

Side chairs, individually or as part of a parlor set, followed many styles. The balloon-back side chair was still going strong in the 1880s, forty years after first achieving a prominent place in the bedroom, the parlor, and the dining room. Decorative details carved into the frame of the balloon-back or other side chairs in-

These pieces by Nic Nichols complete a typical rococo-style parlor set with a lady's and gentleman's chair and a marble-top center table. From the collection of Jack and Shirley Bloomfield.

cluded fruit and vegetable motifs and finger rolls which looked like slanted knuckles. Side chairs might follow the midcentury rococo style with curvy frames and cabriole legs, or they could be done in the more angular Renaissance Revival style. Louis XV styles featured the cabriole leg, and Louis XVI depended on the straight, turned, or fluted leg. Both, of course, recalled French influences.

The director's chair developed during the Victorian period although it never was common in homes. It was a campaign or military field piece and when adapted for home use was made with either canvas, carpet, or needlepoint slings. Swivel chairs were popular in the mid-1800s and there are several miniature versions available for use with heavy desks. Folding, convertible furniture was common beginning in the 1860s when patent chairs appeared. They were often stationary rockers on a platform and were especially popular in the 1880s.

While various revivals were influencing furniture, some bastardization of historical style brought curule chairs back, this time heavy with tassels and the carving of the Middle Ages rather than delicate like the classical curule. Egyptian motifs were used from 1802 on through the century, but Victorian interpretations were most common during the 1860s and 1870s. Chairs and other pieces bore carved or painted animal feet and gilt or brass highlights. The sphinx, the lotus, and the palmetto were among the designs used. Another historical recollection saw heavy Jacobean chairs with high backs facing many Victorian tables.

By the 1870s upholstered-back dining chairs were gaining favor and during the third quarter of the century many chair frames in the bedroom and the parlor were hidden underneath ravenous upholstery and seats made deeper to accommodate heavy springs.

In contrast to these were the Mackintosh chairs of the late nineteenth century. Designed by the Scot Charles Rennie Mackintosh, these chairs were tall, their backs sometimes five feet high, straight and angular. They were most frequently made of dark oak or painted black. Although not common here, they were important as a reflection of the dissatisfaction of many craftsmen, first in England and later in America, with the machine age and its lack of personal involvement with the product. The Arts and Crafts movement was the result: it had its roots in Britain and developed here in the late 1870s and 1880s. During the last twenty years of the nineteenth century over thirty organizations were promoting the themes of the Arts and Crafts movement in this country. They were interested in handmade furniture and often reverted to quasimedieval styles, making heavy, square chairs, settees, benches, and tables with simple joints and little surface decoration. As with almost everything, there were exceptions and on some Arts and Crafts pieces we see a more delicate touch featuring rosewood and ebony with brass and ivory inlay. Ironically,

Arts and Crafts furniture, which was to reunite the man and his work, was too expensive for the working man.

The Arts and Crafts movement foreshadowed the familiar Mission furniture and the work of Frank Lloyd Wright and his ilk. The style is examined further in Chapter Six. Also combined with Arts and Crafts was the new aesthetic awareness of people like John Ruskin and William Morris, a preface to the Art Nouveau of the 1890s which returned to natural motifs of human figures, animals, and plants. Many Art Nouveau chairs were light-colored

Platform rocker with simple turnings on a stationary base. Among other things, this rocker was designed to save wear and tear on the carpeting. The rocker is from L. M. Kenyon.

This is a Morris chair c. 1866 by Franklyn J. Morley. This type of chair was first made by William Morris in 1860 and remained popular through the first part of the twentieth century. Notice the recliner feature, controlled by the extension at the back. The leather upholstery is typical. This chair can go from the Victorian era through the years of Arts and Crafts and Mission influence. *Photo courtesy of Franklyn J. Morley*

These three pieces with their gentle
curves are quiet expressions of the
Art Nouveau style. Note the hardware
particularly. Virginia Hultberg crafted
the set.

The brass bed is an especially fine
example of the Art Nouveau style
with its wavy lines and airy aspect.
From the collection of Robert Milne
of Milne Miniatures.

with swirling, tendril-like designs. Other pieces had smoother, more open curves. Art Nouveau influences in this country were more evident in accessories—lamps for instance—than in furniture. The style was short-lived and is usually assigned the years 1890 to 1910.

Another departure from the standard heavy Victorian fare was bentwood furniture, a great deal of which went West. Although there was a bentwood chair made by Samuel Gragg early in the nineteenth century, the bentwood we think of today was developed by Michael Thonet. It was not seen much in this country until after 1850 and the celebrated bentwood rocker appeared in the 1860s.

Turning from the most innovative nineteenth-century chairs to survivors from the eighteenth century we have the Windors. Victorian types generally had thicker spindles and flatter seats than their predecessors but were still identifiable as Windsors. Arrow-backs were popular in most areas and joining the arrow-back as the Victorian period opened was a round-seated fan-back. Later, after the Civil War, we get the "firehouse" chair, a low spindle-back chair recalling the low-back Windsor of the eighteenth century.

The Windsor settee or deacon's bench, either mounted on rockers or on six to ten legs, was a standard in the country from the first years of the period until the Civil War was over. Many were stenciled and many were found on porches and in gardens. The holdover wagon-seat settee lasted until 1850—longer in the

A stained-glass panel by Dan Nyberg. The two Art Nouveau lamps are from Donna's Dollhouse. The table with Art Nouveau carving is an antique made at the turn of the century.

A mirrored hall stand and cabinet that express the straight-line construction so often favored by pre-World War I designers. The applied decoration reminds us of Art Nouveau styling. These miniatures were made early in the twentieth century.

Two chairs by Emily Good of Heirloom Replicas. At left a stenciled fiddle-back chair (c. 1840–60) with a cane seat; on the right a chair with pierced cornucopia slat and rush seat. Both chairs fall into the fancy chair category. *Photo by Emily Good*

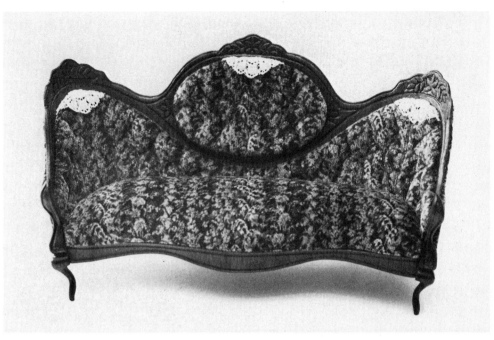

A medallion-back sofa on almost impossibly tiny cabriole legs by Nic Nichols. The rococo-style sofa has tufted upholstery and the omnipresent antimacassar, now reduced to a decorative vestige, used because it has become part of a style rather than for its practicality. From the collection of Jack and Shirley Bloomfield.

Stan Lewis made this medallion-back sofa with floral carving on the crest. This piece has traces of several types of sofas from the tête-à-tête to the chairback settee.

West—and in some rural areas farmers sat on traditional settles until after midcentury.

There was of course much fancier seating for the formal parlor and an entirely new form that appeared in the 1850s was the tête-à-tête, an intimate settee for two which often was S-shaped. Usually in a rococo style, some tête-à-têtes were part of the parlor sets as were other settees, love seats, and sofas. One of the most famous sofas was the medallion back which came to the fore in the 1850s. Still another form was the chairback sofa with a backless connecting portion. It looked like two chairs linked by a short bench.

Many sofas and settees took a special look from the celebrated designs of John Henry Belter. Working between 1844 and 1866, Belter is synonymous with deep, pierced carving on rosewood frames for chairs and sofas. This extremely ornate carving was made possible because Belter developed a special lamination process that made the wood easier to work. By his death in 1866, Belter's pieces were being made almost exclusively for the carriage trade because they had grown so expensive. A Belter parlor set, with lady's chair, gentleman's chair, side chairs and settee, is a magnificent addition to a miniature house although it is harder to acquire than the simpler forms.

The Empire Grecian sofa, in a heavier version, also made it into Victorian homes. One form was the meridienne, a short sofa that was higher on one end than the other. Late in the period the large, overstuffed Chesterfield sofa appeared. There was also another new parlor piece, the ottoman, which was a circular or octagonal sofa with a center post. It was popular after the Civil War and fit perfectly with the late-nineteenth-century fad for Turkish, Moorish, and other Oriental and Near Eastern styles—a fad that owed much to foreign exhibits at the 1876 Centennial.

Falling under the Turkish influence many Victorian families of the 1880s erected cozy corners. Plushly upholstered, these were corner sofas at right angles, often tufted, braided, and deeply fringed as were all Turkish pieces. Sometimes the cozy corner was almost an enclosed room with walls of shelves extending up from

These wonderfully expressive Victorian pieces are reproductions of antiques in the collection of Mrs. Linda Hamelsky and were made by Emily Good of Heirloom Replicas. The chair combines Renaissance Revival-style legs with a really marvelous rococo back. *Photo by Emily Good*

(Above)
Nic Nichols made these two mid-Victorian tables with marble tops. The floral arrangement on the left comes from Posy Patch Originals; the one on the right combines a plant by Wilma Thomas and a cachepot by Deborah McKnight. From the collection of Jack and Shirley Bloomfield.

(Below)
This deeply tufted, heavily fringed confection by Nic Nichols is a perfect emblem of the Turkish delights devised in the last quarter of the nineteenth century. *Photo courtesy of Nic Nichols*

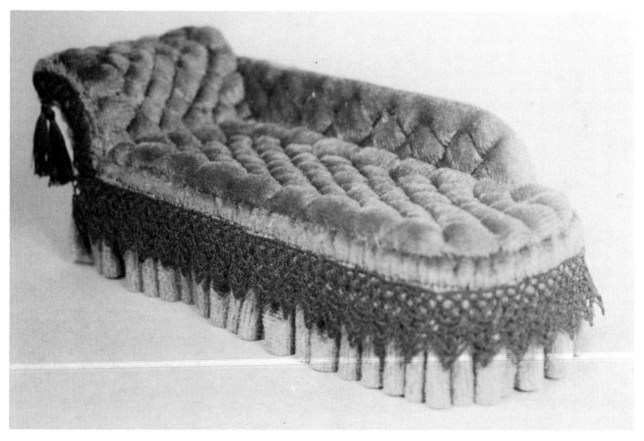

the sofa. Heavy drapery was hung where convenient on the cozy corners and oversize pillows completed the scene. Other Turkish delights included screens, small brass tray tables, and pierced or inlaid small tables.

Most Victorian tables were not so delicate, however, especially dining tables which were massive drop leafs or huge circular pedestal tables. Many Victorian parlors featured a center table as part of a parlor set. Usually these tables were heavy and circular with marble tops. As the 1870s passed, the ottoman replaced the parlor table in many fashionable homes.

During the Victorian era the tiered table used for serving dessert in colonial homes made a comeback. Additional hold-overs from previous periods included the tea table and the basket-table, a work or sewing table for ladies that had galleries surrounding its tiers. Pier tables with the heavy scrolls of the John Hall designs replaced the more delicate Federal table and the influence of John Henry Belter could be seen in richly carved center and side tables. For the first time bedside tables were routinely set next to beds. Smaller still were the pedestals which bore statues and fancy vases, particularly after the Civil War.

The lazy-susan table was a popular country piece especially in Pennsylvania, and favorite colors for it were blue and green. Another country piece was the harvest table, which we often associate with an earlier time but which was a provincial form of the nineteenth century. It was long and slim with narrow drop leaves running the length of the table.

This Wells Fargo patent desk was made by Hermania Anslinger and is in the collection of John M. and Ellen Krucker Blauer. *Photo courtesy of The Miniature Mart®*

If your dollhouse is modeled after a wealthy family home—especially if you have a Southern plantation home—consider reserving some area for the private tutelage of the children. Many youngsters learned at home and would have felt comfortable studying at this c. 1840 child's desk from the family of Emily Good who made all the items pictured here. The c. 1845 cane-seat chair is a very familiar early- to mid-Victorian type. This one is a replica of an heirloom in Mrs. Good's husband's family and is now in the collection of her sister-in-law Mrs. Ethel Hartman. *Photo by Emily Good*

Case pieces drew on earlier inspirations but again with the heaviness of the Victorian makers. The slat-top desk, out of vogue during the Federal period, returned. In 1874 the new and spectacular Wooten desk was patented. Also known as the Wells Fargo desk, it was sometimes six feet high, a complete office full of cubbyholes behind doors that themselves had more shelves and storage space. A Wooten desk won't fit every room, certainly not the bedroom of a refined lady of means, but one could go appropriately in a home office. Another, earlier desk—also massive and not for the parlor—was the partners' desk. It was a solid rectangular piece with drawers on both sides and a top large enough to serve two people. At the other end of the scale there was a plethora of small ladies' desks.

Secretaries were squared and by the end of the century nearly a foot taller than during earlier years. They often had glass doors, especially during the middle of the century and, after the Civil War, they featured cupboard doors on the bottom.

The desk by Martha Dinkel has a drop-down lid which becomes the writing surface and which hides an assemblage of pigeonholes. Its galleried top is a favorite touch in Eastlake design. Blackham's Studio produced the marble-top table. From the collection of Jack and Shirley Bloomfield.

The corner cupboard lost favor in the cities during the 1840s but remained a popular piece in the country. The Welsh dresser was found in many country kitchens and dining rooms and in city kitchens as well. Bedroom dressers were distinguished by their swinging, often tall, attached mirrors. Marble tops were popular especially during the last quarter of the century. Also in the bedroom was the familiar blanket chest with its bottom drawer, lidded top well, and bracket feet. A cheap and easy-to-produce plain chest of drawers in a golden chestnut was the preferred storage piece in bedrooms in middle-class homes.

A piece that fits in almost any Victorian bedroom is the commode. A departure from previous styles, it was a chest with room for a pitcher, chamber pots, a washbowl, and smaller toilet articles. Very often it took the form of a chest with two doors and a small drawer. It was frequently given a marble top and a splashboard. Commodes featured racks on the side for towels. The plainer lift-top commode had a well for storage in addition to the cupboard space below; it was not topped with marble and suited less affluent families. Simple washstands with a towel rack, a basin, and a lower shelf also served many nineteenth-century bedrooms. More information on this subject is given in Chapter Five.

Victorian sideboards were stout pieces, their back grown tall and often covered with mirrors. Corners were rounded and bases reached to the floor with shelves fixed to the sides or backs. In the South, up until the Civil War at least, were found the familiar sugar chests so often linked to Kentucky.

Victorian case pieces had a variety of drawer pulls including the carved-leaf pull popular from the 1860s, white porcelain knobs (usually a mark of a cheap or kitchen piece), glass knobs, which were on furniture throughout the period, and the fancy metal pulls that were added to better furniture.

In the dining room, parlor, or bedroom we find the omnipresent étagère. There are many miniature versions of the étagère or whatnot in various sizes and styles but all share the common trait: shelf space for bric-a-brac. The étagère appeared in a relatively

This sideboard, despite its batwing brasses, dates from the post-Civil War period and is a good example of how elaborate the backs of these pieces became. Notice the incised and gouged carving and the marble top. The sideboard was made by the late Woody Marceil. *Photo courtesy of Mary Pace*

167

This probably would be a good bed for a replay of "The Princess and the Pea," judging from the height of the mattress. The high-paneled back looks like a church and is done in the Renaissance Revival style. Notice how the back of the commode chest is a modified imitation of the headboard. The factories of Grand Rapids, Michigan (and other centers), turned out an endless harvest of furniture that looked just like this. Fran and Don Meehan designed and built the room; the furniture was made by the Master Craftsmen of Fantastic Merchandise. *Photo courtesy of Fran and Don Meehan*

small form with the Federal era but it was an absolute staple in Victorian homes of all areas and degrees of affluence. The words *étagère* and *whatnot* are used interchangeably although the latter usually refers to a somewhat smaller version of the piece. Miniaturists can load their étagère with all the odd small accessories that accumulate in any collection—statues, vases, and glass and china items. Many étagères were simply shelves strung together on posts but more were impressive pieces as tall as a person with mirrored backs and fancy carved shelves and supports. Glass curio cases also held the inevitable mixture of knickknacks while glass-enclosed bookcases lined many library walls.

The Victorian hall had its own distinctive appointment: a hall stand with a mirror, hooks for hats, receptacles for umbrellas and canes, and a seat that opened to hide boots. The hall stand is another item readily available in miniature, although smaller hallways may have to settle for wall-mounted or standing hat racks. Many hat racks were of metal or bentwood.

In the hallway and parlor, dining room and porch, Victorians placed plant stands holding palms, ferns, and other greenery. Late in the nineteenth century the aspidistra was so popular it gave its name to the aspidistra stand: a bamboo or imitation bamboo stand with a hole in the top in which the plant sat.

Victorians lavished attention on beds and they came in a great variety of styles. After 1850, the coil-spring mattress changed sleeping habits forever, replacing the rope-strung supports and wood slats of earlier days. The canopy bed of the colonial and Federal eras faded in popularity after about 1830, although collectors who like the look of the canopy bed can still use one in Victorian settings without violating history, certainly until the end of the Civil War. Posts generally were wider and more heavily carved and, in the South particularly, the half-tester was popular. The half-tester featured draperies hanging from a canopy that extended only from the posts at the head of the bed. In the South, mosquito netting was used on many beds. Another bed that was

H. Preston Cochran made this tall-post bed based on a Maryland model.
Photo by Russel Werneth

A Victorian bed with ball finials on the posts by Hermania Anslinger. As was frequently the case, the carving on the posts at the foot of the bed is much more detailed than that on the posts at the head of the bed. From the collection of Constance Simone. *Photo by Ross Klavan*

more popular in the Victorian homes of the South than the North was the sleigh bed of Empire inspiration.

The single bed was more common during the Victorian period than earlier and even three-quarter-size beds were used. Twin beds grew in importance during the 1840s and beyond and by the 1880s were made in iron and brass. Other metal beds began appearing in the 1850s. Something called a cannonball bed was stylish from the beginning of the period at least until midcentury. The cannonball was a four-poster with turned posts and large ball-shaped finials. It had a shaped headboard and nonmatching blanket-rail at the foot. Just as sideboards and étagères grew tall to match the high Victorian ceilings, so did the headboards. By the end of the period, some headboards were eight feet high, heavily carved with pointed, arched, or flat tops over solid, carved, or paneled fields.

The Victorian era gave us a special bed style that was totally new and quite different from anything before, the spool bed. The primary feature of the spool bed was the spool-turned post. At first these posts were perpendicular to the cross railings and of the same height head and foot. About 1850 the posts started to curve to join the crosspieces, thus creating the Jenny Lind bed. Tall-post spool beds were especially popular in Texas and the South, the posts five and half to seven feet high. The "hired man's" bed was often a spool-turned bed with slats supporting whatever minimal mattress was laid. Spool-turned bedside tables are a good accompaniment for the miniature spool bed.

The brass bed with its well-suited and elaborate dressing is by Barbara Bunce of Butterflies and Buttercups. From the collection of Jack and Shirley Bloomfield.

Franklyn J. Morley made this child's crib (c. 1850) with stick-and-ball turnings in the sides. It is of the Renaissance Revival style, epitomized by the tall headboard with its curved top crest. *Photo courtesy of Franklyn J. Morley*

(Above)
Emily Good made both the adult four-poster and the child's crib. The high-post bed has Jenny Lind styling in its turned bottom rail and dates from the mid–1850s. The crib is c. 1865–70. *Photo by Emily Good*

(Below)
Jenny Lind bed from Carlisle Miniatures. *Photo courtesy of Robert Carlisle*

From the 1850s to the 1880s many country and common bed-rooms were filled with cottage furniture. Made of cheaper woods, these beds and tables were often spool-turned, but the most common identifying mark of cottage furniture is its plain, light enameled surface with either hand-painted or transfer-printed floral or scenic designs. Cottage furniture was mass-produced and a bedroom suite in the cottage style is an ideal addition to a middle-class dollhouse.

The relatively minor Elizabethan Revival of the 1840s to 1860s featured spiral twist turnings and needlework upholstery and was closely related to the spool turning of the cottage furniture, although strictly Elizabethan Revival furniture is somewhat more grand.

In general there was a lot of painted furniture including some pieces with geometric or free-sweeping designs, simulated grained effects, and scenics. There was a certain primitive look about these pieces that takes them far away from the grander painted and gilded city furniture.

Among other furniture fashions that deserve special note are the animal-derived pieces that appeared after the Civil War. These include chairs made of antlers, elephant-leg umbrella stands, and chairs with animal-hide upholstery fastened to wood, metal, or horn frames. These styles lasted into the twentieth century and were popular in the East and the West, where there was more of a reason to use them because there were more buffalo, elk, and other large animals available.

Wicker enjoyed a vogue after the Civil War and by the 1880s

This set of horn furniture is in a style made in Texas c. 1885. It was expensive and rustic in name only. Susanne Russo made these pieces.

Wicker furniture by Iphegenia Rose is pretty, delicate, and very busy. Furniture like this was extremely popular in the late nineteenth century and early twentieth century. *Courtesy of Dearring-Tracy, Ltd.*

most fashionable homes had at least one or two items—settee, table, or chair—made of wicker or rattan. Cast-iron furniture was usually kept outdoors, although during the 1850s it came inside, often taking the form of hat racks or beds, sometimes chairs or settees. The material lent itself to a rustic interpretation that imitated raw wood and we find chairs and tables mounted on iron frames cast to look like tree branches. Other rustic furniture was made of wood, its chief aim to look like something in nature.

In poor country homes furniture was nearly as sparse as during colonial days, the most common pieces including corner cupboards, dough trays, dry sinks, hutch tables, plain chairs, beds, and tables. The most common wood used was pine.

Miniaturists who want to integrate some of their colonial pieces into a Victorian home can use the Centennial Exposition of 1876 as their excuse. The Centennial awakened interest in the eighteenth century, although absolute fidelity to the older styles did not always follow. The exposition inspired a great many pseudo-colonial sofas and chairs but it also inspired a small group of Victorians who began collecting the real thing. It is to these people that modern collectors owe a great deal for they preserved furniture that would have been lost forever. It can be said that the current antiques craze began during the last quarter of the nineteenth century.

The 1876 Centennial Exposition also brought us the Japanese craze. After the exhibition, real or imitation bamboo suddenly became very fashionable and a large amount of Oriental-style furniture and accessories, including thousands of bamboo-turned chairs, found its way into better homes. Japanese tiles were very popular as decorative additions to furniture and by the 1880s tiles in general covered many pieces, Japanese and otherwise.

Beginning in the 1860s, the Englishman Charles Eastlake tried to reform the decorative arts and in doing so resorted to what he at least envisioned as a medieval style that relied largely on straight lines and shallow or incised carving. In this country the Eastlake style was the rage from the early 1870s to about 1890. Interestingly enough, Eastlake himself was known to eschew the American interpretation of his precepts, and indeed in America, "Eastlake-style" often meant only that the manufacturer produced something square that he had the presence of mind to call "Eastlake." Hallmarks of the style here include the same geomet-

A family of bears romps on a hat rack and an ashtray by Susan Gentsch. These pieces fit in a man's study, a game room, a lodge, or even a heavy city hallway. They seem especially suited for the rustic furniture vogue of the mid- to late 1800s. *Courtesy of Susanne Russo*

This late Eastlake-inspired room by John Blauer also brings us some Art Nouveau touches in the two sensuous statuettes, the easel with its flourishing crest, and the clock. The furniture is Eastlake with horsehair upholstery, oak finish, and short spindles. The fireplace is decorated with tiles as was the fashion late in the century. The wallpaper was inspired by the Arts and Crafts movement, the cattails repeated in a vase on the center table. Despite the late date, the pilasters on the walls recall earlier classical motifs. A gas lamp hangs from the ceiling and an unusual straight-back chair that harks back to the Arts and Crafts movement stands at the left near the fireplace. *Courtesy of The Miniature Mart®. Photo by Ellen Krucker Blauer*

ric construction and incised carving of the English prototype along with decorative turned spindles and galleried shelves on cupboards and mantelpieces, inlay and inset tiles, gingerbread aprons on tables, chamfered edges, and natural oak finishes with occasional painted models with black surface and gold trim. Manufacturers often used leather upholstery, heavy hinges, and drop handles on case pieces.

Among collectors of antique miniatures, there is some interest in Biedermeier furniture. It was a German style and because the Germans were such prolific producers of dollhouse furniture it is not surprising that here in this country attention was paid to the style despite the fact that it was not a distinctly American fashion. Biedermeier was a middle-class style, a sort of "homied up" Empire if you will. It was often painted in green, blue, or brown and featured painted detail in black and gold. Biedermeier was made in light bland woods as well as mahogany and fruitwoods and carried relatively simple lines. Dates are disputed but it appears to have closed out the Federal period and lasted until the Civil War.

ACCESSORIES

WHEREAS considerable restraint is needed when placing accessories in colonial homes, less is needed for Federal era dollhouses and still less in Victorian houses. This is not to say collectors have carte blanche with the nineteenth century, but they have greater license because of the sheer number of objects in the home as well as their variety.

Victorians are thought by twentieth-century collectors to have been enamored of clutter and the reputation is deserved although with some qualification. In general, accessories took on a more frivolous nature as the century progressed. Frivolous does not mean valueless; it only means that during the early years most things seen "lying about" would be things you could *use*, like a lamp, a cooking implement, or sewing materials. But with more money, time, and a greater inclination to "decorate" on the part of homemakers, Victorian rooms became more crowded with objects meant only to please the senses like those famous knickknacks. Again as a general guide, the height of the cluttered look, which we usually associate with the Victorians, came during the 1880s. By the late 1890s there was a reaction against such clutter (even earlier among the avant-garde) and it diminished by the turn of the century.

Contributing most to the crammed-full look was the profusion of knickknacks found in the home. Étagères were packed with treasures of the day. This complicated the scene not only because there were so many of them arrayed together, but because they were often so complicated in and of themselves. Consider the frequent arrangements of wax flowers or the collections of shells, sometimes made into objets d'art by leisured ladies. Imagine then a glass dome placed over these trifles and you have but the beginning of an assemblage that cries out for attention. Everywhere there were statuettes and figures of plaster or ceramic or bronze or marble. Many were sculpted to tug at the heart of the sentimental Victorian—by presenting either a scene of young lovers or a dramatic vignette torn from the history books. There even were statuettes grouped to represent incidents in everyday life as with the famous Rogers groups manufactured by John Rogers and popular from 1860 to 1890. Literary figures were evoked in small bronze statues as were heroes of ancient and recent history. Many of the commemorative busts swathed in classical drapes would have been an embarrassment to the men they honored. Presiding over these there was often a blackamoor or two who might bear a sumptuous candelabrum.

Victorians took an interest in archaeology, sometimes to the point of obsession. In fact overanxious investigation ruined many grave sites. We find the spoils littering table and shelves in the form of fossils, figures, geodes, ornamental fragments, and other

An ageless piece from China that would look very much at home in a Victorian parlor or porch. This is a Chinese fishbowl with a stand. The stand is by Donald C. Buttfield; the dish by Deborah McKnight. From a New York collection.

bits and pieces of the past. As if to prove that two are better than one, and three better than two, Victorians were constantly massing items together for the most impressive display. A half-dozen or so witch balls (colored glass balls) would sit in a bowl in the middle of the table. And if one possession could somehow make it necessary to add another, so much the better. Take for example the watch, which demanded a watch holder. The watch holder hung on the wall or sat on the outside table. It might be anything from an elaborate hook to a tiny cathedral ready to guard the gentleman's huge pocketwatch through the night. A gentleman also might need a snuffbox just as a lady would need a dressing table full of delicate perfume bottles and potpourri jars. The boudoir also was home for a range of bandboxes and hatboxes in cardboard or thin wood, often highly decorated. Ladies' hatboxes were at the height of their popularity from the second quarter through the midcentury years.

The same lady who lived among the bottles and boxes also might devote some part of her day to adding to the family's store of objects by creating some of her own. Many Victorian women learned to do quillwork, making delicate flowers out of paper. In the Midwest a similar kind of craft gave us the grain wreath, an arrangement of dried grass formed into flowers and framed under glass.

In the 1880s grand homes adopted suits of armor to lend dignity to their halls as arrangements of peacock feathers lent color and delight to the parlors. Birds complete with feathers chirped from fancy wood, metal, and wicker birdcages. The birdsong was captured, too, in music boxes that were great favorites with Victorian collectors.

Tabletops held albums, first carrying pages of verse and drawings, later crammed with the severe photographs of the day. The first photographs were of course daguerreotypes, perfected in 1839. Often the daguerreotype was nestled in velvet and protected by a decorative cover. Development of the daguerreotype spelled the end of the itinerant painter traveling from place to place to do primitive portraiture, although such vagabonds were not cut down in one fell swoop. Similarly, silhouettes slowly fell from favor as photography made the drawing and cutting of the small shadowed likenesses obsolete.

Victorians saw the fruits of a range of artistic techniques including etchings, lithographs, oils, and watercolors in realistic, Romantic, and Impressionist styles. The most significant advances in nineteenth-century American art followed the Civil War as did a rage for Japanese prints and Japanese accessories in general; fans and screens were added to many parlors. Samplers had slipped in popularity after the 1830s but there were still a lot of needlework mottoes framed and hung in Victorian homes. Hanging anything in a Victorian home was an exercise more in finding wall space than in finding an appropriate background. Pictures,

These accessories could grace any home. The painting of the hunt was done by Linda Wexler-Dube and could well have stood in a parlor or library on an easel just as it's presented here. The china cachepot and stand are from Lionel and Ann Barnard and hold an airy fern from Posy Patch Originals. Braxton Payne did the other plant which is in a cachepot by Deborah McKnight. The plants and their stands are from the collection of Jack and Shirley Bloomfield.

some suspended from long cords, hung side by side, often in ogee-molded frames or, especially after 1850, in massive gilded ones. Family portraits, charcoal sketches, photographs, pastoral oils, and flowery watercolors shared the same walls or even floor space. It wasn't unusual, especially late in the century, to find pictures standing propped against a wall. The famous Currier and Ives prints appeared during the era, but while they hang in the White House today, in the nineteenth century they were the common man's art, found in the parlors of middle-class homes, hotels, and other public places. Between 1840 and 1900 some 7,000 plates were made, not all with Currier's name, however, because he did not become a partner until the 1850s.

Practically every sitting room had its easel with a painting propped against it. The easel was often as not also draped with fabric adding, as was the Victorian wont, just one more irresistible adornment.

Late in the era, during the Turkish craze, many walls flashed with Oriental knives and sabres and a further adventuresome note was struck in a number of gentlemen's studies where a pair of crossed snowshoes testified to a vital spirit. More delicate were

The two clocks pictured here were made by Kent Halsted and span the Victorian era. The clock on the left is in a case with an ogee molding and dates to the 1840s. The clock on the right is from the 1880s and has some Eastlake detail in its incised carving. *Courtesy of Mini-Fab*

the wall pockets, often in needlework, that hung in various rooms holding papers, letters, or even sewing equipment.

Clocks hung on the wall, sat on tables, and stood on floors and shelves. Grandfather clocks—and the Victorians were the first so to refer to them—continued to be used. Smaller clocks became more prominent, for instance in the form of the carved oak and walnut shelf clocks that are such staples of today's antique shops. The famous Gothic steeple clock, one of many wooden-case shelf clocks, came in during the 1840s to be followed shortly by the beehive clock. No longer were clocks the exclusive luxury of the wealthy as the trend toward mass manufacture which began in the Federal era put clocks within the reach of simpler homes.

Victorian lighting went through many changes over the years. Some lighting tools survived from more than a hundred years earlier. For instance, the betty lamp still shone in the Midwest in the 1870s and in farm and frontier homes through to the end of the period.

Candles gave a soft albeit limited light to some homes and were seen frequently in the bedrooms of houses that had more advanced lighting in public rooms. The famous dolphin candlestick graced homes from the beginning of the era to about 1870. Victorian candelabra were often lavish with bases of human or animal figures in opulent gilding. Candelabra of glass, metal, or china were often used *en suite* with two or more matching holders, perhaps a wall sconce, a tabletop candelabrum and a hanging branch.

It's been estimated that until kerosene appeared, the most

common form of illumination remained the candle, but most early Victorians of any means resorted to oil lamps. The Argand lamp of the previous period set the stage for a variety of Victorian lamps, which improved as the fuel and technology improved. Lamps often were sold in multiples and it was stylish to deck the mantel with lamps in twos and threes. Oil lamps of the day ranged from simple glass- or metal-reservoir fixtures to elaborate crystal and colored glass affairs dripping lustres of cut glass. Pairs of lustres were especially popular on midcentury mantels. Astral lamps were favorites of the affluent early Victorians. Like their Federal predecessors, the Victorian astrals were valued because they did not throw heavy shadows. Although styles varied, a typical astral lamp had a pinched-top glass shade on a columnlike base made of brass or some other metal. Many had one or two arms projecting from the base. The green-shaded student lamp, popular from the 1870s, was of this kind.

Many Victorian dollhouses are replete with Gone-with-the-Wind lamps; these are popularly associated with the Civil War era but in fact the name is a misnomer—the elegant flowered-globe style did not come into fashion until 1880.

Through the period, glass lamps came in a variety of sizes, shapes, and colors including red, green, blue, amber, brown, and purple. Lamps might have brass, bronze, or other metal bases and shades of glass, metal, or fabric. Many shades, particularly on hanging lamps, were fringed with lustres.

The elaborate candelabra is by Phyllis Tucker of the Happy Unicorn who entwined the base in foliage. The china three-tiered server from Paul McNeely is emblematic of the fussy tableware that was popular at the time. The small tabletop blackamoor is a holdover from the previous era. Note the Federal eagle crowning the piece which is from Eugene Kupjack.

There were also lanterns ranging from pierced tin boxes to fancy glass inverted domes sparkling enough for a front hallway. Hanging lamps generally had smoke bells suspended above them to protect the ceiling from the inevitable smudges.

Kerosene lamps became immediate favorites after 1860. They were usually larger than oil lamps, and had tall glass chimneys. They were cheap enough so that at last there could be a lamp in every room—even in the homes of those who were not so well-to-do. Kerosene was phased out in the cities by about 1900 but was still used in rural areas long after that. Lamps fueled by oil and kerosene were quick to get dirty and the daily cleaning and filling was a messy job. You might be interested in arranging a vignette around this—gathering all your lamps on a kitchen table and perhaps arranging other parts of the house to represent the daily "once-over" with such items as feather dusters and stove black.

To go with the lamps there was a match holder, a utilitarian receptacle of glass, wood, metal, or china which hung within reasonable reach of lamps that had to be lit. Match holders were also mounted next to stoves and fireplaces.

In addition to gas table lamps and wall sconces, gas chandeliers—gasoliers—were popular (in fact more so than chandeliers had been during the age of candles) and were installed in all sorts of rooms including those in which there would not have been a chandelier in previous times. The gasoliers came with the earliest gas service but their peak popularity extended from about 1875 to the First World War. Gasoliers were maintained with the help of pulleys which allowed them to be raised and lowered. An interesting by-product of the enthusiasm for the gasolier was a surge in popularity of *oil*-fueled hanging fixtures.

A distinction between the electric light fixtures and earlier gaslight fixtures—which often look the same otherwise—is the downward turn of the arms that bore the light bulbs from wall sconces, ceiling fixtures, or table lamps. Oil and gaslight, by their nature, depended on fixtures that ended in upturned burners that did not spread the light as effectively as the electrical devices. The inverted gas burner turned gaslight downward, too, but it was not developed until the very end of the century. Its development gave gaslight a resurgence in the early twentieth century. Many earlier lamps were eventually converted to electric lamps.

In this discussion of light bear in mind that during the Victorian period rooms were much dimmer than what we are used to. The light—from the candle to the electric bulb—simply wasn't as powerful as what we have now.

Federal and colonial dishware including redware and other rough potteries continued to be used. The Victorian era was also the heyday of the gray stoneware trimmed in cobalt blue that is so popular among collectors of country things today. During the period Rockingham (Bennington) ware (see Chapter Three), with its mottled, often tortoise-shell glaze, was seen everywhere. Good

PLATE 16: These are tiles copied from the nineteenth-century creations of the Minton Company. The animal-figured tiles depict Aesop's fables. From the Steak Family.

PLATE 17: Sabre-leg chair with eagle splat by Ibes and Annabell Gonzalez of Miniatures by Ibes. The wallpaper is "Winterberry Document #1," a late eighteenth-century style. It is a Katzenbach and Warren, Inc. Williamsburg wallpaper in miniature by Millie August Miniatures, Inc.

PLATE 18: Two Federal chairs (*right*) from Miniatures by Ibes. The wallpaper is "Jasperware" from the Schumacher Wedgewood Collection by Millie August Miniatures, Inc.

PLATE 19: This dower chest (*right*) by Jim Ison is of a type common throughout the nineteenth century. It is dated 1815 and monogrammed, as was the custom. The stylized tulips remind us of the Pennsylvania-Dutch influence. Lee-Ann Chellis-Wessel of Demi-tasse Miniatures made the figures drawn from chalkware models of the nineteenth century, including the very popular "compote" type in the midst of the people and animals. Chalkware pieces like these were of molded plaster painted in vivid colors. Called the "poor man's Staffordshire," chalkware figures were often sold by peddlers from at least the late eighteenth century.

PLATE 20: These two pieces of furniture (*left*) are sparkling examples of painted furniture popular in the early to mid-nineteenth century. Jim Holmes made the New England table (c. 1825–40) as well as the cupboard which echoes the painted decoration known to have been used in Vermont (c. 1825–35). The basket was made by Roberta Partridge of the Bird House and the dried grass came from Dover Miniatures. Lee-Ann Chellis-Wessel made the pottery pieces including a blackware coffee pot (c. 1825), a chalkware cat, a redware pitcher, a Pennsylvania-Dutch sgraffito tea caddy (1800–30), a spongeware pitcher, and a spot-painted small pitcher (1810–20).

PLATE 21: (*above*) The sink is from Jim Holmes, the table from Barbara Davis of Country Cottage Miniatures, the fruit from Wise Miniatures, and the copper sifter from Dover Miniatures. Crockery is by Lee-Ann Chellis-Wessel of Demitasse Miniatures, except for the dish in the sink, which was done by Carolyn Nygren Curran.

PLATE 22: A serenade in blue (*below*) for two young girls sharing an Empire bedroom and all the fancy dreams that fit the room and the era. This room is in Madelyn Cook's Lagniappe. *Photo by Jim Cook*

PLATE 23: This is a version of General U.S. Grant's dining room in the Galena, Illinois, house where he spent part of his private life. It is a melange of the kind of late Victoriana that might be found in the home of the sturdy midwestern middle class. Note particularly the mammoth storage unit in the corner and the typical accessories from the shells and fruit-under-glass arrangement on the mantel to the plethora of table servers including cruets and covered butter dish. The lighting fixtures include matching kerosene lamps on the mantel and a large chandelier over the table. The rather simple cane seat chairs seem almost to clash with the heavy draperies with their gilt pediments and the black (possibly *papier mâché*) tilt-top table at left. The room was made by Kupjack Studios of Park Ridge, Illinois. *Photo by Jay Kupjack*

PLATE 24: This chair and marble-top table by Stan Lewis are the very epitome of Belter-style furniture.

PLATE 25: A study in blue (*right*) featuring some delicate pieces. Mary Grady O'Brien made the washstand, based on one made in Maine in 1829 which is in the Henry Ford Museum. She also made the small chest which was inspired by a New England piece (c. 1820–40) now found at Historic Deerfield. The hat is from Susanne R. Strickland; the flowers by Rosemary Dyke; and the wallpaper is "Hospitality," from the Schumacher Collection, by Millie August Miniatures, Inc.

PLATE 26: Center table (*above*) by Hermania Anslinger. The rug was worked by Marie Friedman in silk thread in a pattern from Mini Magic Carpet. Marie Friedman also made the cup and saucer. The astral lamp was made by Ellen Krucker Blauer of the Miniature Mart®. The open book is from Chestnut Hill Studio and is from the collection of Constance Simone, as are the lamp and table. *Photo by Ross Klavan*

PLATE 27: Guy and Tom Roberts created this late-Victorian amalgam (*right*) focused on the tiled Eastlake fireplace in the parlor. Notice the exotic wallpaper and feathers massed in a vase. *Photo by Ellen Krucker Blauer*

PLATE 28: This bedroom by
Tom and Guy Roberts gives
us an example of the rustic
style with the chair
constructed to look as
though it were made from
tree branches. *Photo by Phillip
F. McPherson*

PLATE 29: Turn-of-the-century kitchen by Tom and Guy Roberts. *Photo by Phillip F. McPherson*

PLATE 30: Through the window we see the paneled parlor of an eighteenth-century home built by Edward Norton for Rose Barell (*above*). The Martha Washington chair by Roger L. Gutheil, Inc., puts us in the Federal period although the fielded paneling indicates the house itself may be earlier.

PLATE 31: A back-porch laundry and storage room (*left*) by Tom and Guy Roberts. The washtub and wringer were made by the late Chris Mickey of the Miniature Mart®. *Photo by Phillip F. McPherson*

PLATE 32: Here is an array of Victorian pieces (*above*) by Kent Halsted against a background of wallpaper from the Schumacher in Miniature Collection, by Millie August Miniatures. The pattern is "Pennington."

PLATE 33: Victorian fussiness at its height (*below*) in a room built and outfitted by Nic Nichols of Nic's Creative Workshop. Some special details here are the molding designed for hanging pictures, the shawl-like cloth cast over the center table, and the fringed mantelpiece visible in the room off to the right. The room is in the collection of the Miniature Museum of Kansas City. *Photo by Warren Fowler*

domestic porcelain was available after the Civil War which meant that more people had porcelain dinner sets. The less fine but still lovely creamware and other ceramic porcelain substitutes also filled Victorian homes. Blue remained a favorite color and the famous Flow Blue with its clouded effect came onto the popular markets after 1825. You have a wealth of patterns from which to choose. The designs are much less restricted than before when most good dinnerware was trimmed rather simply with red, green, or blue rims. By the last quarter of the nineteenth century

Items in this photo span the nineteenth century against a background of Millie August wallpaper which was copied from Theodore Roosevelt's childhood home in New York City. The hanging light fixture is from Illinois Hobbycraft. It represents electric light with its downturned globes (or possibly the later improved gaslight fixture). At the other end of the century is the double-wick camphene lamp by Studio B. Such lamps were dangerous because of the volatility of the fuel. The pretty Victorian cast-iron fireplace is especially suited to a bedroom with its delicate proportions. It is from Sussex Crafts. On the mantel there is a Meissen china piece copied by Robert Olszewski. Meissen, sometimes called Dresden, was a good china imported from Germany. Its "best" period was the mid-eighteenth century.

china painting was a fad producing a lot of dizzyingly decorative dishes. In the 1880s the homey nesting hen in pottery or glass was fashionable along with other animal motif dishes.

Glassware ran from plain tumblers to marvelous etched and cut patterns. American Bohemia ware with its cut and colored glass was in vogue from the 1840s. The famous Sandwich (Massachusetts) glass factory opened in 1835 and two years later its owners saw the possibilities in the new molding process then being perfected. The result was the pressed glass with which we identify the era.

Pressed glass carried through the entire Victorian era in some 2,500 patterns, including the very lacy effect of the 1830s and 1840s. The often-reproduced hobnail glass made its appearance in the 1850s and was especially popular during the 1880s. Also enjoying late popularity was milk glass which is reproduced in miniature in both plastic and real glass.

The end of the period saw development of the spectacular art ware exemplified by Tiffany glass. Although not the first such, the Tiffany glass experiments, begun in the 1870s, were the most famous. The illustrious Favrile glass they produced was a highlight of the 1880s and beyond.

During the last quarter of the nineteenth century commemorative pressed-glass platters and pitchers in a variety of colors became popular. In fact color was a wonderful detail about Victorian glass: not only was there a quantity of plain and exotic clear glass, there were pieces in every color of the rainbow and sometimes in combinations. Fancy glass decanters, cruets, and all other manner of exhibition glassware dotted sideboards in Victorian homes throughout the country.

The glass cruet sets shared sideboard billing with metalware of all sorts, too. Silver plate and Britannia ware were much used

This assortment of Victorian glassware was made by Ferenc Albert. From left to right, Diamond Thumbprint decanter and pitcher (c. 1860); Boston and Sandwich Company clear decanter typical of those made throughout the century; and an old English hobnail decanter and goblets (c. 1880). What these pieces illustrate, in addition to the considerable artistry of the craftsman, is that it is important to get seemingly small details right in order to ensure an authentic look.

in this country, the latter especially until the Civil War. Pewter was not so popular although it was produced at least until the war. You would be more likely however to find painted tinware than pewter as the art of decorating toleware had turned into an industry. Victorian hostesses relied heavily on plated ware and factories churned out elaborate patterns in hollow and flatware. A good addition to the miniature dining room is a silverplated ice water pitcher swinging in its own bracket. Silver styles were both angular and rococo. Repoussé, initiated during the previous era, was still produced and flower and vegetable designs were applied to silver of all types. Some tea services had two teapots along with a coffeepot or urn, a sugar bowl, creamer, and waste bowl. Afternoon tea was still a ritual in some homes but less so than in colonial households. The important thing is that now even the poorer country folk had the advantage of, if not china and silver and crystal, at least a somewhat acceptable compromise.

The less affluent aped high society in other ways, too, inundating their sofas with fringed pillows. Fringed shawls hung over tables and chairbacks and there were rugs thrown over tables as there had been in the seventeenth century. Many modern collectors will remember being in the home of an older relative (or perhaps even a young couple on a restoration binge!) sitting in sofas and chairs protected with embroidered or crocheted antimacassars. These swatches originally kept the backs of chairs from being soiled by the macassar oil men used to dress their hair.

With all miniaturized fabric, the difficulty is to get the material to lay right or, in the case of curtains and draperies, hang right. The Victorian dollhouse gives you plenty of space to experiment because its full-size ancestor was swathed in drapery. We've already seen it on furniture and easels and of course the Victorian dining-room table with its tablecloth. Turning to the window, we might need two or three different materials to achieve a properly enveloping look. The typical Victorian window wore a lace slip, a filmy curtain hanging under the heavier drapery which might be made of tapestry, velvet, or damask. The lace curtain showed when the drapery was tied back, usually with matching fabric or a cord with fringe and tassels.

Topping the drapery we might find a valance or lambrequin of the same or different fabric. Cornices like great gilded frames slung themselves over window tops. Deep colors were favored for draperies as were heavy materials. The heaviest materials came down in summer, however, to be replaced by the lighter cotton or silk, perhaps in some instances not to be replaced at all. There were some windows that did not have the formal valance or lambrequin but were curtained with panels that hung from rods. Eastlake preferred this treatment to the fancier styles and his favorite curtain rod extended beyond the window frame. Its spear-shaped tips made it an ornament in itself. Victorians, besides obscuring their windows with draperies and swags and festoons of voluminous material, also developed the shade. The shade roller much as we know it was perfected in 1864 which gave great impetus to the manufacture of shades. The Roman shade which pulled up to a bunched crinkle at the top had preceded the roller shade by many years, but it can't be decorated with pictures as the roller shade can. Miniature windows would do well now and then to show off a decorated shade because they were very common and bore designs from the unskilled to the highly artistic. Scenics were especially popular but you can include flowers and free-form patterns as well.

Windows weren't the only openings that were festooned however. As mentioned earlier, curtains often separated rooms and trimmed archways. Like draperies they were heavy in winter, often lighter in summer. Valance-like hangings also dropped from radiators and fireplaces, some of which were covered with what looked like altar cloths.

The fireplace itself probably held a coal grate or brass andirons. Fenders with sides often were used as were fire screens. The latter were borrowed from an earlier day but were finished in the Victorian manner with turned members in the frame and heavy needlework designs. There were even some glass fire screens. When a coal fire was in order, as was the case more and more during the nineteenth century, the fireplace was mated with a coal hod, sometimes painted in a gaudy design. During the summer we still find fireboards sealing unused fireplaces. Alternatively, a housekeeper might put an arrangement of flowers in the fireplace opening, especially late in the period. Of course by the late Victorian era, fireplaces were out of fashion in many homes and were either gone altogether or bricked up. Bricking up a min-

Rosemary Hansen did the needlework on this Kent Halsted fire screen. It's definitely a Victorian piece and because of its spiral turnings would be especially comfortable in a home with Elizabethan-style furniture.

iature fireplace is simple enough to do with a few scale bricks and it could produce an interesting effect.

At the hearth we find the hearth rug which started a fashion for scatter rugs that lasted through the Victorian era. Hooked rugs, which entered Federal era homes toward the end of the period, remained favorites although they lost some of their unique character during the last third of the century when businessmen started turning out commercial patterns; this meant that the lady of the house no longer had to invest much imagination in the enterprise. Hooked and braided rugs on painted floors were common prior to 1850; after that the middle class embraced the Kidderminster or ingrain carpet in both appealing and not-so-appealing florals. Carpeting was bound to spread because in 1839 the steam-operated loom started making it available in some form to even modest homeowners. Imported Aubusson carpets, ravishing Orientals, along with the Axminister and Brussels, still softened the steps of visitors to wealthy homes. Some Victorian decorators presaged the layered look of recent years by slinging an animal skin complete with head over a massive Oriental. That was particularly fashionable after the Civil War with the polar bear rug a special favorite of the 1890s.

Miniaturists who want to carry authenticity to the ultimate degree or who are thrilled with knowing some secret decorating facet of their dollhouses others may miss, might want to toy with undermatting. For Victorians undermatting was usually made of paper or straw. The trick is to match scale so the rug itself doesn't look bulky. Carpeting for stairs is not always easy to perfect, but if you are going to attempt it, you may be helped by two facts: Victorians often used stair rods of brass or wood which make it easier for you to anchor your carpet; and, even in nice homes, the stair carpeting sometimes only went as far as the downstairs eye could see. Eastlake would have objected to such tactics which would have seemed like cheating merely to impress visitors. He also disliked wall-to-wall carpeting and though he approved of "Turkey" rugs, he was very much opposed to the big floral designs so popular in most Victorian homes. In fact, tiled floors, especially in hallways, were popular with Eastlake followers. During the last quarter of the nineteenth century, rugs replaced larger carpeting to a great extent. To make exposed flooring look more impressive, some homeowners laid wooden borders or fixed oilcloth borders of simulated wood design between the rug and the wall. As with draperies, summertime often saw carpets come up in favor of plain or straw-matted floors. (See page 69 for a related discussion.)

Less than ten years after the steam loom put carpeting in middle-class homes, the sewing machine made more clothing available to more people. Elias Howe demonstrated a perfected machine in 1845, but it wasn't until 1858 that he had a practical

A homey aura hangs over the high-button shoes by Sylvia Rountree. The sewing machine comes from the collection of Marie Friedman, and the tray was painted by Mary Grady O'Brien. *Photo by Ross Klavan*

Kent Halsted made the lovely little Victorian footstool that was covered by Rosemary Hansen's needlepoint. Notice the similarity between the base of the footstool and the base of the watch stand, which was also made by Kent Halsted. Halsted made the zeotrope too, an 1880s moving-picture machine (spin the metal top to see the pictures move). The stool and watch stand date to the 1890s. The hats, created by Suzanne R. Strickland, are also late-Victorian styles. The plumed hat was popular in the 1880s and 90s while veiled styles like the hat on the right were fashionable from the 1870s to the turn-of-the-century.

machine going. There was a lot of patent infringement between then and 1870 as sewing machines proliferated.

Other conveniences that dawned in the Victorian day included the typewriter, which was developed in the 1840s but was not practical until the mid-1870s. Even then it didn't catch on right away and the typewriter boom didn't come until the 1880s. The Bissell sweeper, which looked quite a bit like today's model, appeared in 1876 and the motor-driven vacuum cleaner in very bulky form closed out the century twenty years later. Sometimes two people were required to run it: one to guide the hose, one to power it by treadle!

In the servant-staffed Victorian home the lady of the house would know the vacuum cleaner only by reputation, and if you are equipping a house with maids and butlers, it would be well to include the convenience of the bell pulls, speaking tubes, and a downstairs call board.

Electric fans began spinning in 1882, four years after the pho-

A room by Tom and Guy Roberts to close out the nineteenth century but one that bears an accumulation of items from the last quarter of the century. Notice the phonograph with the large horn-shaped speaker, the dried flowers under a glass dome, and the lamp in the window with lustres hanging from the shade. The tiled fireplace with the shelved overmantel is reminiscent of the Eastlake style as well as of the Renaissance Revival which appears in the furniture. There is a stove in front of the fireplace. *Photo by Phillip F. McPherson*

A late-nineteenth-century upright piano by Emily Good. The piano is made of ebonized wood with gilt trim. The oil-on-ivory portraits are of Mendelssohn and Beethoven. *Photo by Bill Good*

nograph was patented. The earliest records were of the cylinder type. In the late 1880s we had discs, but it wasn't until the 1890s that many homes had the phonograph with its big horn speaker. For those of you who have a phonograph with the famous dog trademark, he first appeared in 1898.

In the 1890s people also got their first small folding cameras. Stereoscopes, of which there are several in miniature, were popular from the 1850s. Less spectacular, but perhaps more affecting, improvements in daily life included the safety pin (1849) and the paper bag (1852). Dwarfing almost everything else of course was the telephone. The first telephone was still experimental in 1876, yet two years later the first commercial switchboard was plugged in. Telephones came in various styles. Some were nothing more than plain wooden boards on the wall with attached appliances that served as both ear- and mouthpiece. It was not at all unusual for the speaking and listening device to be the same although of course there were also models like the familiar wall box that carried separate devices and loudly ringing bells.

Stepping back from the advanced realm of the telephone we

find that some areas of life had not advanced. Pest control was a big problem and the fastidious dollhousekeeper might consider following the lead of the nineteenth-century prototype by strategically placing bowls of water to catch flies. (Victorian bug hunters put cobalt in the water, but that might be carrying things too far in the quest for authenticity in miniature!) Dozens of such small touches can give not only a real look to a dollhouse but a liveliness that directly expresses the interest, care, and diligence of the collector.

A few more of these small touches might include leaving a bicycle on the porch or tucked away in a back hall. Bicycling in postwar America might be compared to the present-day jogging boom. A metal-wheeled baby carriage also fits well in a Victorian dollhouse. After the Civil War youngsters went on a savings binge promoted by a procession of toy banks. Their modish parents may have strung Japanese lanterns in the parlor or sitting room during the late-century Oriental fad.

More books were becoming available and together with colorfully covered almanacs they were an important and colorful part of the décor of many houses. Magazines spread news and fashion during the era with the premier fashion magazine, *Godey's Lady's Book*, first appearing in the 1830s. By the mid-1840s there were a number of fashion magazines and before the war there were also illustrated news and feature periodicals. Many nineteenth-century publications including newspapers have been cheaply and accurately reduced to scale

Miniaturists with an otherwise reasonably calm attitude tend to lose detachment at Christmas time. The Christmas tree is one Victorian delight that is frequently crafted to scale—both poorly and properly. (The Christmas tree came out of a German tradition that was brought west through England by Queen Victoria's consort, Prince Albert.) It is well to remember however that Christmas trees didn't proliferate in this country until about 1850, rather later in our national life than many collectors suppose.

FIVE

AMERICAN KITCHENS AND BATHROOMS

COOKING

FOR 200 years following the arrival of the Pilgrims, the fireplace was the core of the kitchen. As we noted in Chapter One, the first fireplaces were built of brick or stone with wide openings, sometimes accommodating two fires. Firebacks were set in some fireplaces to protect the masonry and reflect heat, although they were less common in fireplaces used solely for cooking. Some fireplace interiors were whitewashed.

During the whole of the seventeenth century, fireplaces were equipped with lug poles of wood or metal suspended inside the chimney above the hearth. Trammels hung from the lug pole and it was from these trammels, many of which were made adjustable by ratchets, that cooking pots dangled directly over the fire. In the early eighteenth century, cranes were fixed in the side or back wall of the fireplace, an addition that was a great convenience for the homemaker because the cranes swung away from the flames and made cooking somewhat less hazardous. Pots were hung on the cranes and trammels by small S-shaped hooks.

Another change effected over the turn of the eighteenth century involved the oven. Ovens appeared in the back walls of fireplaces in the mid-seventeenth century but by about 1720 they had moved to the side wall and finally, during the middle of the eighteenth century, to the front wall beside the opening. These ovens ordinarily had wood or metal doors, some simply had unattached covers with handles in the middle. Below the oven was another niche, the ash well, where ashes were saved for later use.

In some fireplaces a special corner area was reserved for keeping hot water at the ready. A metal-lined reservoir was sunk in a

This rather cleaned-up version of a kitchen dependency is based on the kitchen of the Governor's Palace in Williamsburg, Virginia, and is in the Thorne Rooms Collection of the Art Institute of Chicago. The furniture is simple but handsome, particularly the finely arched slat-back chair and the large cupboard. The large fireplace has both a side-crane and a hanging ratchet trammel suspended from a lug pole hidden from view high up in the chimney. There is not a great variety of cooking implements in the room but there are some important ones including the tin kitchen at the right of the hearth, the long-handled pots hanging to the left of the fireplace, the pot on the trivet visible under the center worktable, and the churn near the ladder. The ladder leads to a loft storeroom where the kitchen slaves slept. *Courtesy of the Art Institute of Chicago; Gift of Mrs. James Ward Thorne*

solid waist-high brick projection built into one corner of the fireplace.

During the eighteenth century colonists reduced some of the tedium of cooking (and made the operation more efficient) with the addition of jacks to the fireplaces. The jacks rotated the spits for even roasting. Depending on their type, the jacks were attached inside the chimney or outside the fireplace, on the mantel, or above the lintel. Smoke jacks resembled small windmills and were hung inside the chimney so that the rising smoke and heat turned the paddle wheel that was attached by a line to the spit. The more sophisticated clock and spring jacks hung outside the fireplace and were wound like clocks. Jacks of this type were used from their first appearance in about 1750 into the nineteenth century.

Because they are so intricate it is difficult to find miniature jacks but it is not so hard to find the other accessories to make the miniature fireplace look real. There is a great variety of andirons (also called "dogs") available although many are too fancy to use in kitchens, especially the earliest kitchen. Plain iron andirons

Sussex Crafts makes the brick water-boiler with its metal liner. A fire would be built in a small opening (hidden by the cover) in the bottom and hot water could be kept at the ready. Such reservoirs might be built into the corner of a fireplace or left freestanding. They were used until quite late—some were still operating in the early twentieth century. At the right is a coffee roaster dating from colonial times by H. G. Littwin and an open saltbox by Martha Dinkel of the Mouse Hole.

This is a late-eighteenth-century vertical roasting oven, really a sophisticated form of the tin kitchen. It is complete with a jack—a "bottle jack" in this instance—that rotates the hook on which the meat hangs, thus ensuring even roasting in front of the fire. Many jacks—smoke, bottle, and clock—hung from the fireplace itself causing a spit to turn. From Studio B. *Photo courtesy of Studio B*

This late-eighteenth-century Pennsylvania German kitchen is in the Thorne Rooms Collection of the Art Institute of Chicago. The room is based on the 1752 home of Jerg Muler of Millbach, Lebanon County, Pennsylvania. Note the painted chest, flax wheel, and cupboard to the right of the massive fireplace as well as the carved peasant chair near the Dutch door and the wooden shoes. Next to the wainscot chair is a standing betty lamp. There is a potentially dangerous situation which a careful colonist would likely correct: the gun and powder horn would be better hung away from the open fire. *Courtesy of the Art Institute of Chicago; Gift of Mrs. James Ward Thorne*

work well in such scenes and you may find some with hooks on the front in which you can lay a spit. When using such spit-dogs be sure to place a drip pan underneath. During the eighteenth century a sophisticated spit came into use, complete with its own metal oven. It was called a tin kitchen or roasting oven. In some homes another roaster, a coffee roaster, was used along with a coffee grinder. During the Revolution some andirons were melted down to make weapons so fires were laid using stones or green logs to support the burning logs. Metal baskets held the coal fires that were used as early as the eighteenth century but only in a few kitchens.

When the fire was going out for the night, a few colonial homemakers followed the English custom of using a curfew—a domed metal cover—to enclose the last embers, thus protecting the rooms from a potential fire and protecting the last of the fire from dying out completely. It is appropriate to have bellows at the miniature fireplace as it is to have a small brush for sweeping up ashes from the hearth. Every home also had a saltbox placed conveniently near the cooking area—usually hanging on the wall—along with a spoon rack.

Utensils used by seventeenth- and eighteenth-century cooks include peels for taking baked goods from the oven, skewers which usually hung on a rack near the fireplaces, trivets, kettles and caldrons, long-handled frying pans, skimmers, spoons, and a

This display of kitchen accessories focuses on colonial implements, some of which survived well into the Victorian era. The two tin kitchens come from Studio B. You can see from examining the one on the right how they worked, although the spit design would vary. This small one has a spit which would have taken up to six small fowl, probably birds. The door opens to permit basting (and checking). Jim Holmes made the larger set of skewers and Martha Dinkel crafted the long-handled peel. Al Atkins, the Village Smithy, made the large ratchet which would hang from a lug pole so that pots could be suspended over the fire at various heights. J. S. Powel of Miniatures of Merritt made the three fireplace tools—poker, tongs, and shovel. Notice the three-legged pot which has its own built-in trivet and griddle which has a hook to mate it with the crane of ratchet.

few long-handled meat forks, graters, copper molds, and small footed grills with handles. Many pots were also footed, among them the Dutch oven which was a lidded pot. The cook set it in the burning embers, placing some of the embers on the top of the lid for thorough cooking and baking. Most pots and kettles were made of iron although copper and brass were also used. To compensate for the considerable weight of some kettles there was a device called an idleback. Like the curfew, it was used less here than in England. In essence it was a metal armature that attached

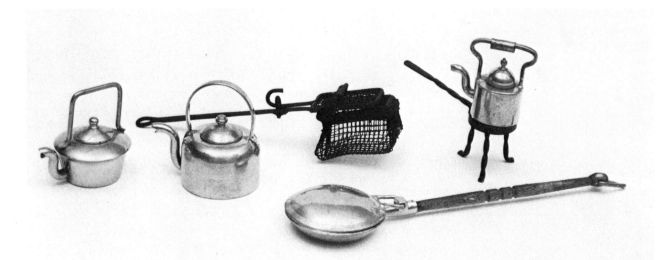

(Above)
A gathering of kitchen implements from Sherwood Interiors. The kettles hang on the fireplace crane or sit nearby on the hearth, usually, as here, supported on a trivet. The bed-warmer awaits the last embers of the fire with which it will warm the family beds. The wire-mesh contraption is a popcorn popper.

(Below)
These fireplace implements for the colonial hearth include a set of long-handled cooking utensils by J. S. Powel of Miniatures of Merritt, a revolving toaster by Jim Holmes, a chain to hang from a lug pole by David Usher, a footed cooking pot, and a tripod-base roaster by Jim Holmes; fowl was fixed on the prongs and the stand was moved in front of the fire.

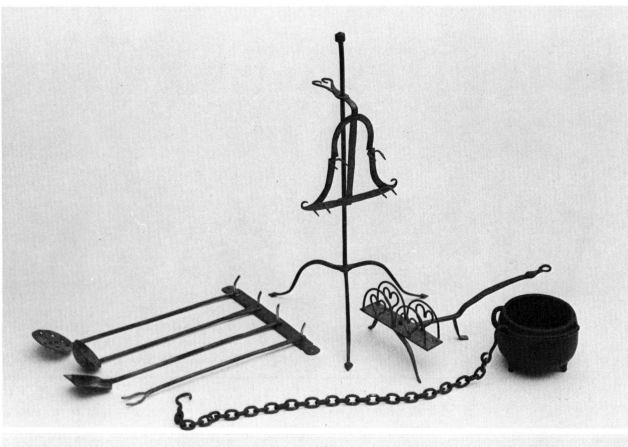

to the kettle so the cook could pour from the kettle without lifting it off the crane. The entire hearth, which might extend several feet into the room, could be used as a stove. Cooks frequently placed footed pots at various spots on the hearth, packing them from underneath in hot embers from the fire.

Among other utensils were ale warmers (shoe- or cone-shaped metal cups placed in the fireplace coals to heat a toddy), rack-like toasters on long handles, scales, plate warmers, waffle irons, and copper molds.

There are other accessories that while not directly used for cooking were typically placed near the colonial fireplace. Wall-mounted pipe boxes were needed for the long-stemmed clay pipes gentlemen smoked; the boxes usually had a small drawer for tobacco. There, too, were the tongs on a long-handled extension apparatus used to pluck hot coals from the fire for lighting pipes. Warming pans and small foot warmers were also kept near the fire and metal or wooden candle boxes were hung on the adjacent wall. Light was provided by the fire, candles, and lanterns.

During the seventeenth century and in rural and western frontier areas on through much of the nineteenth century some utensils were fashioned from gourds. Many more of the utensils and plates used by colonists were wooden. Pewter began to take over by 1750, though of course there had always been some pewter, the amount depending on the wealth of the family. Pewter was

The c. 1760 New England Windsor is from Studio B and the refectory table is from Warren Dick. On the table are some basic kitchen implements and accessories: a hanging cupboard from the Hoffman Collection, a large dough stirrer and dough knife by T. C. Cottrell, Jr., and a chopper, an apple-butter scoop, and a bowl by J. S. Powel.

not used for cooking however because it was soft and easily ruined by heat.

Nearly all homes had mortars and pestles ranging in size from very small to very large; in the Governor's Palace at Williamsburg there is a mortar with a pestle that would take two hands to manage. Dough trays or boxes were often mounted on their own stands. The dough was kneaded on the flat top and set to rise in the boxlike section. Colonial homemakers kept staples like flour in wooden bins while barrels of different sizes also were used for storage.

One thing to remember when equipping your colonial kitchen is that each item, every skewer and pot, had a purpose. They were not for show. As collectors we all have succumbed to the temptation to display every accessory we own, but a seventeenth-century cook would not have laid out every plate, pot, and spoon on the table any more than you would take everything out of your kitchen drawers. There is a fine line between accurately portraying a working kitchen and cluttering it up. Bear in mind that each piece should have a reason for being there. Sometimes when we carefully cover a hearth or table with too much we obscure the individual trees by building a forest.

Of course personal taste is a key factor and your own enjoyment of your miniatures should be the final guide. But sometimes the dictum "less is more" operates very effectively and has the added advantage of economy. It may be a cliché, but choosing one fine piece rather than buying three inferior ones is a good rule and you should not feel that you must sacrifice quality so that you can afford to "load up" a hearth. If you are still determined to show an entire collection of pots and skillets rather than a few select pieces, you could establish your kitchen around meal preparation—say a Thanksgiving dinner for a host of relatives and Indians. This will allow you to disrupt the usual order in the same way that erecting a candlemaking scene does (see Chapter One).

Another vignette that gives you a chance to exhibit a special set of accessories involves dairy operations, vital to the family that depended on home resources for milk, cream, butter, and cheese. The kitchen utensils discussed thus far have been of wood or metal primarily but for processing dairy products a great many ceramic pieces were used, even during the seventeenth century. Made of earthenware, these include wide shallow bowls in which milk was set to allow the cream to rise. Ceramic pans, collanders, jars, and crocks were also used and are available in miniature. Stoneware, a less porous ceramic, began to replace earthenware during the eighteenth century when the use of ceramics spread beyond the dairy. Also necessary were butter churns, mostly of the broomstick variety, in wood or stoneware. During the nineteenth century the broomstick churn was often replaced by the paddle churn, a crank-turned barrel laid on its side in a holder. To squeeze the remaining moisture from the new butter, colonial

These pieces are from the dairy. Phyllis Howard made the stoneware lipped milk pan, collander, funnel, batter jug, crock, and bulbous jug. The small churn was made by Jean Tag and the wooden item on the far right of the table is a butter stamp by Carol Hardy used to put recognizable patterns on a crock of butter (like a trademark or brand name—for instance if a farmer were to sell the dairy products at market). Betty Valentine made the table which is of a stretcher type made in the eighteenth and nineteenth centuries. The table has unusually delicate, turned legs and is nicely finished with breadboards at the ends of the top.

and Victorian homemakers worked the churned product with small wooden paddles or "hands." Large quantities of butter were worked with paddles or rolling pins on trays curved to facilitate the run-off liquid. The butter was packed into convenient-sized earthenware or stoneware crocks and stamped with the familiar wooden butter mold now so often exhibited at antique shows. These molds or presses have convex designs carved in them, the design sometimes serving as a brand mark for producers who sold their butter.

Another specialized food-processing routine was meat smoking. Outfitting your miniature homes with a smokehouse would mean a departure from the standard dollhouse but it can be done without drastic alterations. A small smoke oven can be built into the chimney at the attic or cellar level. The typical chimney smoke oven was constructed with a lug pole set three or four feet above the hearth, with an opening in the chimney perhaps a foot or two off the floor. The opening, which was often not very large, led to an interior chamber that could be as big as the kitchen fireplace interior (which, in the case of the cellar smoke oven, would of course be above it). Meat was hung over a smoky fire until cured and then rehung in the attic loft. This procedure was followed from the seventeenth century on into the twentieth century. Very often large smokehouses were built as dependencies outside the house itself. This was particularly common in the South where, as we have mentioned, the kitchen was usually also a separate building on homesteads where there were servants or slaves. The separate outdoor kitchen was like the indoor kitchen in its appointments and might have a wooden, stone, or brick floor. Servants and slaves slept in a loft over the kitchen. Perhaps reflecting a lack of regard for servants and slaves, builders often made kitchens with only very small windows or none at all. In those cases the only light and ventilation came through the door. In Dutch homes this door was a double "Dutch" door.

Some colonial homes had separate butteries for dairy functions within the house. There also might be a larder for cooling and storing food and a pantry for keeping dishes and other household goods. These might be nothing more than corners of a room or roughly partitioned lean-tos built in the slant-roofed addition that identified the saltbox.

Furniture in the seventeenth-century kitchen—which frequently served as the major or only room in the house—was sparse, ordinarily including a dresser or cupboard, a table, a hutch table, a stool or two, and perhaps a chair. During the eighteenth century furniture grew in quantity with more chairs, tables, and cupboards. Many colonial cooks created extra storage space by using the ceiling. Often we find meat, fowl, vegetables, and fruit hanging from poles suspended from the ceiling. Chandelier-like mounts with metal hooks were also used to hang meat and fowl. Some dried fruit and vegetables hung like swags from the fireplace itself and a few colorful strings of peppers, apples, and pumpkin rings would enhance the authenticity of the seventeenth- or eighteenth-century miniature kitchen.

The nineteenth century added some furniture types like the dry sink and the water bench which were usually consigned to the back porch. It comes as a surprise to many miniaturists that the dry sink—ubiquitous as it is in scale—was not a kitchen staple until so late. The dry sink, which was often zinc-lined, represented the first common indoor sink and was used by homemakers without water connections well into the twentieth century. Before indoor plumbing, water was carried inside in buckets and poured into a bowl which was set in the dry sink. The first kitchen pumps came in about 1850 and quite soon became common over a wide range of the country. At the same time we see the first iron sinks replacing wooden dry sinks in some homes. The familiar white enameled sink was largely a creature of the turn of the century.

Throughout the Victorian era sinks were also made of soapstone and granite in addition to wood and iron. Most early sinks had wooden drainboards; don't forget that any drainboard should slant slightly toward the sink.

If you have built your dollhouse or miniature settings to suit a particular area, it should not be difficult to determine when indoor water connections were effected with a letter or call to the local historical society, library, or sanitation department. Running water was established in homes soon after 1800; nevertheless, the date for your area may be later than you imagine. Philadelphia had a new waterworks in the 1820s, but even in New York, where indoor hookups came with the 1840s, only a minority of the city's homes enjoyed public water service a full four decades later. Any number of urban communities were providing some degree of running water during the period immediately following the Civil War.

Much earlier there were innovative builders who designed indoor sinks with their own waste drains. The Hyland House in Guilford, Connecticut—built gradually during the seventeenth and eighteenth centuries—has a soapstone sink that drains into the backyard. Interesting, too, is the Jethro Coffin House built in Nantucket in 1686. It has a sinklike limestone slab mounted on a crude, waist-high stand. Rainwater was filtered through the limestone to purify it. A number of soapstone sinks have been found

Jim Holmes made this piece with pump and metal-lined sink. The baskets are from Roberta Partridge and the churn is by Jean Tag.

in Federal era homes. Some kitchens had deep, brick-lined holes in the floors that served as wells.

Just as the dry sink presaged the modern sink, the fireplace gave way to the stove. Although the first recognizable kitchen ranges made their appearance in the 1840s, some Franklin-type stoves were used for cooking (or at least heating water) in the late 1700s. By the 1850s there were many kitchen ranges, commonly built into the old kitchen fireplace or on their own brick foundation. There were many different ways of constructing these stoves: in one case a metal oven was built into a brick wall with a standing water tank by its side. If you have an inferior kitchen range you sometimes can disguise its faults by bricking it into a kitchen fireplace.

In kitchens without fireplaces, builders would often erect a range breast—a sort of mantel-like surround establishing a recess for the stove. In some kitchens the cookstove or gas range was surrounded not by fireplace (real or fake) but by a wall that was either tiled or painted with black enamel, the object being to make things easier to keep clean. Next to the stove there might be a table with a zinc covering, ready to receive pots, pans, and platters still hot from cooking. There might also be a special soapstone sink reserved for pots and pans.

From the 1850s on, stoves were made with shelves for drying and warming food and some had special toasters and waffle irons

A close-up of the sink shows one of the "hidden" authentic touches that can make a piece extra special. The two pipes are for the pump and the drain; there's been a leak, too, as we can readily see from the irregular stain on the cupboard bottom.

As was common by midcentury, this cookstove is placed in a fireplace. The stove, with its spigot and ash drawer, was made by Sussex Crafts as was the surround and shelf. The large crock on the left is really a pottery church (without the dasher) by Carolyn Nygren Curran. The slipware platter and Pennsylvania Dutch-style *sgraffito* plate are from Deborah McKnight. The other ceramics—two preserve jars, a mold, a covered pitcher, and a jug—were made by Lee-Ann Chellis-Wessel. The red peppers hanging on the right are from Wise Miniatures. The bricks are Tom Thumb bricks from Binghamton Brick Co.

designed to fit into the range-top openings. These openings, corresponding to burners, were ordinarily covered with lids. Because they were relatively small, the big pots and pans of the colonial period were replaced by smaller models.

Kitchen ranges of the 1840s and 1850s were primarily squarish boxes of cast iron with doors and lids over internal fires. They were not as ornate as the subsequent big black cookstove of the late nineteenth century. Those larger cast-iron ranges we see reproduced so often in miniature came in with the 1860s.

Kitchen ranges were wood- or coal-burning so of course somewhere near the range you will want to put a woodbox or coal scuttle and shovel. Small tin match holders were nailed to the wall near the ranges, especially from the 1850s when an effective friction match became widely available. There was a great variety in style and decoration for ranges but from their introduction until past the turn of the century, nearly everyone of them held a big hot water kettle more or less around the clock.

The small icebox with a draining spigot is by Evelyn and Frank Gerratana from an icebox of the last quarter of the nineteenth century. The wooden coffee mill is by J. S. Powel. The larger coffee mill is for heavier use. The chair from Reminiscence has the pressed back popular at the turn-of-the-century.

The first gas stoves came in at the close of the Civil War but obviously these could be used only in cities with gas connections and they were seen infrequently enough so that at the Centennial Exposition in 1876 gas stoves were an absolute sensation. Gas cookers were essentially an 1880s phenomenon. Rural areas of this country did not get their first gas stoves until after 1910 and there were many established communities that did not have universal gas connections until the 1920s. In some homes gas cookers were used only as warm weather substitutes for the wood or coal stove.

The electric range was a stunning feature of the 1893 World's Columbian Exposition which also exhibited an electric iron. Around 1910 there were some electric ranges that had eye-level ovens above the tablelike range surface, but electric ranges were not popular until the 1920s and 1930s. In addition to the kitchen range, the "electric age" brought in a number of separate electrical pans, ovens, boilers, and broilers.

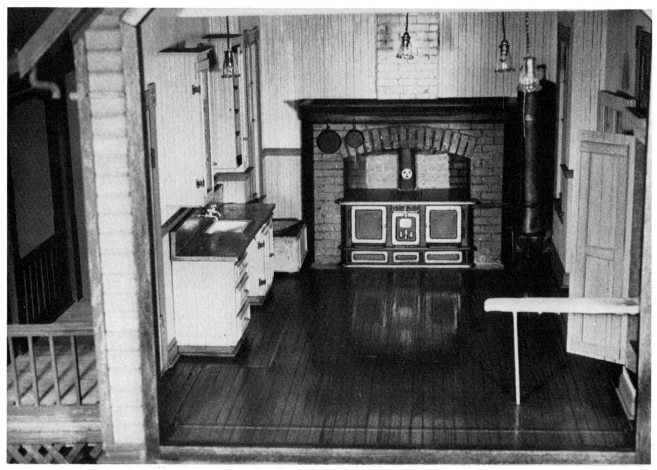

This kitchen made by Noel and Pat Thomas has several special features including an ironing board that folds into the wall; a cylindrical hot-water tank next to the stove; a large range vented in a fireplace; and, to the left of the fireplace, a woodbox. To make it more convenient to fill the box from the outside woodlot, it is built like a drawer and when pushed in on the kitchen-side, opens on the outside.

Rural families of the early decades of the 1900s depended on ice houses and attic lofts to preserve food while their city cousins were enjoying the advantages of the electric refrigerator. The electric refrigerator was making inroads against the older icebox during the years preceding World War I with the oak refrigerator being a special favorite. Iceboxes, if in a rudimentary form, date from at least the early nineteenth century. A patent was granted in 1803 for a small insulated wooden box on short legs. Ice was laid in the bottom and the food on top of the ice. By midcentury such chest-type iceboxes were fairly common, having been given a boost by the development of the commercial ice machine in 1825. The common midcentury icebox was zinc- or tin-lined and rested on the floor. Later models varied in style and some were boxes on pedestal bases. During the 1850s a switch was made and the ice was put above the food rather than underneath it. The first practical compressor-type refrigerator was developed in the 1870s. By that time both upright and lower chest types were well-established. The electric refrigerator went on the domestic market in 1913. Many Victorian homemakers kept their iceboxes in a pantry or on the back porch—well away from the roaring cookstove.

There are a few accessories that go with the icebox, most notably ice itself. Ice was delivered to homes in chunks weighing 12½, 25, 50, or 100 pounds. Homemakers put a small sign in the window with the appropriate number so that the iceman making his rounds knew how big a piece to take into the house. The iceman needed huge tongs but most family kitchens had smaller ones. Kitchens were also equipped with ice picks and ice shavers.

Another food storage item which is frequently made in miniature is the pie safe. The first of these appeared about 1800. Pie safes or cupboards commonly had punched-tin panels and while the punched designs might look nice when pierced from the outside in, they are more efficient when pierced from the inside out. The resulting jagged exterior edges make it harder for the flies to get in. Pie safes came in all sizes and some were suspended from the ceiling, especially when used in cellars where damp floors threatened the stored goods. You could also put your basement pie safe on a mounting of wooden planks or bricks.

Nineteenth-century kitchens also had apothecary-type chests

These two items are from the Tin Feather's nineteenth-century collection of country pieces. The pie safe was made by Renée Bowen as was the delightful Shaker herb chopping table. It has a metal chopping blade fitted to the shallow, demi-lune-shaped bin top. Note the chute that funnels chopped herbs into the container. *Photo courtesy of The Tin Feather*

for the storage of herbs, some of which would be growing on the windowsill. There was also a variety of dressers and cupboards including many built-in cabinets with glass doors. You may want to station a rolling tea cart in the kitchen since they were used to carry food and dishes from the kitchen to the dining room. A comfortable addition to the Victorian kitchen is a rocking chair and many people today recall rocking chairs in early twentieth-century kitchens, too.

Some kitchen tables had marble insets for pastry making. Homemakers sometimes made cleaning easier by covering table tops and shelves with wipable oilcloth.

This large, almost formal kitchen table is too imposing for an ordinary kitchen and belongs only in a rather grand house—preferably in the city. The table is from It's a Small World. The accessories include an earthenware bowl from the Steak Family and a wooden cutting board with a handy, open side. Laurence St. Leger made the woodenware: at left is a butter stamp or print and the other item is a pastry or pie crimper, also known as a pastry wheel, dough trimmer, or jigger. The woodenware and the pans are from the Steak Family. The stockpot is copper with brass handles while the saucepan and jelly pan are brass with iron handles. Generally speaking, earlier pans had iron handles and later pans had brass handles.

In 1869 Catharine Beecher's *The American Woman's Home* was published and it had a great impact on kitchen design. Beecher suggested setting plants around and using light, white curtains or none at all. Mrs. Beecher was also very convenience-minded, advising her readers to rely on built-in shelves and dressers arranged close enough together to save steps. Another step-saver was the dumbwaiter that opened into many kitchens.

Kitchen rugs were unknown during the seventeenth century, rare during the eighteenth, but quite common by the Victorian era. A braided rug will add color to your Victorian kitchen which, if it is true to the trend of the day, will have decidedly colorless walls.

Most kitchen walls were painted white or some light color. A dull mustard yellow or green apparently was *de rigueur* in many kitchens from at least the 1840s. There were exceptions, however, and if you want a bright kitchen wall you can have it and still be accurate. Some kitchens had plain vertical wainscoting of stained or painted wood while others used tiles or wallpaper. You might put a plate rail above the wainscoting or higher up on the wall near the ceiling.

It might be well to fix a towel rack to the wall, especially one with projecting fingerlike rods. There were also some indoor lines on which to hang towels.

Most kitchen floors were of the wooden plank type, and were sometimes painted. Linoleum, that staple of kitchen décor, first came to American kitchens in the 1860s and 70s. There also were tile floors and tile splashboards. Plain or patterned oilcloths were laid in front of stoves and almost without exception homemakers would put some special, heat-resistant flooring—perhaps a zinc pad—under the stove.

Some designs for Victorian kitchens show kitchen suites that included a main kitchen, a pantry for storing dishes and some food, a larder, a scullery where the pots were kept and the dirtiest work done, and a summer kitchen which was used for cooking during the warmer months. Some summer kitchens were separate buildings while in some families the men simply moved the stove outside during the hot season. For a real summer look, add a screen door to the porch.

Many homes had pantries and a dollhouse pantry can, among other things, diminish kitchen clutter. Pantries were often lined with shelves or dressers for dishes. Food staples like flour and sugar might be kept in barrels and buckets on the floor. Brooms, sweepers, aprons, and towels were hung on hooks.

You can design a fancy pantry with built-in glass-doored cupboards, cup hooks, felt padding for dishes and linen-lined drawers. Add a sink and small icebox to complete the picture.

Victorian kitchens were illuminated by lamps hanging over the kitchen table and by wall-mounted lamps, often backed by reflectors. From the early 1800s when the mass production of clocks made them more available, timepieces began to appear in kitchens and by the Victorian period clocks were very common in kitchens.

Other accessories to consider for your Victorian kitchen are wire and rattan rug beaters, dustpans, and feather dusters, mops, brooms, brushes, pails, and butter churns of the broomstick or crank type. Some churns were even hung from the ceiling.

During the nineteenth century a great deal of energy was devoted to inventing gadgets, particularly highly specialized gadgets, for instance, a grape seeder. An 1803 apple parer probably started the ball rolling. By the mid-1830s there was a procession

The most spectacular item adorning this kitchen fireplace is the rare clock-jack. This Pennsylvania German kitchen obviously belongs in a grand house judging from its fittings including the great variety of spits—each suited for a particular meat or fowl—which are used with either a tin kitchen or andirons. The pots hang from a lug pole. This kitchen is the creation of Madelyn Cook for her famous dollhouse, Lagniappe. *Photo by Jim Cook*

A turn-of-the-century pantry by Tom and Guy Roberts. *Photo by Phillip F. McPherson*

A more sophisticated pantry by Tom and Guy Roberts. Ellen Krucker Blauer of The Miniature Mart made many of the plates. *Photo by Phillip F. McPherson*

A collection of kitchen utensils. The redware plates have a highly glazed finish. The double rolling pin is by T. C. Cottrell, Jr., the masher by J. S. Powel of Miniatures of Merritt and the cabbage shredder (note the blade inserted in the middle of the platform) is from Dollhouse Antics.

of gadgetry eventually to include cherry pitters, meat grinders, cutters, stuffers, and parers. There was an 1848 patent for an ice-cream freezer although the height of its popularity didn't come until the 1880s.

Coffee gained favor following the Civil War and many kitchens had wall- or table-mounted mills. The ones with big wheels were usually used for large households or commercial establishments. Coffee roasters, which had appeared in colonial kitchens, were also common.

Victorian kitchens had the usual assortment of small utensils like graters, wire whisks, chopping or mincing knives, apple peelers and cabbage shredders. Some cabbage shredders were not so small. Sauerkraut was made by the barrel and for that and cole slaw, large shredders or "kraut cutters" were necessary—sometimes mounted on legs like a dough box. Metal potato mashers came in during the 1850s, the modern can opener in the 1860s, and the eggbeater in the 1870s. Screw-top bottles and Mason jars were developed in the late 1850s; previously bottles had had cork stoppers. The crown seal was invented in the early 1890s. Milk bottles as we know them appeared in the late 1870s at a time when homemakers began to rely more and more on glass for storage, particularly in iceboxes. The tin can made life easier after 1831. Utensils were hung out in the open for convenience or stored in drawers and closets. Iron and copper pots and pans were hung on the wall or stored in cupboards.

During the 1870s many homemakers turned to enamelware pots which were much lighter but highly susceptible to chipping. Some enamelware had a mottled finish and was called agateware. It came in gray, blue, black, green, turquoise, and brown. Other enamelware was white with a colored rim. Eventually everything from pans to ladles was made in the lighter material. There were even toilet sets made of agateware. Aluminum pots and pans were produced as early as the 1850s but were not affordable until the late 1880s and not popular for another decade after that.

Wooden boxes—round, square, and oval—were used for food storage from colonial times through the Victorian era. Tin canisters were also frequently used for storage and in the late 1880s, china and pottery canister sets were common.

Gray stoneware with cobalt trim was a fixture in the nineteenth-century kitchen, as were sets of yellowware bowls that were often trimmed with colored bands.

Interestingly, an Indiana housewife invented a dishwasher for home use in 1899. It was a wooden tub with a crank handle that powered "air plungers" that forced water over and around the dishes. An electric motor replaced the crank in 1914.

The first real effort at decorating kitchens came with the twentieth century. White was still a favorite color but more attention

This table with its distressed finish was made by Jim Holmes who included signs of wear on the stretcher. He also made the cutting board with its much-marred, dark center. T. C. Cottrell, Jr. made the marvelous slicer which has a head for a crest. The two jugs are from Phyllis Howard of Butt Hinge Pottery as is a larger crock which is really a stoneware barrel to hold water. Except for the cutting board the accessories are from the collection of Jack and Shirley Bloomfield.

This busy kitchen table is relatively timeless although such white enameled pieces were very popular in the twentieth-century kitchen. Bob Callahan of Dover Miniatures crafted the copper sifter and the peaches are the produce of Wise Miniatures. Jean Tag made the nested yellowware bowls. Yellowware was made in quantity by the 1830s and continued to be popular into the twentieth century. The rooster bowl is a 1910 design copied here by Lee-Ann Chellis-Wessel who also made the other decorated bowl which takes its motif from older Pennsylvania Dutch sources. Food grinders like the one shown were in use from the late nineteenth century.

went to choosing pleasing linoleum or tiles for the floor that also might have cork mats and rugs for weary feet. These would be especially welcome on the concrete floor that was laid in some modern kitchens. Walls were tiled, painted, or covered with glazed wallpaper.

CERAMICS

EARTHENWARE, a soft absorbent pottery that was frequently glazed to make it less porous, was manufactured in this country in the 1620s. During the seventeenth and eighteenth centuries it was usually buff, brown, or red in color and frequently had a green or

This kitchen has typical turn-of-the-century narrow-panel wainscoting which in this case extends to the ceiling. Notice that the wiring for overhead electrical fixtures runs along the ceiling and down the wall. The stovepipe is properly vented and the stove itself sits on a protective metal pad. It is attention to details like this (as well as the extraordinary execution) that puts houses like this Megler Landing House by Noel and Pat Thomas of Open House into a very special category. The miniature version of the house really is an accurate, authentic scale model of a house. While we can't all have such incredible miniature houses, we can learn from them. *Photo by Harry Liles*

yellow glaze. Although decorated pottery was not very common in the homes of early settlers, there was some slipware and *sgraffi-to*-decorated ceramic ware (see Accessories in Chapter One). American-made slipware has been traced to the late seventeenth century.

Some English stoneware was available early and American production began in the late seventeenth century although it did not begin in New England until late in the eighteenth century. Stoneware is nonabsorbent and can be glazed or unglazed. We know that brown stoneware and German blue-gray stoneware with cobalt trim were around during the colonial period but the common cobalt-trimmed stoneware that we find today in antique shops and at auctions came late in the eighteenth century and was

Four pieces of mid-nineteenth-century and later gray and blue stoneware by Carolyn Nygren Curran. Note the number #4—a size classification—on the crock in the middle. Potters generally decorated their larger pieces more elaborately than the smaller ones.

most common during the whole of the nineteenth century. After 1800, stoneware jugs were frequently coated inside with a brown slip called Albany slip.

Delft was a fancier ware that came from Holland and England. It was called majolica in Spain and Italy and faience in France. It was a tin-enameled earthenware which was most often seen in shades of blue and white but could also be quite colorful. There was some delft here during the seventeenth century, when it was highly prized, and it was quite a common tableware during the 1700s. Colonists considered it an acceptable substitute for the much finer Chinese porcelain, which was available to only the wealthiest among them. Chinese export porcelain was most commonly trimmed in blue, red, or gold, but it too could be more colorful and some of it bore fabulous designs. It was encountered here most often after the Revolution when the United States got directly involved in the China trade. We also imported porcelain from Europe. It wasn't until the nineteenth century that porcelain was practically manufactured in the U.S.

Of the plainer ware, creamware and pearlware gave delft serious competition in the 1760s. These better-quality ceramics came in a buff color that lightened to ivory and white over a period of about twenty years. Creamware was often trimmed in green or blue.

Beginning in the 1830s Americans could get quantities of what we might call modern pottery. Multicolored printed designs came on ceramics from earthenware to china. (See the Accessories sections of each chapter for further discussions on the ceramics of each period.)

CHAMBER POTS, PRIVIES, AND BATHROOMS

DURING the seventeenth and most of the eighteenth centuries, personal hygiene was a simple matter, dispensed with in ways that make twentieth-century observers wonder how much hygiene was really involved. The earliest conveniences were not particularly convenient, consisting of outdoor privies (some with two or more seats) and indoor chamber pots made of metal or ceramics. Some early chamber pots showed a definite disregard for delicacy, painted as they were with humorous and bawdy inscriptions. Not every colonist had his or her own chamber pot; like dishware, these items were often shared.

During the eighteenth century a little more sensitivity appears

All that's missing here is a fire to cozy up to. This array of bathing accessories features a copper hip bath by Bob Callahan of Dover Miniatures; a colonial basin stand by Lou Murter, and a painted hip bath in a popular brown and cream combination. The china chamber pot is a Limoges piece and the white chamber pot, pitcher, and basin are by Lee-Ann Chellis-Wessel of Demi-Tasse Miniatures. Herbert and Jennifer Bennett made the item that looks like a rolling pin on legs: it's a footwarmer which kept colonial toes off cold floors. The kettle would have been used to heat water to warm the bath. The chair is a late inheritor of the rod-back Windsor style.

to have crept in; now chamber pots in genteel bedrooms were often concealed in tiny cupboards or within bed-steps. In wealthy colonial homes there were also bidets, but even though we find them in eighteenth-century Williamsburg and nineteenth-century New Orleans, bidets were not generally found until after the Civil War. Even so, their vogue was short-lived because they never caught on in America.

At about the middle of the eighteenth century the basin stand appeared. There are several types and names for basically the same contrivance: basin stand, wig stand, and powder stand. As discussed in Chapter Two, a basin stand was a small stand with a hole in the top to accommodate a bowl, usually a tiny drawer for toiletries and wig powder, and a small platform near the bottom for a water ewer. In addition to using them for ordinary washing, gentlemen would re-powder their wigs over them, shaking the excess over the basin and rinsing their hands before going on public view again. The basin stand was bedroom and dressing room furniture. During the eighteenth century more elaborate versions of the basin stand became popular. These washstands were square or triangular (to fit in a corner) and had the same basic equipment as the basin stand—drawers and shelves—except that they were larger. Some washstands were tables with their own tanks, spigots, basins, and mirrors. There also are some lavabos—wall water tanks with spigot and bowl underneath—recorded as being used

This walnut Victorian washstand by Kent Halsted conceals its basin in the cupboard under the marble top. Marie Friedman made the towel bars and the elaborate high splashboard of tiles. *Courtesy of MiniFab*

in eighteenth-century bedrooms. A rare pewter lavabo is in Philipsburg Manor in North Tarrytown, one of the homes of the Philipse family of New York.

Washstands, about which more has been said in Chapters Three and Four, developed into substantial pieces of furniture during the nineteenth century. Many were bulky chests with cupboards below and lift tops concealing deep wells. Other Victorian commodes had marble tops, their own mirrors, and attached towel racks. In a maid's room oilcloth probably served in place of marble. Eventually the back splashboard was raised and tiled. On commodes that had no splashboard, a strip of cloth tacked to the wall behind it protected the wallpaper.

The chamber set that accompanied the commodes was essentially the same as before with a basin, a pitcher, a slop jar, a chamber pot, and miscellaneous small containers. A supply of copper and other metal buckets and cans was kept handy for conveying water to the bedroom.

In fact, washstands and chamber pots were common appointments even in early-twentieth-century homes that lacked indoor plumbing. Some rich people had indoor plumbing by the 1830s, and in fact, some had a form of running water soon after 1800. As mentioned earlier in the section on cooking, there was some city water service in the early decades of the 1800s but when you look at the whole country, only a handful had hookups.

Although some chamber pots were hidden behind the bedroom door, there were also very ornamental cupboards for them which, by the Victorian era, were parceled out usually one to a customer. Outhouses of course continued to be the usual daytime recourse and there still were backyard outhouses in major cities in the later nineteenth century.

It may surprise you to learn that the flush toilet goes back to the Elizabethan times in theory but only rarely in practice. A patent for an improved water closet was granted in England in 1775 and there followed a succession of technical advances. In the United States, as early as about 1800, there was a small number of indoor toilets with flush apparatus. They did not of course look like the flush toilets we know today, but more closely resembled boxes with holes in them. The "flushing" was more like "dumping" in most models.

Victorian toilets (of which there were, relatively speaking, not many) were often enclosed in wooden cases until late in the century. Sometimes they were really boxes with lids, the lids occasionally padded and pillowed. On the other hand, other early bathrooms show fully exposed pipes connected to toilets and sinks that were little more than thin slabs suspended like platforms with holes in the middle for basins.

In 1860, an Englishman invented the earth closet, a not-very-serious rival to the toilet or water closet. As its name implies, it used dirt instead of water and had to be emptied rather frequent-

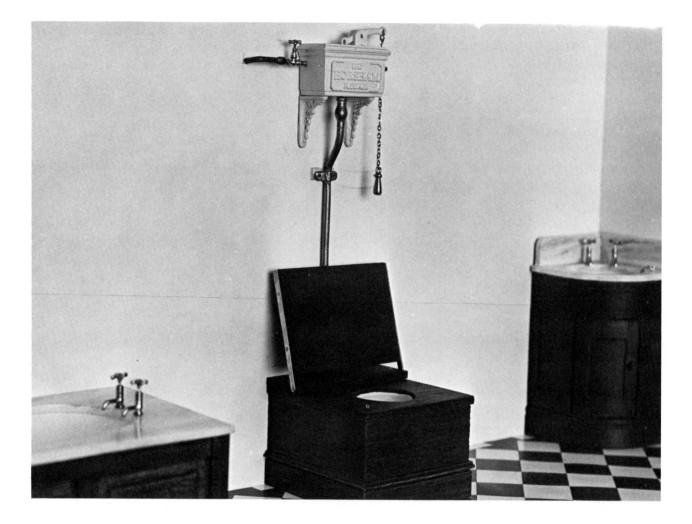

These nineteenth-century bathroom fixtures come from Sussex Crafts. Note the pipes: if you're going to put a toilet in your house, you should consider the plumbing, too. The wooden-cased tub and sink effectively hide their imaginary pipes.

ly. It looked like a wooden box with a thick wooden back from which dirt was spilled, as necessary, into the box enclosure. It may not be surprising that the earth closet never gained the popularity of the water closet, especially considering that contemporary pictures show it vented, like a stove, at a window or fireplace chimney.

Some toilets had overhead tanks while others had lower or no visible tanks. The hopper was often very fancifully designed featuring transfer-print landscapes, decorative patterns, and even historical scenes! Eventually porcelain hoppers were embossed and prettily painted. Toilets were imported until the beginning of domestic manufacture in the 1870s. This fostered a spread of the use of toilets indoors as did the increasing availability of running water.

The separate bathroom as a standard feature of common residences was a post-Civil War phenomenon although there were some antebellum exceptions in wealthy homes. If you want to be really authentic in putting a bathroom in your older Victorian house, you might do exactly what the Victorians did and eke a bath out of a bedroom. You can do this by dividing a large bedroom with a new wall. That will leave a telltale sign found in many Victorian homes: three of the walls of the original bedroom will have fancy molding and other decoration that disappear into the plainer partition that is obviously an afterthought. In other words, in both the bedroom and the bathroom there will be one of the four walls that doesn't have the same architectural detail as the others because it's newer. Remember, too, that *bath*room sometimes meant just that, and had only a sink and a bathtub. The toilet would be in an adjacent room (or it might not exist at all). Generally by the 1870s the toilet was in the same room although it might be hidden by a screen or room divider.

Once bathrooms developed and water was run through pipes, many sinks were encased in marble and wooden cupboards. These cabinets followed the prevailing furniture style which was often, as in the Renaissance Revival, massive and extremely elaborate. There were also vanities or lavatory cabinets with two sinks.

Bathtubs themselves closely followed the development of sinks. During the seventeenth and eighteenth centuries bathing was not very ceremonial: on those rare occasions when it was considered appropriate to bathe, wooden or tin tubs were pulled in front of a kitchen or bedroom fire. One well-to-do Philadelphia matron is quoted as saying she never had every part of her body wet at the same time. She was not the only one.

During the nineteenth century there developed a greater though certainly not consuming passion for cleanliness. The tin tub was often painted and one house might have several tubs. These were pulled up to the kitchen fire or stove or positioned in front of a bedroom fire; some perhaps had their own special bedroom alcove. Most tubs were small, round or oval metal affairs of the so-called hip bath size. There were also some slipper baths, shaped like boots, which all but enclosed the bather, preserving both warmth and modesty. Other tubs were made of porcelain.

If you are putting a tub in use in your dollhouse bedroom you may want to station some metal cans nearby for the water and also put a drop cloth underneath the tub as did nineteenth-century homemakers. During the 1840s and 1850s, when separate bathrooms first began to appear in affluent homes, tubs themselves started to become larger and more elaborate.

The cast-iron tub with claw feet was popular beginning in the 1880s at which time some baths had hooded shower enclosures. Earlier, during the midcentury period, there were some tubs that already had built-in showers. Before that a rudimentary shower had appeared, for instance, the contraption at Gore Palace in Waltham, Massachusetts. Built between 1802 and 1804, one of Gore's rooms had a hole in the ceiling above a lead tub through which servants poured water down on the master.

By the 1840s, showers were slightly more sophisticated and there were several different kinds. Examples include the adapta-

Bathroom by Tom and Guy Roberts
with tiny hexagonal tiles on the tub
enclosure and floor. The room is
wainscoted and wallpapered. Note
the rustic treatment on the washstand
at right. *Photo by Phillip F. McPherson*

tion of the hip bath by attaching pipes to support a new overhead
tank. There was also a sort of high-sided round pan with an overhead tank and a curtain. Sometimes the tank was fed from a lower
reservoir using a handpump.

Many nineteenth-century bathrooms were large, elaborate
rooms with wainscoted, wallpapered, or tiled walls, curtains and
stained-glass windows, and carpeted, painted, or tiled floors.
Some were large enough to accommodate dressers, chairs, and
sofas and some had heaters in the wall.

As they grew more common, they became somewhat plainer so that at the turn of the century, bathrooms were not only more numerous, they were smaller. Most had white enameled metal or wood furnishings including cork-seated chairs and hanging cabinets. The sink, tub, and toilet were less heavily decorated.

Separate stall showers, while not common, were known, and there were glass-doored stalls. Even though the rooms tended to be plainer than their elaborate Victorian predecessor (Art Nouveau-influenced bathrooms being an exception) there still was room for some interesting design on basins, shiny tile dadoes and

Bathroom of the c. 1890 Megler Landing House by Noel and Pat Thomas. Like many Victorian rooms it's somewhat oddly shaped (check the ceiling) and in fact could have been shaped by "stealing" from another large room or from an area carved by a staircase. The footed tub is right at home with the etched mirror on the door and dark wood molding. *Photo by Harry Liles*

friezes, wallpaper and the ubiquitous, tiny matte-white hexagonal floor tiles. Other choices for floors included linoleum, cork, or even oilcloth. Because square corners caught dirt, some bathrooms were built with curved corners.

An accessory you'll want to include is toothpaste. From the 1870s to the 1890s, when the toothpaste tube was marketed, toothpaste was made in solid blocks packed in pottery or metal containers. Razor strops hung in many bathrooms and though the safety razor was available in the 1880s it was not well accepted for a number of years. Perforated toilet paper was an 1880s invention that we still enjoy.

WASHDAY

As we go from washing bodies to washing clothes it becomes evident that more energy was expended on the latter than on the former. In addition to a caldron of hot water on the fire, the usual colonial washday accoutrements were a tub (or tubs), a washing stick, and wash dollies. Washing sticks were the forerunners of the familiar washboard with its wooden, metal, or ceramic slats. Interestingly, the washboard wasn't a factor until the mid-nineteenth century. The washing sticks were thick wooden slats with ridges carved in them. The dollies were primitive agitators, essentially clothes beaters that were about three feet long and had several short legs or a stump at one end and a crosspiece that formed a handle at the other.

Soap, in solid or liquid form, was made at home out of fats and ash. A related small laundry accessory which should not be hard to make is the lye box, a small wooden container with holes in the bottom. The homemaker laid straw and muslin in the bottom, then filled the box with ash. Holding the box over the washtub, the laundress poured water into it. The water filtered through the ash, taking with it the lye which was considered a good cleanser.

It is fairly simple to recreate a colonial washday scene in miniature if you put a caldron of water on the fire, station a washtub near the hearth, and place a washing stick and a lye box nearby. Sometimes the washing stick was used to fish the clothes out of the water, or there might have been a wooden laundry fork, a long forked stick, or a pole. Clothes were hung on a line using notched clothespins. Some homes had drying racks which lowered from the ceiling or stood near the fire.

You can construct essentially the same scene for the nineteenth century, too. To get the full effect it should be fairly elaborate with several tubs (probably on legs), one for each of the separate operations: soaping, bluing, starching, and rinsing. Add a washing stick, fork, clothesline, clothes bag and baskets, pails, dippers, and kettles.

Well-equipped colonial homes had irons to smooth the

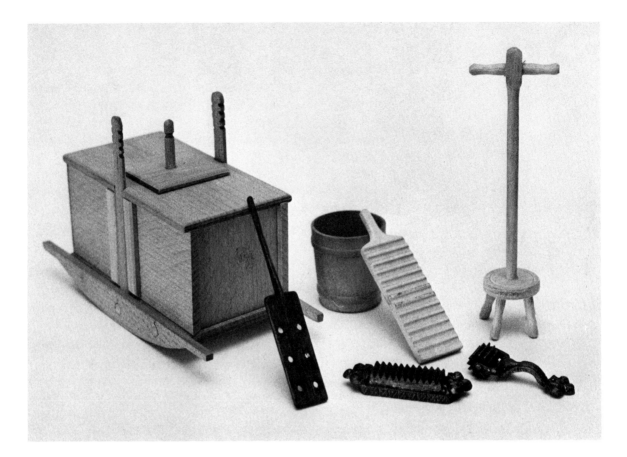

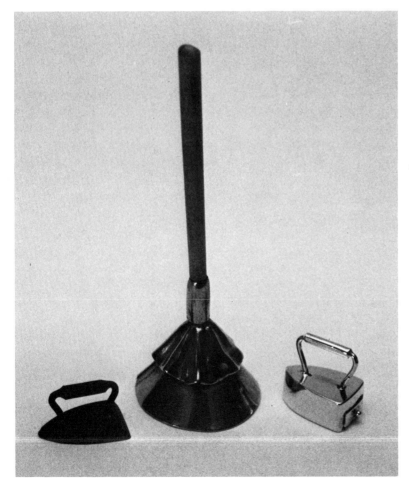

(Above)
It's easy to see why wash-day was never referred to as wash-hour when looking over these implements. From the left they are a washing machine by J. Weinberg which relied on a combination of rocking and plunging action for cleaning clothes, a washing stick by Barbara Davis, a multi-use wooden bucket, a washing board by J. S. Powel, and a washing dolly. The two-piece contraption is a fluting iron by Al Atkins, the Village Smithy. It is of a type that gained popularity in the 1860s. Washing machines on rockers were being made fairly early in the nineteenth century and some models were still being developed in the 1880s.

(Left)
Here are some more wash-day implements. Chet Spacher made the wash dolly and Lesli Rahmatulla made the irons. At left is a flat or sadiron, called flat for obvious reasons and called sad as a reference to its being solid or heavy (although it's evident that many a sad hour could be spent hefting the thing!). The other is a box iron with a small drawer in which a homemaker would put a hot slug that would heat the iron.

clothes after washing. Seventeenth-century irons were hollow boxlike contraptions that held hot coals or metal slugs. The solid sadiron or flatiron, developed during the eighteenth century, was heated at the hearth or on a stove. Most homemakers had two or more irons so that as one iron cooled, another could be reheated and ready to use.

Some Victorian cookstoves had special pyramid-shaped iron heater units that fit on the top. There were also some separate heaters designed specifically for this purpose and used in big households. Victorian cookstoves also came with metal boiling tubs for clothes washing.

There were several specialized types of irons. Very narrow pointed tally irons were for finishing sleeves, cuffs, and collars. There also were fluting or crimping irons used to make ruffles and pleats by a process also known as goffering. These irons depended on a corrugated surface to produce the desired effect. They developed from the late-seventeenth-century wooden crimping board—a small, corrugated slab on which the cloth was laid and over which the laundress then passed a corrugated roller. In the nineteenth century, more sophisticated iron fluting irons were constructed of corrugated rollers arranged like miniature wringers.

In the late eighteenth century some colonial dames turned to mangles—rollers under pressure—to smooth laundry. The mangle remained a common laundry appointment through the Victorian era. In the mid-nineteenth century some women used a box mangle, a six-foot-long weighted box with a crank and a flywheel to power the box over clothes wound around rollers. The linen press was used to smooth flat linens such as tablecloths. It is identified by the screw-turn feature that held linens tightly between flat wooden surfaces. Though it seems very late for a very logical idea to come to fruition, it was not until the 1890s that the folding ironing board appeared. Prior to that ironing was done on tables, some of which were very elaborate with storage space below for irons, trivets, and sleeveboards.

There was a gas iron by the 1876 Centennial Exposition at which all gas appliances were considered the newest rage. Fuel-fed irons were a menace to safety, however, and went out of favor relatively quickly. An electric flatiron was exhibited as early as 1882 but it was more than a decade before it was ready for home use and then it was still quite heavy. In 1913 the electric iron with its own rest was introduced, eliminating the need for a trivet.

Washing machines developed steadily from early patents granted during the period between 1797 and 1805. The accent was on "washing" rather than "machine," however, and early washing machines were essentially tubs with dollies on board beaters attached to hand cranks. Some of the washing machines of the mid-nineteenth century were set on their sides on rockers which presumably made them easier to operate. In the 1850s roller-type wringers were added to the washing machine tub. Other wringers were attached to tables or mounted on their own stands.

The electric washing machine went on the market in 1906. One 1908 model featured a washtub with wringers on legs. The early twentieth century also introduced gasoline-powered washing machines.

Amid all this progress it is well to remember that from the seventeenth century through the twentieth, clusters of isolated rural homemakers washed clothes by hand in hollowed-out logs filled with water that was heated on kitchen or yard fires.

SIX

SPECIAL CASES

THE NEW CENTURY

THE year 1900 brought a new century that, in many ways, was also a new age. But the twentieth century was attached to the nineteenth and much of what was Victorian crossed over the year 1900. This juxtaposition of old and new gives us a most interesting period and it also provides the miniaturist with a choice of direction. You can repeat much of the style of the late Victorian era in furniture and interior design or you can break off into the new approaches hinted at at the close of the nineteenth century—Art Nouveau and the Arts and Crafts movement—or you can refine your own blend of old and new.

We treat only a short period before World War I—just seventeen years—but it is a period when you can show how America was pulling out of the nineteenth century into modern times. You can fit enough transitional elements into your rooms to effect a very interesting and expressive setting. In your choice of furniture and accessories you can show how America was bursting through the Victorian fetters and speeding toward a faster, sometimes freer lifestyle that would prove to have its own complications. The leisurely pace of the earlier life is ending. As the century opened, agriculture—the family farm—still employed more workers than any other occupation but city life was encroaching. New waves of immigrants were arriving, bringing new blood and new cultures to American life. In 1900 the average American family had 4.7 people and no car. There were in fact only 8,000 cars in the country and 150 miles of paved road. But that would change quickly and during the pre-war years the growth of the automobile changed the face of the country and incidentally provided a model for the dollhouse enthusiast who wants to do something a little different.

As roads multiplied, many homeowners along the way decided to take advantage of the situation, turning front parlors into tearooms for motorists and their weary passengers. You might consider turning one of your dollhouse parlors into a neatly appointed tearoom served by the family. This also would mean some changes in the kitchen which would have to be efficient enough for preparation of a good deal of food and drink. Essentially that would involve getting more and bigger kitchen utensils and other accoutrements.

As for the style of the early-twentieth-century dollhouse, you have much to choose from. Victorian styles, sometimes much sim-

This early-twentieth-century living room setting was made by Helen Dorsett. The unusual billiard table-settee in the Mission style was taken from a 1909 issue of *Popular Mechanics,* reproduced in miniature for the Scale Cabinetmaker (vol. 3, no. 2). The table with early Victorian pillar-and-scroll styling at the left of the fireplace was taken from a 1914 Butler Bros. catalogue as was the leather rocker. Kathy Sevebeck made the rug and Francis Whittemore made the lamp with its opalescent art-glass shade. The wallpaper is from Joe Hermes. *Photo by Don and Cindy Massie*

This is the living room showing the table turned into a settee. *Photo by Don and Cindy Massie*

plified, still sheltered many families. Tudor elements, most affecting the exterior, were popular in the first two decades, while many a wealthy businessman requested his architect to draw a Georgian mansion for his suburban lot. In California and Florida, the Spanish hacienda and Mission styles were fairly common. The less sophisticated pueblo of the Southwest Indian influenced building in that area which went from territory to statehood during the period. Of course there were some overblown imitation European chateâux and castles that camped along Fifth Avenue and various other fashionable city and country addresses.

But a new architecture was afoot in the land, building on a revolution begun in the late years of the previous century. To those of us now, the most famous exponent of the new style was Frank Lloyd Wright. He and his fellow architects were devoted to an "earth" architecture, an organic, ground-hugging style that emphasized horizontal lines over vertical, and spread houses on the land rather than massing cupola upon tower upon bay upon porch.

As there were new styles, so, too, there were whole new kinds of houses—houses to suit the masses, the working people, the finally servantless middle and lower middle classes. Single-story bungalows with porches sprang up in towns and suburbs all over the country. If you are just starting or haven't much money to put into a dollhouse, such a small house might be a very good option. The houses took the form of a basic prefabricated box without the molding, cornices, and decorative niches of older, more substantial homes. This means that you can take a less expensive simple dollhouse shell and work it into a dollhouse of character. A dollhouse with living room, dining room, kitchen, bath, and one or two bedrooms is more than adequate for this project. Another working class option was the semi-detached or double house. The treat here is obvious to the dollhouse collector who sees a chance to do two kinds of houses with two different styles of interior and furniture. You can double your fun without doubling your expense.

Many working families had large homes, however, that were two or three stories high, as America's towns and towns-that-are-now cities bear ample witness. We enter one such home by a front porch with turned posts and perhaps a simple railing. The basic floor plan lacks an entry hall and instead brings us into the parlor. It is the smallest of the three first-floor rooms and is separated from the dining room by a large, doorless opening. The kitchen at the back of the house is the biggest of the rooms, sporting new plumbing and an old stove (for more about the stove see Chapter Five). There is linoleum in the kitchen but wide-board floors in the other rooms. The walls are painted and redone each year. The plain mahogany stairway runs straight from the parlor to a

A turn-of-the-century bedroom by Helen Dorsett with furniture from the Scale Cabinetmaker Guide V. The lace curtains hang as simple, straight panels. The pictures are from Don Massie, the wallpaper from the Calico Print Shop, the crazy quilt from Mimi Ayers, and the washbowl and pitcher from Barbara Epstein. *Photo by Don and Cindy Massie*

small landing and turns to empty onto the second-floor hallway. Arranged at either end of the hall are bedrooms one and two with three others opening as railroad cars off one side of the hall. The only room carved out of the other side of the hallway is a bathroom, recently taking the place of an outdoor privy. In fact the washstands are still neatly arrayed in the bedrooms. The attic, with its sloping ceiling, stores household goods, clothing, family treasures, and food. Dozens of apples—each one laid out on the floor and carefully separated from the others—await the next baking day. At the other extreme is the cellar; it has an earthen floor and hides a coal bin that opens to the outside through a chute. The coal will feed the cookstove and the stoves that warm the parlor and dining room. Each of the three ground-floor rooms contains some built-in cupboard or closet space for dishes, food, books, and the few knickknacks the family has accumulated.

It is easy to see the large family—perhaps a family of Irish immigrants making their way in the New World—the father reads his newspaper in the kitchen, the mother cleans up the dinner dishes, the children sit at the big round dining-room table doing homework, and everyone waiting for the priest who is expected momentarily and who will be the excuse for using the parlor this evening.

Not so far from that simple homestead stands a remnant of earlier, more lavish days: a Victorian mansion. This edifice can be brought out of the nineteenth century whole by the collector who wants to add only a few turn-of-the-century touches. Or, it can be transformed into a true twentieth-century house the way a twentieth-century family might have changed it, encouraged by pacesetting books and magazines that urged alteration of the old houses to suit the new life. Here is an ambitious and rewarding project for the collector who must overcome the architectural faults of an eclectic Victorian. Twenty-five years earlier we might have gloried in the house's dark, narrow hallway, its high ceilings, and misplaced windows. Now, however, we tackle these old-fashioned wonderments with an updated hammer, saw, and paint brush.

Let me repeat a warning from a previous chapter: I in no way encourage the alteration of an *antique* dollhouse. I believe that these houses should be restored—with the advice of experts and a kind hand—as close to their original condition as possible. The house I am suggesting for change is not a custom-designed work of art, either. It is rather an ordinary reproduction either newly built or newly bought that lends itself both aesthetically and structurally to alteration. As we examine some of the aspects of interior design that marked the era, you will see ways to change the Victorian house or to build authentic elements into your twentieth-century house.

The term "living room" came to replace the word "parlor" although not everybody approved. In large homes the living room was a family gathering place as opposed to the drawing room which remained largely a ceremonial room for guests. In many houses, however, the drawing room disappeared altogether. Dining rooms were still used but there were fewer "cubbyholes" hidden off hallways or attached to larger rooms. The floor plan was more open, easier to move around in and sometimes complete with such amenities as sun rooms—usually protruding from the house with three walls of windows—and sleeping porches for the summer. In general porches and dormers were popular.

Remembering that telephones were not really widespread, you

A dining-room setting inspired by the Arts and Crafts and Mission styles constructed by Helen Dorsett with furniture from Scale Cabinetmaker Guide V. This room leans heavily on the style advanced by the Green Brothers with its paneled dado, beamed ceiling, and bay for the buffet. Note the intricately paned glass. Helen Dorsett made the lamp and, along with Kathy Sevebeck, the dishes in the china cabinet. On top of the cabinet a brass vase and bowl from Clare-Bell and a wooden tray and stemware by Brant Keyes. The rug is from the Keshishian Collection, the centerpiece is by Kathy Sevebeck, and the palm is from Rosemary Dyke. *Photo by Don and Cindy Massie*

might want to take up the arrangement of some fine homes that had their own separate telephone booths, presumably in a somewhat exaggerated and snobbish desire for privacy. Often these booths with their table, chair, and window were tucked under a stairway. Despite generally less-pigeonholed interiors, there still were shallow niches and bays carved out of walls to accept pieces of furniture such as a sideboard.

Wall treatments were myriad, so you have a large choice. There was some paneling still being done as well as stenciling and painted wood-graining. Dadoes still were evident in some homes but in most there were no dadoes. Wall surfaces might be done in anything from a matte-finish paint to a lacquer gloss and with wallpaper as cheap as five cents a roll, many homemakers chose to paper their walls. Here alone there is considerable variety available as wallpapers could be had in reproduction styles made from old blocks, scenics, silver and gold designs, Oriental patterns, grasscloth, or the more prosaic, though generally by now smaller, florals and geometrics introduced in the previous century. There were some rather avant-garde advisors writing books during the early years and one even recommends using butcher's brown wrapping paper! This gives you some idea of how much imagination you can use without going totally wrong historically.

Of course there were also the marble walls of the great railroad magnates' rooms rising to meet gilded ceilings. Much more likely, though, the papered wall of the doctor's or teacher's or grocer's house would reach a ceiling lower than its Victorian predecessor, lighter in color than the wall and finished with paint, paper, or plaster relief work. There also were some beamed or paneled ceilings and this treatment was especially popular among decidedly twentieth-century stylists building Arts and Crafts inspired homes. Some of the more poetic decorated their beams with floral or geometric designs.

Sliding downward again we find pine and hardwood floors of great variety including parquets and planks measuring from a few inches to a foot wide. Many floors were painted—some were painted white in very sophisticated homes—and some were stenciled. On the other hand, a worker paying off a four-room bungalow might come home to a concrete floor that was waxed over for effect.

Windows drew on more styles than at any time in American history with the modern thrust being toward the wider, bigger-paned window. Frank Lloyd Wright tried to get more light into his houses by using wider windows and he also, as did others, designed decorative windows in colorful stained glass, sometimes mixed with clear glass. The designs might be starkly geometric or airily Art Nouveau. Other decorative light-admitting windows wound their way around exterior doors or were cut into the door itself. French doors led to fine terraces. The one-over-one sash window which is so familiar today was very common. But there were some odd twists on the sash window as well. People who were taken with the Georgian Revival might slap a colonial-style window on an otherwise Victorian house, thinking that fixed the look. It was not rare to see one of the stately *grande dames* of the late nineteenth century dotted with six-over-six or—for the builder who was schizophrenically trying to live in both worlds—six-over-one sash windows. Casement windows were popular with these colonial enthusiasts, as they were with more modern types like Gustav Stickley, the furniture maker, who suggested casements as a fine complement to a fireplace (which he would surround with built-in settees, bookcases, and shelving).

The fireplace, which had been de-emphasized during the previous era, made a comeback in some homes. The premier decorator of her day, the fabled Elsie de Wolfe, thought no drawing room complete without one. Stickley felt the fireplace added warmth, literally and figuratively. Fireplaces might protrude, as they had in the nineteenth century, or be very sparse and flush with the wall, the brick-lined well recessed.

In addition to the brick and wood fireplaces of old there were cement fireplaces now, and many fireplaces decorated with glazed tiles and glazed brick. The colors were greens, blues, browns and ochres tinged with other earth-color glazes. The tiles were both plain and fancy with some marvelous designs molded into them.

Followers of the Arts and Crafts movement were particularly taken with the tiles and stained glass and sometimes put thick friezes of tiles as a border at the top of the wall. They also liked paint and paper borders near beamed or paneled ceilings.

Less artistic certainly were the company houses being built

A mirrored sideboard and a dining set in Golden Oak by Carlisle Miniatures. The pressed-back chairs were found almost by the handful in many late Victorian and early-twentieth-century homes. *Photo courtesy of Robert L. Carlisle*

during the turn-of-the-century decades for poor workers in mills and mines. Just as the middle class was beginning to cast off Victorian styles, the Victorian mire was filtering down to the worker's family, who were trying to accumulate what they saw as the badges of the middle class: the cluttered parlor and the fringed portiere. They bought furniture on time and stashed most of it (including a bed or two) in the front room of what probably was a two- or perhaps three-room house. Fabric hangings were room dividers and doors; the valanced mantel, crowds of pictures and cheap carpet all contributed to the old-fashioned feeling which the residents interpreted as the new fashion.

The furniture people put in their homes ran the gamut from good eighteenth-century pieces salvaged by the growing number of antiques enthusiasts—who frequently mixed colonial and Federal styles in so-called colonial rooms—to the most modern cantilevered tables and chairs imaginable at that time. If you're doing a twentieth-century dollhouse you can mix all sorts of pieces together, even updating some older pieces along the way. After all, a good bit of older hand-me-down furniture was butchered to meet a family's stylistic and practical needs. For instance, many a homebound carpenter took a saw to the fretwork of Grandmother's table, shortened the legs of an old bureau, removed the mirror on an aged sideboard, or stripped a center table of its marble top for use somewhere else. I don't suggest you cut up antique dollhouse furniture, but you can only improve some of the worst of the current commercial production with some judicious editing, including repainting.

Pillar-and-scroll furniture was quite popular in many homes, as were surviving Eastlake and other mid- and late Victorian furniture. There were painted peasant styles, and some recall Biedermeier pieces from turn-of-the-century parlors.

Frequently you can achieve the desired transition to the twentieth century by reupholstering pieces. The choices in material include velour, corduroy, damask, velvet, brocade, silk, tapestry, cotton, linen, denim, haircloth, leather, and needlework. Slipcovers of linen print or chintz hide ugly furniture and give a sense of the era. You should include at least one bed of brass or iron as the metal beds were eclipsing wooden beds in popularity and you will certainly want to put a willow chair or two somewhere.

Built-in furniture—cupboards, settles, seats, chests, bookcases, tables—was fashionable among the stylish, often combining Art Nouveau touches with the harder-edged products of the Arts and Crafts tradition. The Arts and Crafts furniture (first referred to in Chapter Four) was based on theories of honest construction. That often meant rectilinear lines, a flat surface with little decoration, and forthright if not massive hardware. It was architectural furniture, often to the point of being designed right along with the house and built in to suit the designer's idea of unity in décor. The Arts and Crafts people saw furniture as integrated to its background. Leather upholstery and decorative tiles usually came in browns, blues, greens, and rose colors. Though occasionally swayed by Oriental influences, Arts and Crafts proponents tried at all times to reform what was left of the nineteenth century's typically overladen Victoriana.

Inheriting the Arts and Crafts mantle were people like Wright and the brothers Charles and Henry Greene, whose furniture is easy to signify in miniature because they put ebony pegs over the screws that held their pieces together. Designers in this tradition squared things off. Charles Rennie Mackintosh exemplifies this in his tall back chairs (see Chapter Four). These straight, sometimes lightly ornamented plank seated chairs did not yield their straight lines even to the sitter's back. Popular designer William Bradley gave us rectilinear lines in his furniture that were relieved with colorful painted surfaces, often recalling Art Nouveau motifs.

The Arts and Crafts movement opened the way for Mission furniture—so named not only because it reminded people of the furniture of the Spanish missions, but because it was indeed furniture with a mission. It was to bring a new, simple, straightforward and above all honest craftsmanship to a wider range of people than did the generally expensive Arts and Crafts pieces. Mission furniture was boxy, sturdy, and most of it was made of oak. Gus-

A Golden Oak dresser-desk-bed combination by Ida Stearns Fritsche of Ipso Facto Studio. *Photo by Ross Klavan*

Bill Burkey is the craftsman who furnished this bedroom in turn-of-the-century pieces which include a copy of a desk made (c. 1901–08) by the Larkin Company of Buffalo, New York. The desk was priced at $2 but the company would throw it in free if a customer spent a certain amount on its other home and health-care products. There are some things in the room which predate the desk by many years—the braided and hooked rugs and the bedside Argand lamp (which would be replaced by kerosene in most homes in the absence of gas or electricity). *Photo courtesy of Bill Burkey*

tav Stickley, probably the most famous of its manufacturers, described it as being beautiful to the extent that it fulfilled its purpose. It was given to square posts in the seat back and leather or canvas upholstery. Fittings were copper and iron and the finish generally was natural.

A lot of Golden Oak furniture was an offshoot of Mission although it often diverged in style. Golden Oak now refers to that undistinguished body of furniture produced in factories to sell cheaply to the masses. It relied on massive forms, relatively coarse carving and lines that blurred depending on what style the factory might be remembering. Grand Rapids, Michigan, was a hotbed of Golden Oak and fed the nation a steady diet of bastardized styles.

Many people, especially outside the cities, found their furniture in the pages of the "Wish Books," those thick catalogues from Montgomery Ward and Sears Roebuck. Collectors, who are finding more miniature Golden Oak available each season, have only to leaf through one of the inexpensive turn-of-the-century catalogue reprints currently available to see exactly what it was the homemaker was wishing for.

The great advances in lighting were made during the nineteenth century leaving us with a wide choice of illumination for the twentieth century, dependent really on how modern the town is where you are locating your dollhouse. Some farmhouses still used kerosene lamps while many towns had gas hookups and bigger towns and cities could provide electricity. As suggested in Chapter Four, you might consider building a kitchen or pantry vignette out of lamp cleaning: each day the homemaker would line up those lamps that were fuel-burning and clean the sooty glass chimneys.

The student lamps were especially popular with Mission furni-

A turn-of-the-century parlor done in "catalogue" style with furniture straight from the Montgomery Ward catalogue. Notice how the dado has disappeared. The fireplace is of oak with green-glazed brick. The lace curtains hang perfectly straight, their panels amply accommodated by the wide windows. The parlor is made by Helen Dorsett; the furniture is from the Scale Cabinetmaker Guide V. The rug is from the Keshishian Collection. The plants are by Rosemary Dyke; the glass lamp, bottle, and vase by Francis Whittemore; the portrait from Don and Cindy Massie; the book on the center table by Jane Bernier of Borrower's Press; the pewter candlesticks from Lilliput; and the wallpaper from the Calico Print Shop. Compare this room with the dining room from the Scale Cabinetmaker Guide V which is influenced by Arts and Crafts and Mission models. *Photo by Don and Cindy Massie*

ture enthusiasts and Tiffany lamps were the *crème de la crème* with the Arts and Crafts crew as well as with less *haute* homemakers. You also can convert a vase or even a coffee canister into a lamp if you wish. One decorating advice book recommends wiring such receptacles to get a truly distinctive and original lamp and to avoid the "mortification" of seeing the same lamp you bought in somebody else's house!

In general, table and floor lamps were used as were chandeliers and wall sconces. A bedroom light near the door would be quite an extravagance in many homes which found it cheaper to string the wiring through the attic—and thus to a ceiling fixture—than to carry it down the wall to a sconce conveniently near the door.

Remember to drop a pull string from your center ceiling fixtures and, if you're interested in complete accuracy, don't forget the exposed wiring itself where appropriate, in conversions from gas to electric lighting.

The light shone down on a great variety of rugs and carpeting in the twentieth-century home—from braided rugs enjoying a rebirth of popularity to patterned straw, hemp, and jute mats imported from China and Japan. In many homes rugs replaced carpeting, continuing a trend begun during the last quarter of the nineteenth century. Where carpeting prevailed, solid colors were newly fashionable; another modern touch was the Navajo design rug.

Linoleum had just about done away with floorcloths and oilcloths although some oilcloth borders with phony wood designs were still made to fill in the plain wood spaces between the edge of a rug and the wall. You might also find oilcloth mats placed strategically in the kitchen and of course oilcloth protected many kitchen tables.

Portières were still in use in some homes as were window shades in plain colors and prints. Draperies hung over thin undercurtains or curtains hung alone. The materials were echoes of upholstery materials: silk, velour, corduroy, velvet, brocade, damask, poplin, cotton, linen, chintz, burlap, denim, and crewel with linen, silk, lace, and swiss under curtains.

Pictures were hung with somewhat more restraint than in earlier years. It was no longer necessary to cover every inch of wall space. Photographs were very popular, as were prints and paintings. Though sentimental oils were sold, modern art was taking up its cudgel with more confidence and the 1913 Armory Show featuring Cézanne, Matisse, Duchamp, and Picasso woke American artists to new possibilities. It also spurred the growing controversy over modern art: art students in Chicago burned a Matisse, fortunately in effigy.

Art was not confined to the canvas. Great craftsmen of the day worked their magic on glass as they had begun to do in the nineteenth century and art glass—of which Tiffany's product was but one expression—filled the homes of appreciative audiences. The colored glass in opalescent and opaque finishes brought all the colors of the rainbow and nearly all imaginable shapes and sizes into everyday use. Art pottery also filled many homes.

A new voice was heard from earnest decorators, however, warning against too much bric-a-brac. One even warned against leaving any glass or china "set out" in the dining room. Collectors furnishing twentieth-century dollhouses may take a note from one design advisor who suggested changing the exhibit, as it were, by rotating the accumulated knickknacks of a lifetime so that most pieces were in storage awaiting their turn to be shown.

The turn-of-the-century household was learning to live with convenience. Electricity was really taking over by about 1910. By 1913 we had hand-held hair dryers much like the modern versions and there were both canister and bag-type vacuum cleaners. Victrolas with massive cases and built-in speakers entertained whole families as did the first modern 35-mm. camera which came along in 1914. The first dial telephone also appeared in 1914. The proliferation of central heating fixed radiators in almost every room.

In the midst of all this modernity speaking tubes were still being installed in affluent homes so that mistress and servant could communicate. If you want to add a tiny but evocative note, put a miniature ice block in a china bowl and set it on the dining room table. That was a circa-1900 anti-fly device. You might add some copper and glass accessories which were popular as everything from candlesticks to decorative pots. Screens tidied room corners or divided rooms. Some were plain glass panels, others decorative Orientals. An especially fine screen might hang on the wall. Your living room should probably have at least one musical instrument, a piano or an organ for the ambitious, or even a guitar. Almost every family of means wanted to be sure somebody could play something.

A less cheerful recollection can be dredged up if you attach a quarantine sign to the door. Diphtheria and typhoid were still major causes of death and it was not unusual to see a house in the neighborhood under quarantine.

Some people say regretfully that America lost its innocence in this age of the Gibson girl but that may be a too rueful approach. As the homemaker picked through the old and new styles that faced her, the country was making choices, too. America was learning to make its own way in a world with many promises but only one assurance: that it would not be the same as the old.

HOME ON THE RANGE

In 1814 the United States government offered 160 acres of land to veterans of the War of 1812. Some of them accepted the bonus, which was as much a challenge as a gift since it meant pioneering virgin land. That began the rush from East to West which was to turn from the initial trickle into a great flood following the Civil War.

The Western settlers lived a life that would, except for the terrain, have been quite familiar to the seventeenth-century Pilgrims. Most of them couldn't take very much when they left their Eastern homes: perhaps a cookstove, a bedstead, and some chests or boxes that would become the first storage and seating pieces. Many pioneers had their furniture shipped but it was so expensive that some had to wait a year to save the money to pay off the freight bill. Eventually of course Eastern and Midwestern mass production provided quite stylish furniture for the Western trade which—with certain impositions, such as primitive sanitation—provided quite stylish homes in which to put the pieces.

Prior to the Civil War, however, frame houses on the frontier were a rarity and were reserved for the prosperous who were able to make the transition from the much more common log cabin, celebrated in American folk history. It usually is considered a frontier fixture, but in fact the first log cabins were built by Scandinavians on the East coast in the seventeenth century and by the eighteenth century some Eastern Indians had adapted the cabin style with bark roofs and dirt floors. American slaves lived in log cabins for generations.

The frontier log cabin took the Eastern model West. The earliest cabins might not have a fireplace but rather a hole in the roof. The fire was built on a rude open hearth. Better and later cabins did have stone or brick fireplaces with stone, brick, or log chimneys. Instead of iron andirons, big flat rocks were often used to support the firewood.

A typical settler's cabin had a beamed ceiling and a dirt, plank, or wooden slab floor. Some planks concealed a hole under the floor for storing such staples as potatoes. Food was also stored in cloth pouches hanging from the ceiling beam.

Though unpainted woodwork and exposed rafters were commonplace, some interior walls were plastered, paneled, or whitewashed. There were shelves and/or pegs for household goods and clothes. If there was a sleeping loft, pegs protruding from the wall might form all the ladder there was although some houses with second floors went so far as to have real stairs. Windows were not glazed ordinarily and shutterlike batten doors were common.

The cabin itself could be from one room, perhaps sixteen feet square with one door, to several rooms. Extra rooms were added as needed and sometimes they were added without benefit of connecting doors. In such cases the settlers had to go out one door to the outside and back in the exterior door of the other room. This little peculiarity makes it very easy for miniaturists to use some of

The chair at left by Renée Bowen is a plain slat-back with a splint seat which is of the kind found in many frontier homes (this particular chair is a Shaker chair which, for our purposes, we'll assume was sold to a settler before the move West). At the right is a piece of stick furniture, as close as some hard-pressed pioneers could come to the Windsors they remembered. The bench hewn from a split log is by Tom Latané. The hanging lantern and the hatchet were fast company for the homesteader.

the small cubes sold as rooms and simply stick them together without having so much as to lift a saw.

You might however find the dogtrot arrangement more imaginative. In this layout a long outside hallway separates the two rooms. Some of course had porches and more than one fireplace. Alternatively, there might be a cookstove.

Other types of rugged housing which persisted on the Western frontier even after there were cities in the West were the dugout and the sod house. The dugout, reminiscent of the earliest shelter of some English settlers in New England, was holed out of the side of a hill or cast in a ravine. There were no windows, the floors were tamped dirt and the facades were often made of clay. An average size for a dugout was eight by twelve feet. Although there would be little recognizable furniture—mostly boxes or chests—there might be an iron stove and a stuffed mattress.

Sod houses had sod walls and windows covered by skins or blankets. The one room might be divided into living and sleeping areas by a quilt hung from the ceiling. Stoves burned grass or chips and sometimes wood.

Adobe brick construction was common as well, sometimes

A typical roughly made table and bench by Tom Latané. The bench is made from a split log, the table from unevenly hewn boards. The treenware bowls are by Jim Holmes.

with stucco laid over the adobe. Some two-story adobe-brick houses in perfect Eastern style exist to this day.

Whatever the style of the home, it was likely that the Conestoga wagon that brought the family to it was part of the construction. If the wood of the wagon itself wasn't torn apart for some use, the box part of the wagon might be attached whole to the side of the house, perhaps for storage.

Furniture in Western houses and cabins was simple, consisting of corner cupboards, wooden slab and trestle tables and blanket chests with iron or wooden hinges. Long benches of wood or hewn logs and three-legged stools provided a great deal of the available seating although there were also some slat- and splat-back chairs with splint, rush, and hide seats. There were many modified Windsors on the prairie, some no more than stick chairs. Families that did without closets also for the most part did without clothes presses or wardrobes, although you will find a few. Many homemakers used baskets for storage. Pie safes and food cupboards were fairly common.

Perhaps most attention was given to the bed. There were pallets and four-posters, spool beds, and plain narrow boxes. Most of the bedding was homemade and a flat mattress on a rope support was as much comfort as most pioneers had. Sheets were in short supply so a quilt or two might serve. Home spinning wheels and looms provided what bedclothes there were for most people though some frontier women had sewing machines. The washing of the resulting homespun was accomplished at outside hearths with wooden tubs. Pewter and wooden plates and utensils were standard as were utensils carved from gourds. If you are going to put a miner in your cabin or shack, remember to include scales to weigh the day's find.

Furniture had to be utilitarian and the woods used to make it were oak, hickory, walnut, cherry, maple, and a great deal of pine. There was some attempt at fancier fare and occasionally a poorer piece was mahoganized with a red stain and black smears.

Interestingly enough, the rustic organic furniture was a rich man's fad and a poor man's necessity. Rural and poor families couldn't afford to buy fine furniture and to them the loglike tables and real tree chairs came naturally. Their furniture tended to be understandably less elegant: tender tree branches supported a chair much better in cast iron on a New York terrace than in reality in a sod hut on the prairie. There "rustic" more often meant hollowing out a tree stump into a table or chair. Westerners used everything they could get their hands on to furnish their homes, including old barrels and packing crates.

When they did have time to devote to making furniture, the early settlers copied the Empire style which prevailed in the East at the time of their departure. Much furniture was homemade throughout the nineteenth century although even in the 1820s there was some good furniture in the West and we should not overlook the fact that many Westerners eventually established elegant homes.

In some frontier areas, particularly in the upper Midwest, there were enough stores and traders by the 1850s to put fine furniture, glassware, china, and carpets in the homes of the affluent settlers and military officers. It was not unusual for a log home or shanty with its almost empty interior to sit fairly near a fashionable Georgian or Greek Revival home with damask in the dining room, china in the cupboard, and silver on the sideboard.

By the late nineteenth century the home of the colonel's lady, the cattle baron, or the "high falutin' " madam had many of the amenities of gentler Eastern establishments. For those kinds of homes you can refer to Chapter Four.

THE SOUTHWEST AND CALIFORNIA

THE Southwest and California, although they share a common Spanish heritage, present totally different lines of development of furniture style and decoration. Decorative style is inextricably linked with the history of this area.

Spanish expeditions arrived in Santa Fe as early as 1550 and by 1610 had set up a settlement there. The settlements in the Southwest retained their sixteenth-century Spanish cultural patterns for a long time. Unlike settlers in other parts of the country, the Spanish were quick to use native Indian colors and materials which they combined with their own designs to develop a characteristic style.

The settlers' tools were crude, modeled after tools that had been used for centuries. The local wood was primarily ponderosa

Some of the things we might find in a Southwestern adobe home including baskets, kachina dolls, and pottery. From a New York collection.

pine and, until the middle of the nineteenth century, was hand-adzed. The mortise and tenon joint was common and, most often, the tenon passed through the mortise making an exposed tenon. Some doweling, including square doweling, was occasionally used. The hardware was simple as there was a scarcity of iron, so leather or very simple iron hinges were common.

Pomegranates, scallops, and shells, done in deep relief by gouging, and heavy grooving and cut-outs on rails were typical motifs. Bright colors obtained from the Indians were used to decorate and the combination of carving and paint was striking.

The houses themselves were frequently built around a central open patio with several outbuildings. Verandas ran the length of the house. The houses were made of sun-dried adobe brick and the walls were whitewashed over a mud plaster. To prevent the whitewash from rubbing off onto clothing, many Southwesterners papered the walls in calico or muslin to a height of five or six feet. The floor was smooth dirt or mud covered with woven woolen squares in a black and white checkerboard pattern called *jerga*. The windows had panes of mica and were shuttered with carved panels. Along one wall there was often a benchlike ledge or *larima* built as part of the adobe wall.

There was a corner fireplace in every room but it contained no andirons; logs were arranged in a conical fashion to be burned. The kitchen fireplace featured a big, swollen, bell-shaped chimney. Baking ovens in the familiar beehive shape were built outside on the patio. Fireplace chimneys had small niches for carved figures. A mantel shelf curved around the fireplace and held decorative and utilitarian objects. Later kitchens had bulky stone ranges. Cooking smoke was vented through holes in the flat roof.

Furniture was sparse in both the haciendas of the wealthy and the *jacales* (huts) of the poor. In the early years the only piece brought overland was the chest, often made of rawhide.

In the late seventeenth and early eighteenth centuries, mattresses stuffed with wool and spread on the floor served as beds. Rolled up against the wall and covered with *chimayo* blankets, they acted as seating during the daytime.

Chests containing the family's clothing, grain, and other foodstuffs were set against the wall. The early chests stood about twenty inches high, were about forty inches long and had a depth of twenty inches. Some of them stood on simple rectangular frames with open tops and a stretcher on each side joining the square post legs.

An *alacena*, a cupboard embedded in the wall, was also useful storage space. The *alacenas* were roughly thirty-five inches high and sixteen inches wide. The doors were carved or slatted, reminders of the English livery cupboard.

A *reprisa* or hanging shelf was a handy addition to a room. It had a decorative edge to keep objects from falling off. Mirrors were hung in pierced tin frames, and crucifixes, religious paintings, and figures known as *retablos* and *santos* decorated the walls. A rod on which the family's extra blankets hung was suspended from the ceiling.

Dining was done picnic-style and family members held their

This formal nineteenth-century chair has a lineage going back to ancient times. It was made by Barbara Jean of Innovative Ideas in Miniature. *Photo courtesy of Innovative Ideas in Miniature*

This c. 1800 chest has a happy look with its lions and rabbits. Chests were extremely common—indeed necessary—pieces of furniture in the Spanish Southwest just as they were in the East. This chest was made by Betty Libo and Mary Brady of the Original House of Miniatures. *Photo courtesy of the Original House of Miniatures*

Here are two pieces that would have been used from the late eighteenth century to the mid-nineteenth century and beyond. The chip-carved chair was especially common around the turn of the nineteenth century. Furniture makers, however humble, typically ornamented their pieces with some kind of painting and/or carving. The execution ranged from crude to brilliant. These pieces come from Betty Libo and Mary Brady of the Original House of Miniatures. *Photo courtesy of Original House of Miniatures*

plates on their laps. Small, three-legged stools called *taramitas* provided extra seating.

In the early eighteenth century the *sala* of the hacienda contained several chairs and tables. The chairs were dark and heavy, narrow and formal looking. They were not designed for comfort and any sitter was forced into an absolutely erect posture. Along the wall was a *vargueña*, a Spanish chest filled with drawers and compartments. It stood on high, carved legs and was inlaid with ivory and nacre.

The bedroom contained a bed or a pallet with a thin mattress covered by a spread with a *clocha* embroidery. A plain worktable for the lady of the hacienda and a chair where she could sit to do her handwork would also be there.

In the kitchen the family ate at a homemade, unfinished table. Typically, the round top would have a diameter of thirty-two inches and would be set on a square frame. Wide stretchers were carved with cutouts on the bottom. The side chairs had solid seats with a wide skirt and stretchers. Copper pots and pans, wooden utensils and bowls, majolica from Mexico, pottery from the pueblos, and even Chinese porcelain could all be found there. Silver

A sideboard with carved supports reminiscent of those on many Eastern pier tables. This piece is from the Casa Collection made by Barbara Jean of Innovative Ideas in Miniature. It belongs in a hacienda rather than in a more modest dwelling. *Photo courtesy of Innovative Ideas in Miniature*

Called a *trastero*, this cupboard was the "closet" of Spanish America. The painting would have been in vivid colors according to the makers, Betty Libo and Mary Brady of the Original House of Miniatures. This particular piece dates to the second quarter of the nineteenth century. *Photo courtesy of the Original House of Miniatures*

Living room taken from the Soberanes House in Monterey, California, c. 1850–75, in the Thorne Rooms Collection of the Art Institute of Chicago. This house is not the hacienda of a Spanish don but rather a home tended by Yankees come West from New England. It gives us an example of how Easterners adapted the Spanish architecture to their heritage and shows us what they felt comfortable with. The room also illustrates the fact that the clipper ship and overland transportation kept the West from being totally isolated from Eastern style. *Courtesy of the Art Institute of Chicago; Gift of Mrs. James Ward Thorne*

was the pride of the Southwest and every hacienda had quantities of it, some from Spain but most from Mexico. Candles in iron or wooden candelabra provided the usual lighting.

In the last quarter of the eighteenth century an important piece of furniture made its appearance. This was the *trastero,* a seven-foot cupboard of narrow depth that stood on legs. It had shelves for storing books, dishes, silver, and other valuables. The sides and solid panels were usually heavily carved and gaily painted. Doors on the early *trasteros* were carved spindles set in a frame.

With the advent of the Santa Fe trade in the nineteenth century, the *jacales* changed very little but the haciendas became luxurious. A table and possibly a chair might be introduced into a *jacale.* The chairs were wooden side chairs with a low seat of laced rawhide thongs. The tables were serving tables only a little over a foot high. The stretchers on the legs were at different levels.

In the haciendas the windows were now curtained with crimson worsted and Brussels carpets covered the floors. Large tables topped with marble, gilded framed mirrors, oil lamps, and other American-style furniture of the period were used. On the walls one still found *retablos* and crucifixes.

California's ties to Mexico ended earlier than did those that bound areas of the Southwest to the motherland. Ship traffic from the Orient and the East coast of the United States brought furniture and other decorative articles quite soon in California's development. After the early part of the eighteenth century, during which the furnishings of a room looked much like those in the Southwest, California began to use the same kinds of furniture found on the Eastern seaboard with a heavy sprinkling of objets d'art.

When the army came to the Southwest in the mid-nineteenth century, soldiers brought tools that were different and modern, including the level. The establishment of permanent forts throughout this area brought settlers as well as army dependents. The territorial style was established and the Boston rocker made its appearance on the front porch, ultimately uniting West and East under a Victorian banner.

SHAKER

MANY collectors feel confident in identifying Shaker pieces because the form is so distinctive and in fact it is not difficult to pick out the low Shaker slat-back chair or the angular black Shaker stove. Neither is it difficult to find them because there is a number of excellent Shaker reproductions in miniature. But faced with so many pieces in natural finishes, we too often limit our vision when equipping a Shaker home, not thinking to include a blue cupboard or red chair. The truth is that all Shakers did not live exclusively with unfinished furniture. Mustard yellow, dull red, dark green, and blue were all used.

One important thing to remember when building a Shaker setting is that for the first time in our study of interiors we are not dealing with a home for a single family. The Shakers lived a communal life and a dozen or more sisters and brothers shared one domicile. Generally these community lodgings were built on a dual framework, with separate doors, stairs, and dormitories for men and women. Even common rooms had their men's and women's sides.

Once past the typically hooded doorway we find a large house with white plastered walls lined with pegboards: the head-high strips of woodwork dotted with pegs that followed the walls of rooms and hallways. Clothes, mirrors, candleholders, small cupboards, even extra chairs were hung on the pegs, out of the way but conveniently close. Some pegboards were run under windows where small accessories like scissors might hang close to a sewing table and a chair set near the light from the window.

The plank floors were painted or stained to a yellowish hue and woodwork might have a reddish or brownish-yellow tinge.

Simple frames surrounded the doors and windows which had blinds or shutters rather than shades. Sometimes a short white, blue, or green curtain was hung on the window.

The narrow halls, steep stairs, and small rooms of the earlier Shaker lodgings gave way eventually to wide halls and larger rooms, made more spacious by the clean look of built-in cupboards and minimal furnishings. Most Shaker dwellings were heated by unadorned, rectangular black stoves, spare and efficient in their design.

Indeed, "spare" and "efficient" describe much of the Shaker culture including the furniture and the lifestyle itself. The modern dicta "form follows function" and "less is more" were given practical expression by Shaker craftsmen who were guided by strict religious principle. Cleanliness of mind and body was translated into cleanliness of line, and dedication to God led to the development of furniture production techniques that were not

Shaker room c. 1840 by Jim Ison. The stove is a distinctly Shaker design and like so much of the Shakers' work, is spare and functional, almost sculptural in its lines. *Photo by Rich de la Mar Associates*

Sisters' bedroom from the Hoffman Collection. Notice the built-in chest and cupboard and pegboard strips with mirror, wall chest, hanger, candleholder, and shelves hanging from pegs. The room is in the collection of the Children's Museum of Indianapolis. *Photo courtesy of Mary Pace*

merely symbols of praise to the Almighty but actual worship. To make a chair was to work for God and the community, and the grace and strength of the table or cupboard were components of prayer more than matters of individual pride. The identifiably Shaker characteristic of plainness and perfection of simple forms also was a logical extension of the backgrounds of early Shaker converts who were themselves plain country people.

They did not bring to the community any family history of fancy cabinetwork or a background of richly decorated chests and chairs. Shaker carpenters drew from the plain work they had learned in their youth—a general direction in woodworking that was, through the teachings of the new religion, perfected into a canon of craftsmanship that was austere without being rigid.

After the Civil War, a time that saw the beginning of the decline of Shakerism in this country, Shakers slowly fell prey to many of the same stylistic excesses that already attached themselves to those working in the outside world. There was, in the 1870s and 1880s, a degeneration creeping into the product of some Shaker craftsmen as they borrowed embellishments from outside the community and allowed such decadence as linoleum, pianos, and platform rockers. It is generally agreed that the best of the Shaker furniture was being made during the heyday of the sect from about 1800 to the Civil War.

Led by an Englishwoman, Mother Ann Lee, the Shakers came to America in 1774, establishing their first community two years later near Albany, New York. Eventually there were Shaker communities throughout New England, in Kentucky, and as far west as Ohio and Indiana. By 1850 there were about 6,000, the most there would ever be in this country.

Early on they had rejected some of the standard forms of the eighteenth century: the highboy, the lowboy, the canopy bed, the Windsor chair, banister and splat-back chairs, and any show of the cabriole leg. Rosewood and mahogany were out; the Shakers worked with pine, walnut, hickory, maple, cherry, and other fruitwoods.

Most of their chairs were of the slat-back style; the three-slat ladder-back was popular in the North while Southern communities often made four-slat ladder-backs. In addition there were one- and two-slat dining chairs, easily pushed under the table when not in use. The seats were rush and splint for the most part until the communities were better established in the nineteenth century when cane or woven seats in checkerboard patterns were introduced. Interestingly, but not surprising for the times, women's chairs were frequently lower than men's chairs. Chairs meant for use in looming or ironing were taller than usual however and leaned forward slightly.

The modest adornments on these chairs consisted of acorn- and mushroom-shaped finials and knobs. A cushion rail was added to some chairs, including the many rockers that dotted Shaker domiciles. It is sometimes called a shawl rail but its initial purpose was to provide a top rail to which a back cushion could be attached with a short tape. A uniquely Shaker chair mechanism was the tilter. After 1800, the Shakers developed a ball-and-socket foot which, fitted on the back legs, permitted the chair to tilt without the rubbing associated with rockers. The tilter saved wear on the floors and the few rugs the Shakers allowed themselves.

Although the Shakers had sworn off the Windsor chair there were some spindle-backs, including a few revolving spindle-backs. There were also some bentwood Shaker chairs although they were considerably more restrained than the Thonet version we looked at in Chapter Four. There were some double-armchair settees but they were relatively rare. Shakers also made good use of benches for seating.

Many meals were eaten at long trestle tables, sisters at one, brothers at another. A good deal of ironing and other work was done at a kitchen sawbuck table. Of course there were also the four-legged types with squarish tapered or lightly turned legs without feet. Ordinarily Shakers did not put chairs at the ends of the dining tables, leaving that area open for serving.

Other utility tables included candlestands and sewing stands (which were essentially candlestands with a drawer or two added). There were bigger tailoring tables with deep drawers and dozens of worktables for kitchen, laundry, and other rooms that usually were at basement level. It was not unusual for a Shaker domicile to have several drop-leaf tables, distinguishable because they had only one rather than two drop leaves.

A Shaker rocker with a tape seat in the checkerboard pattern and top rail designed for a small pillow that could be attached by short tapes. From a New York collection.

There were several types of desks as well, most of them of the desk-on-frame construction. Others had chestlike supports and there were some small lap desks. There were also some severe secretaries with plain, shelved cupboards on top of the writing surface.

Other cupboards were built-in, hung from the pegboards, or set on the floor. There were not very many corner cupboards or pie safes although a few examples of each exist. Perhaps the cupboard we most often associate with the Shakers is the tin cupboard, a tall, narrow piece with shelves and doors, designed to hold tinware and other utensils.

Clothes were ordinarily folded and stored in chests of drawers or hung on tiered hangers. There were some wardrobe cupboards, particularly in Kentucky.

Dressers also might be built-in and some were so tall that stepladders were used to reach their top drawers. The Shakers had the usual blanket chests and in the South kept sugar chests as did non-Shaker Southerners. Dressers and cupboards were often kept in the hall. Drawer pulls were made of turned wood or white porcelain. The dictates of Shaker life pronounced against brass hardware and there are cases of chests being "purified" by the removal of original brasses.

Shaker beds were of the low-post type with short headboards. The bedstead was often painted green and might have had a white or blue spread. Shaker beds commonly had large wooden casters, another evidence of the carpenter's functional bent.

Most Shaker furniture was made to serve two people at a time. Desks, dressers, and worktables are the best examples of double-sided furniture, some for instance with duplicate sets of drawers.

Putting accessories in a Shaker domicile isn't very hard because there wasn't the variety you find elsewhere. Obviously the Shakers needed the same pots, pans, and irons as other people who had to eat and keep their clothes in order, but who else among our forebears were told that they could have a mirror if it were no bigger than 18 by 14 inches? Shakers were allowed one glass lamp to a room, although more could be secured if really needed. Clock cases, whether for tall, shelf, or wall clocks, were uniformly plain (although the faces were not always so plain).

There were some hooked and braided rag rugs on the floors as well as plain striped carpeting but color selection was minimal. Two or three colors were allowed with the emphasis on green and gray. Some red, brown, and blue geometrics turn up in the long, shaggy pile of crinkled fibers that make up Shaker ravel-knit rugs.

Following the Shaker passion for cleanliness, you can put mats and metal boot scrapers at doorways and wood boxes with a brush and dustpan near the stove. You can easily see where Shaker efforts were concentrated when you examine a list of the inventions with which they are credited: the clothespin, the flour sifter, the dish drainer, the circular saw.

Many of us who have storehouses of colonial and Victorian furniture have avoided getting involved in buying Shaker items because we are afraid to start yet another style with its investment in space and money. However, many of us have also wanted to buy an especially pleasing piece or two and there's no reason to resist. You can do a small setting that features a corner of a room—two or three pieces of related furniture will fill it and you can have the Shaker feeling and craftsmanship without starting a whole new collection.

You also can integrate a few Shaker pieces, mostly chairs, into your established nineteenth-century setting because the Shakers did a very busy furniture sales business, even setting up a booth at the 1876 Philadelphia Centennial Exposition. The first recorded sale of a piece outside the community is 1789 but such sales were sporadic until the 1850s, when the Shakers began to realize they were on to something worth exploiting. In the early 1860s the Shakers started advertising, eventually sending out illustrated catalogues. An 1876 catalogue even warns of imitators. The sales were generally limited to chairs, rockers, footstools, and a few rugs and mats. Almost no Shaker case pieces were sold directly to the community.

Whatever Shaker pieces you choose, whether a houseful or a single chair, it is worthwhile becoming acquainted with the style because an appreciation of its combination of discipline and warmth helps to educate the eye for other fine work.

THE FARMHOUSE

THE farmhouse of the early twentieth century presents a special opportunity for miniaturists, many of whom remember such homes from their youth or from visits to grandparents. The farmhouse described here draws its inspiration from a Maryland house of the second decade but is much like those that were operating all over the country during the era.

Doing a farmhouse gives builders and collectors a chance to make good use of two areas that do not receive elaborate treatment in the colonial, Federal, and Victorian periods—the basement and the attic. Many commercial dollhouses have attics although few have basements. But the cellar is so important that it is worthwhile adding a basement level. A perfectly adequate basement can be built as a plain boxlike structure and positioned under the dollhouse. These two sections of the house were vitally important because they were food storage and preservation centers.

You can also add other rooms and wings to the basic house, perhaps building additions in different styles as the needs of the farm called for more space to accommodate hired hands or married children. The eclectic look can be a virtue here, joining generations of styles into one fascinating house that is a catalogue of changing design.

The furniture of the early-twentieth-century farmhouse was much like that of other homes of the time except that most pieces would have been plainer than those in a city townhouse or country estate. Many farmers could not afford fine furniture and what they kept at home tended to be serviceable and well-worn.

When equipping a farmhouse you can use an occasional piece from an earlier era because families depended to a great extent on the legacy of the hand-me-down. Many farms were furnished from mail order catalogues which provided everything from wallpaper to furniture and appliances. There are several reprints of turn-of-the-century catalogues that are good guides.

The kitchen of the typical farmhouse had a cast-iron cookstove, a dry sink, a table, built-in and freestanding cupboards, and as many chairs as fit in the room, for it was in the kitchen that both family and farm workers were fed. A rocking chair is a good addition to a farm kitchen. It seems to be a constant and most people with whom I have spoken recall that a rocking chair was a permanent kitchen fixture. There weren't many iceboxes in rural areas until the 1920s which leaves miniaturists to find other places to keep food. Fortunately the farm provides many, as we shall see.

Among the accessories you can include in a kitchen or adjacent porch or pantry are an ice-cream freezer and a galvanized tin tub for the Saturday night bath. The kitchen was the place where homemakers ironed clothes and the process was long and tedious. An ironing board of course is necessary and it was usual for the family to have at least three sadirons, two heating on the stove while one was in use. The wash itself was done either outside or in the basement.

The basement was divided into front and back sections. In the front there could be a fireplace. The floor would have been wood, cement, or stone. The wash was done in the front room, necessitating a washtub and washboard. Some farmers had hand-turned washing machines as the second decade of the century began.

The back basement area had a dirt floor and was strictly for food storage and preservation. Meat was laid out to cure in salt or sugar on boards set across trestles, a reminder of the first tables used by the early colonists. Meat was stored in crockpots in the basement. Crocks were used for many things and ranged in size from a quart to twenty gallons. As an example, stoneware crocks kept milk and butter. Bins to hold fruit and potatoes were arranged in racks that might take up most of the wall space. Many times a pie safe was also kept in the basement.

Another place where food was stored was in the bedroom. Besides a bed or two, a bureau, a wardrobe, and possibly a washstand, you might find a pumpkin lurking under the bed and sweet potatoes in a barrel in the corner. Sweet potatoes were kept on an upper floor where it would be relatively cool but drier than the basement. Farther up, in the attic, farmers kept dried fruits and grain hanging in canvas bags suspended from the rafters.

Farmhouses built at the beginning of the century often were without fireplaces which had gone out of favor with the emergence of the reliable wood-burning stove. However, these homes did have chimneys which vented the stoves. In rooms on the second floor, holes were cut in the floor and covered over with a wire or metal grate for safety. These registers carried the heat generated by stoves on the first floor to the bedrooms, which explains why it still would have been cool enough to maintain sweet potatoes in the bedroom!

Of course older homes did have fireplaces but often they were boarded up, sometimes with metal sheets. What few closets a farmhouse had were, as in the eighteenth century, often built next to the fireplace.

There were few amenities found in the typical farmhouse; there were very few telephones used by rural families before World War I. Farm wives did have pedal-operated sewing machines and some families were fortunate enough to have record players even in the early 1900s.

Electricity came to farms bit by bit and it is best to check your local historical society or library to find out when electric light made it to the area you want your farmhouse to represent. A kerosene lamp is always a good touch.

If you have the space, you may want to add a summer kitchen to the house. Like the kitchens of the Southern plantations, the summer kitchen was positioned away from the main house, connected by an open or covered walkway. It was usual for families in warm climates to move the stove out to the summer kitchen for the hot season.

The most important thing to remember when furnishing a farmhouse is that it was the center of a largely self-sufficient food production and harvesting operation. That was the cornerstone of farm life and the miniature farmhouse should reflect the hard work that farming meant in its simple appointments and sturdy furniture.

A QUICK GUIDE

The following are general lists of furniture, accessories, and interior appointments according to period. Remember that you can often add to one period from the lists of *preceding* periods. The lists are intended as an outline for your guidance. More detailed information is contained in the text itself, including notes on which furniture and appointments failed to survive from one period to the next.

EARLY SETTLEMENT: 1607–1690

Furniture

BEDS: Four-post, low post, tester, wainscot, box, trundle, pallet, hooded cradle

CHAIRS: Brewster, Carver, Cromwellian, wainscot, Restoration, slat-back, benches (forms), stools

CHESTS: six-board, Hartford, Hadley, Ipswich, chest of drawers, Bible box, spice chest

CUPBOARD/DRESSERS: court, livery, press, *kas,* Settle

TABLES: chair table, trestle, sawbuck, stretcher

Accessories

Andirons
Barrels, buckets
Bracket clock
Candle mold, candle box
Earthenware, stoneware
Floorcloth, straw mat
Glass bottles
Hand tools
Pewter
Rolled samplers
Small mirror
Spinning wheel
Table and bed rugs
Warming pan
Woodenware

Interior

Often one room
Exposed beams
Small casement windows, glassless window holes
Large fireplace
Dirt, plank, stone, and brick floors
Whitewashed and sheathed walls
Low ceiling

Lighting

Candles (sconces, candlesticks)
Candlewood
Grease lamps (betty)
Rushlight
Tinderbox

Kitchen/Bath

Cooking over an open fire with lug pole and back oven
Dutch oven, mortar and pestle
Chamber pots and privies

259

Pots, kettles, caldrons,
trivets, skewers,
long-handled pans
and implements

Styles

Some Elizabethan   Jacobean

COLONIAL GLORY: 1690–1790

Furniture

BEDS: tester, four-post, trundle, press, daybed, hooded or open cradle, pencil-post, low post

CHAIRS: wing, Windsor, benches (forms), stools, banister-back, tall-back, corner chair, slat-back, slipper, back stool, commode chair, cockfighting chair

CHESTS: Hartford, Hadley, Ipswich, Taunton, Guilford, spice cabinet, sugar chest, cellarette, chest of drawers, chest-on-chest, highboy

CUPBOARDS/DRESSERS: *kas,* corner cupboard, Welsh dresser, breakfront

DESKS: secretary, desk-on-frame, slant-front, drop-lid, kneehole

SOFAS: chairback settee, camel-back sofa, Windsor settee, love seat, window seat

TABLES: gateleg, butterfly, tavern table, tea table, serving or mixing table, chair table, Pembroke, candlestand, drop-leaf, handkerchief, drum table, kettle stand, dessert server, spider table, basin or wig stand

Accessories

Andirons	Hand tools
Bracket clock, tall case clock	Knife box
	Nautical instruments
Doorstop	Paintings and portraits
Draperies, panel curtains, venetian blinds	Quilts
	Samplers
Earthenware, stoneware, creamware, slipware, *sgraffito,* porcelain	Silverware, pewter
	Spinet, harpsichord
	Spinning wheel, loom
	Woodenware
Fire screen, fireboard	

Floorcloth, straw mat, braided rug, Oriental, Axminster, ingrain, and Brussels carpets
Framed mirror
Glassware—clear and colored

Interior

Exposed and concealed beams	Mantel-less fireplace
Expansion of the number of rooms (bedchamber, kitchen)	Franklin stove
	Plank, brick, stone floors
Paneled, plastered and painted walls, wallpaper	Plain and ornamental ceilings
Wainscoting	
Sash windows with small panes, Palladian windows	

Lighting

Candles (sconces, chandeliers, candlesticks)	Hurricane shades
Grease lamps (betty)	

Kitchen/Bath

Cooking over an open fire with lug pole and crane, side or front oven	Churn
	Dough tray
Tin kitchen roaster	Chamber pots and privies
Smoke oven	
Pots, kettles, caldrons, trivets, long-handled pans and implements, toaster, platewarmer, jacks, peels, skewers, Dutch oven, mortar and pestle, coffee mill	

Styles

William and Mary	Chippendale
Queen Anne	Chinese Chippendale

THE REPUBLIC: 1780–1840

Furniture

BEDS: four-post, low post, field bed, sleigh bed, twin, trundle, open and hooded cradles, press bed

CHAIRS: shield-back, Windsor, rocker (conversion, Boston), slat-back, fancy chair (Hitchcock), *klismos, curule,* pretzel-back, Martha Washington, wing

CHESTS: chest of drawers, blanket chest, cellarette, sugar chest, spice cabinet, dower

CUPBOARDS/DRESSERS: sideboard, huntboard, Welsh dresser, bookcases, breakfront, armoire, *kas,* corner cupboard

DESKS: drop-lid, secretary

SOFAS: straight leg, open or closed arms, chairback settee, récamier, mammy bench, wagon-seat settee, cornucopia sofa

TABLES: sofa table, Pembroke, pier table, lady's work-table, kettle stand, teapoy, tea table, dressing table, sectional dining table, demi-lune

Accessories

Andirons, grate
Bracket clock, grandmother clock, pillar and scroll clock, tall case clock
Canterbury
China mantel garniture
Curtains, draperies, venetian blinds
Earthenware, stoneware, creamware, porcelain, slipware, *sgraffito,*
Bennington ware
Fireboard, fire screen
Floorcloth, straw mat, braided rug, hooked rug, striped rug, Aubusson, Axminster, ingrain, Brussels, and Oriental carpets
Glassware—pressed, etched, cut, colored and clear

Hat box
Knife box
Lavabo
Mirrors (bull's-eye, constitution)
Paintings and portraits, mourning pictures, lithographs, silhouettes
Quilt, whitework bedspreads, printed bed dressings
Silver, plated ware, toleware, pewter, tea services
Wine cooler

Interior

Expansion of number of rooms (dining room)
Plaster walls, less paneling, stenciling, paint, wallpaper
Fireplace with mantel shelf
Franklin stove

Plank, parquet floors
Larger-pane sash windows, Palladian windows, fanlight
Columns, pilasters, pediments
Oval rooms
Spiral staircase

Lighting

Argand lamp (astral)
Candles (sconces, chandeliers, candlesticks)
Experimental gaslight late in period
Glass and metal oil lamps

Grease lamps (betty)
Hurricane shades
Lustres

Kitchen/Bath

Cooking over open fire with lug pole, crane, and side or front oven
Smoke oven
Small ranges late in period
Tin kitchen roaster
Pots, kettles, caldrons, trivets, toaster, plate warmer, jack, peel, skewers, Dutch

oven, mortar and pestle, coffee mill, long-handled pans and implements
Churn
Dough tray
Ice box, pie safe
Dry sink
Chamber pots and privies

Styles

Federal (Hepplewhite and Sheraton)

Empire

THE VICTORIAN PERIODS: 1830–1900

Furniture

BEDS: half-tester, four-post, sleigh bed, trundle, twin, brass and iron, spool and Jenny Lind, open cradles with spindles, high headboard beds, cannonball bed

CHAIRS: servants' hall chair, fancy chair (Hitchcock), Mackintosh, Boston and Lincoln rockers, lady's chair, gentleman's chair, bentwood, tabouret, gondola, balloon-back, director's chair, swivel chair, patent chair (rocker), *curule,* high-back, firehouse and modified Windsors, horn chair, wicker, Morris chair

CHESTS: trunks, blanket chest, chest of drawers, commode, mirrored clothes dresser, dower

CUPBOARDS/DRESSERS: sideboard, Welsh dresser, bookcases, breakfront

DESKS: slant-top, Wooten, partners', lady's desk, secretary

ÉTAGÈRE: whatnot, curio cabinet, hall stand, hat rack

SOFAS: tête-à-tête, medallion back, chairback settee, Chesterfield, Grecian, cozy corner, ottoman

TABLES: Damascus, circular pedestal, dessert server, lady's worktable, pier table, bedside table, pedestals, plant stands, lazy susan, harvest table, washstand, mirrored dressing table, marble-top table

Accessories

Albums, almanacs
Andirons, grate
Christmas tree
Daguerreotypes, watercolors, oils, lithographs, prints, needlework mottoes, easels
Earthenware, stoneware, creamware, porcelain, Bennington ware
Fireboard, fire screen
Glassware—colored and clear, etched, cut, pressed, Favrile
Grandfather clock, grandmother clock, pillar-and-scroll, beehive, mantel and shelf, steeple clock
Hatbox
Hearth rug, hooked rug, braided rug, ingrain, Oriental, Brussels, Aubusson, and Axminster carpets, animal-skin rugs, wall-to-wall

Knickknacks, figurines, statues, Rogers groups, busts
Lace undercurtains, draperies, shades, venetian blinds, curtains
Large framed mirror
Phonograph
Pillows, shawls, antimacassars
Sewing machine
Silver, plated ware, toleware
Stereoscope
Telephone
Typewriter

Interior

Many specialized rooms, servants' suite
Dumbwaiter
Plastered and paneled walls, paint, stenciling, wallpaper, Lincrusta Walton
Plate rail, dado
Plank, parquet, tile floors
Heavy woodwork
Ornamental and tin ceilings

Large-pane sash windows, bay windows, stained-glass windows, arched windows
Sliding doors
Portières
Spiral and straight staircases
Fireplace with heavy mantel
Parlor stoves

Lighting

Argand lamp (astral)
Candles (sconces, chandeliers, candlesticks)
Electric light (1880s)
Gaslight
Glass and metal oil lamps

Grease lamps (betty) in rural areas
Gone-with-the-Wind lamp
Kerosene lamp
Lustres
Student lamp

Kitchen/Bath

Ranges and cook stoves
Experimental gas range
Cooking over open fire with crane and ovens in rural areas
Pots, pans (enamelware, iron), coffee mills, foodgrinders, corers, peelers, seeders, whisks, eggbeaters, tin cans, potato mashers
Pie safe
Pumps and indoor water connection

Dry sinks
Iron sink
Icebox
Washing "machine"
Chamber pots and privies
Post-Civil War bathrooms

Styles

Pillar and Scroll
Rococo Revival
Elizabethan Revival
Gothic Revival

Renaissance Revival
Louis VX
Louis VXI
Arts and Crafts

BIBLIOGRAPHY

These books were consulted, in whole or in part, during the preparation of *American Period Interiors in Miniature*. Some are very fine resources while others are less reliable; but from each I benefited if only through exposure to a new picture or good bibliography. Those books that I found especially helpful or interesting are marked with an asterisk.

BOOKS

Andrews, Edward Deming, and Andrews, Faith, *Shaker Furniture: The Craftsmanship of an American Communal Sect.* New York: Dover Publications, Inc., 1964.*

Aronson, Joseph, *The Encyclopedia of Furniture.* New York: Crown Publishers, Inc., 1976.

Bailey, Chris, *200 Years of American Clocks and Watches*, Englewood Cliffs: Prentice-Hall, Inc., 1975.

Bates, Elizabeth Bidwell, and Fairbanks, Jonathan L., *American Furniture 1620 to the Present.* New York: Richard Marek, 1981.*

Bealer, Alex W., and Ellis, John O., *The Log Cabin: Home of the North American Wilderness.* Barre, Mass: Barre Publishers, 1978.*

Bishop, Robert, *Centuries and Styles of the American Chair: 1640–1970.* New York: E. P. Dutton & Co., Inc., 1972.*

———. *How to Know American Antique Furniture.* New York: E. P. Dutton & Co., Inc., 1973.

Bishop, Robert, and Coblentz, Patricia, *The World of Antiques, Art and Architecture in Victorian America.* New York: E. P. Dutton & Co., Inc., 1979.*

Bjerkoe, Ethel Hall, *How to Decorate for and with American Antiques.* New York: Avenele Books, 1959.

Boger, Ada Louise, *The Complete Guide to Furniture Styles.* New York: Charles Scribner's Sons, 1969.

———. *House and Garden's Antiques Questions and Answers.* New York: Simon & Schuster, 1973.

Bridgerman, Harriet, and Drury, Eliza (eds.), *Encyclopedia of Victoriana.* New York: Macmillan Publishing Co., Inc., 1975

Burroughs, Paul H., *Southern Antiques.* New York: Bonanza Books, 1967.

Butler, Joseph T., *American Antiques: 1800–1900.* New York: The Odyssey Press, 1965.

———. *Americam Furniture from the First Colonies to World War I.* London: Triune Books, 1973.

Chamberlain, Samuel, *Open House in New England.* New York: Hastings House, 1948.

Cohen, Lizabeth, *Respectability at $5 Down, 20 Months to Pay: Furnishing a Working Class Victorian Home.* Paper delivered for the Victorian Society Symposium on Furniture in Victorian America. Philadelphia: October 1978.*

Coleman, Oliver, *Successful Houses.* New York: Fox Duffield, 1906.

Comstock, Helen, *American Furniture.* New York: Viking Press, Inc., 1962.*

———. *100 Most Beautiful Rooms in America.* New York: Bonanza Books, 1965.

Cornelius, Charles O., *Early American Furniture.* New York: The Century Company, 1926.

Cosentino, Geraldine, and Stewart, Regina, *Kitchenware.* New York: Golden Press, 1977.

Cowie, Donald, *Antiques: How to Identify and Collect Them.* New York: A. S. Barnes & Co., 1970.

Davidson, Marshall (ed.), *Antiques: Civil War to World War I.* New York: American Heritage Press, 1969.

Deetz, James, *In Small Things Forgotten.* Garden City: Doubleday & Co., Inc., 1977.*

Demos, John, *A Little Commonwealth.* New York: Oxford University Press, 1977.*

de Haan, David, *Antique Household Gadgets and Appliances.* Dorset: Blandford Press, Ltd., 1977.*

Dolz, Renate, *Porcelain.* New York: Popular Library, 1977.

Downing, A. J. *The Architecture of Country Homes.* New York: Dover Publications, Inc., 1969.

Downs, Joseph, *American Furniture: Queen Anne and Chippendale.* New York: Bonanza Books, 1962.

Drepperd, Carl W., *New Geography of American Antiques.* Garden City: Doubleday & Co., Inc., 1948.

———. *The Primer of American Antiques.* Garden City: Doubleday & Co., Inc., 1944.

———. *Victorian: The Cinderella of Antiques.* Garden City: Doubleday & Co., Inc., 1950.

Drum, Stella M. (ed.), *Down the Santa Fe Trail and into Mexico: Diary of Susan Magoffin Shelby.* New Haven: Yale University Press, 1966.

Dubrow, Eileen, and Dubrow, Richard, *Furniture Made in America 1875 to 1905.* Exton, Pa.: Schiffer Publishing, Ltd., 1982.

Durant, Mary, *American Heritage Guide to Antiques.* New York: American Heritage Press, 1970.*

Fales, Dean A., Jr., *American Painted Furniture: 1660–1800.* New York: E. P. Dutton & Co., Inc., 1972.*

———. *Furniture of Historic Deerfield.* New York: E. P. Dutton & Co., Inc., 1976.*

Fales, Martha Gandy, *Early American Silver.* New York: Excalibur Books, 1970.

Fowles, Orson S., *The Octagon House: A Home for All.* New York: Dover Publications, Inc., 1973.

Freeman, Dr. Larry, *New Light on Old Lamps.* Watkins Glen: Century House, 1968.

Furnas, J. C., *The Americans: A Social History 1587–1914.* 2 vols. New York: Capricorn Books, 1969.

Gaines, Edith, and Jenkins, Dorothy H., *Woman's Day Dictionary of Antique Furniture.* Princeton: Pyne Press, 1974.

Gloag, John, *A Short Dictionary of Furniture.* London: George Allen and Unwin, 1952.

———. *Victorian Taste.* New York: Harper & Row Publishers, Inc., 1973.

Gorde, John Wood, *Observor's Book of Furniture,* New York: Frederick Warne & Co., Inc, 1974.

Green, Bernard, *Timetables of History.* New York: Simon & Schuster, 1975.

Greenlaw, Barry A., *New England Furniture at Williamsburg.* Williamsburg: Colonial Williamsburg Foundation, 1974.

Grow, Lawrence (comp.), *Old House Plans.* New York: Universe Books, 1978.

———. *The Old House Book of Kitchens and Dining Rooms.* New York: Warner Books, 1981.*

Halsey, R. T. H., and Cornelius, Charles O., *A Handbook of the American Wing.* New York: Metropolitan Museum of Art, 1925.

Hayward, Arthur H., *Colonial and Early American Lighting.* New York: Dover Publications, Inc., 1962.*

Hinckley, F. Lewis. *A Directory of Antique Furniture.* New York: Bonanza Books, 1953.

Holloway, Stratton (ed.), *The Practical Book of American Furniture and Decoration.* Philadelphia: J. B. Lippincott Co., 1937.

Horgan, Paul, *Great River.* 2 vols. New York: Farrar, Straus, and Giroux, 1954.

Hornung, Clarence, *Treasury of American Antiques.* New York: Harry N. Abrams, Inc., 1977.*

Hughes, Therle, *Antiques: An Illustrated A to Z.* New York: World Publishing, 1972.

Hume, Ivor Noel, *A Guide to Artifacts of Colonial America.* New York: Borzoi Books, 1976.*

Kane, Patricia E., *Three Hundred Years of American Seating Furniture.* Boston: New York Graphic Society, 1976.*

Kauffman, Henry J., *The American Farmhouse.* New York: Hawthorne Books, Inc., 1975.

———. *The American Fireplace.* New York: Galahad Books, 1972.*

Kidney, Walter C., *The Architecture of Choice, Eclecticism in America 1880–1930.* New York: George Braziller, Inc., 1974.

Kirk, John T., *Early American Furniture.* New York: Alfred A. Knopf, Inc., 1970.

Kovel, Ralph and Terry, *American County Furniture: 1780–1875.* New York: Crown Publishers, Inc., 1965.

Ladd, Paul R., *Early American Fireplaces.* New York: Hastings House, 1977.*

Lambton, Lucinda, *Temples of Convenience.* New York: St. Martin's Press, 1978.

Lantz, Louise K., *Old American Kitchenware: 1725–1925.* Nashville: Thomas Nelson, Inc., 1970.

Lazeare, James, *Primitive Pine Furniture.* Watkins Glen: Century House, n.d.

Little, Nina Fletcher, *American Decorative Wall Painting: 1700–1850.* New York: E. P. Dutton & Co., Inc., 1972.

———. *Country Arts in Early American Homes.* New York: E. P. Dutton & Co., Inc., 1975.*

Lyon, Irving W., *Colonial Furniture of New England.* New York: E. P. Dutton & Co., Inc., 1977.

Margon, Lester, *More American Furniture Treasures: 1620–1840.* New York: Architectural Book Publishers, 1971.

Mayhew, Edgar, and Meyers, Minor, Jr., *A Documentary History of American Interiors from the Colonial Era to 1915.* New York: Charles Scribner's Sons, 1980.*

McClelland, Nancy, *Furnishing the Colonial and Federal House.* New York: J. B. Lippincott Company, 1947.

McClinton, Katharine Morrison, *An Outline of Period Furniture.* New York: Clarkson N. Potter, 1972.

McClure, Abbot, and Eberlein, H. D., *Home Furnishing and Decoration.* New York: McBride, Nast, 1914.*

Meader, Robert F. W., *Illustrated Guide to Shaker Furniture.* New York: Dover Publications, Inc., 1972.*

Michael, George, *George Michael's Treasury of Federal Antiques.* New York: Hawthorne Books, Inc., 1972.

Miller, Edgar G., Jr., *American Antique Furniture.* 2 vols. New York: Dover Publications, Inc., 1966.

Miller, J. C., *The First Frontier: Life in Colonial America.* New York: Dell, 1966.

Montgomery, Charles P., *American Furniture: The Federal Period.* New York: Viking Press, Inc., 1966.

Moore, N. Hudson, *The Old Furniture Book.* New York: Tudor Publishing Co., 1937.

Morse, Frances Clary, *Furniture of the Olden Times.* New York: Macmillan Publishing Co., Inc., 1926.

Mumford, Lewis, *The Brown Decades.* New York: Dover Publications, Inc., 1955

Norwak, Mary, *Kitchen Antiques.* New York: Praeger Publishers, 1975.*

Nutting, Wallace, *Furniture Treasury.* 2 vols. New York: Macmillan Publishing Co., Inc., 1975.

———. *Furniture of the Pilgrim Century.* New York: Bonanza Books, n.d.

Obst, Janis, *Minnesota Interiors of the 19th Century.* Paper delivered for the Victorian Society Symposium on Furniture in Victorian America. Philadelphia: October 1978.*

Peter, Mary, *Collecting Victoriana.* New York: Praeger Publishers, 1968.

Phipps, Frances, *The Collector's Complete Dictionary of American Antiques.* Garden City: Doubleday & Co., 1974.

———. *Colonial Kitchens, Their Furnishings and Their Gardens.* New York: Hawthorne Books, Inc., 1972.*

Poese, Bill, *Lighting Through the Years.* Des Moines: Wallace-Homestead, 1976.

Presence, Peter (ed.), *Encyclopedia of Inventions.* Secaucus: Chartwell Books, 1976.

Reif, Rita, *Treasure Rooms of America's Mansions, Manors and Houses.* New York: Coward-McCann, 1970.

Reyburn, Wallace, *Flushed with Pride.* Englewood Cliffs: Prentice-Hall, Inc., 1971.

Rogers, Meyric, *American Interior Design.* New York: Bonanza Books, 1978.

Sanchez, Nellie, V., *Stories of the States.* New York: Thomas Y. Crowell Co., 1945.

Seale, William, *Recreating the Historic House Interior.* American Association for State and Local History. Nashville: 1979.*

Snyder, John J. (ed.), *Philadelphia Furniture and Its Makers.* New York: Main Street-Universe Books, 1975.

Stanforth, Deirdre, *Restored America.* New York: Praeger Publishers, 1975.

Stillinger, Elizabeth, *The Antiques Guide to Decorative Arts in America.* New York: E. P. Dutton & Co., Inc., 1973.*

Sweeney, John A. H., *The Treasury of Early American Rooms.* New York: Viking Press, Inc., 1963.

Trent, Robert (ed.), *Pilgrim Century Furniture.* New York: Main Street-Universe Books, 1976.

Vedder, Alan C., *Furniture of Spanish New Mexico.* Santa Fe: Sunstone Press, 1977.

Von Rosenstiel, Helene, *American Rugs and Carpets.* London: Barrie & Jenkins, 1978.

Voss, Thomas M., *Antique American Country Furniture: A Field Guide.* New York: J. B. Lippincott Co., 1978.

Warren, David B., *Bayou Bend.* Boston: New York Graphic Society, 1975.

Way, Nelson, and Stapleton, Constance, *Antiques Don't Lie.* Garden City: Doubleday & Co., Inc., 1975.

Wells, Stanley, *Period Lighting.* London: Pelham Books, 1975.*

Whiton, Sherrill, *Interior Design and Decoration.* New York: J. B. Lippincott Co., 1974.

Whitson, Skip (comp.), *The Elegant Homes of America: 100 Years Ago.* Vol. II. Albuquerque: Sun Books, 1977.

Williams, Henry Lionel, *Country Furniture of Early America.* New York: A. S. Barnes and Co., Inc., 1963.

Williams, Henry Lionel and Ottalie. *How to Furnish Old American Houses.* New York: Bonanza Books, 1949.

Winchester, Alice (ed.), *The Antiques Treasury of Furniture and Other Decorative Arts.* New York: Galahad Books, 1959.

Wright, Lawrence, *Clean and Decent.* London: Routledge and Kegan Paul, 1971.*

————. *Home Fires Burning.* London: Routledge and Kegan Paul, 1964.*

Wright, Louis B., and Tatum, George B., McCoubrey, John W., Smith, Robert C., *The Arts in America: The Colonial Period.* New York: Charles Scribner's Sons, 1966.

Yates, Raymond F. and Marguerite W., *A Guide to Victorian Antiques.* New York: Harper, 1949.

Frontier America: The Far West. Boston: Museum of Fine Arts. New York Graphic Society, 1975.

The Spanish West, New York: Time-Life Books, 1976.

This Fabulous Century: 1900–1910, New York: Time-Life Books, 1974.

Visiting Our Past: American Historylands. Washington, D.C.: National Geographic Society, 1977.

PERIODICALS

In preparing this book I found the following magazines and periodicals helpful and interesting.

Arts and Antiques
1515 Broadway
New York, New York 10036

Americana
American Heritage Publishing
19 Rockefeller Plaza
New York, New York 10020

The Magazine Antiques
551 5th Avenue
New York, New York 10017

Antiques World
122 East 42nd Street
New York, New York 10017

Architectural Digest
5900 Wilshire Boulevard
Los Angeles, California 90036

Early American Life
Early American Society
Box 1831
Harrisburg, Pennsylvania, 17105

Historic Preservation
National Trust for Historic Preservation
1785 Massachusetts Avenue N. W.
Washington, D.C. 20036

House Beautiful's Colonial Homes
717 5th Avenue
New York, New York 10022

Nineteenth Century
Victorian Society in America
The Athenaeum
East Washington Square
Philadelphia, Pennsylvania 19106

Old House Journal
69 A 7th Avenue
Brooklyn, New York 11217

Spinning Wheel
Everybody's Press, Inc.
Hanover, Pennsylvania 17331

Victorian Society in America Bulletin
Victorian Society in America
The Athenaeum
East Washington Square
Philadelphia, Pennsylvania 19106

MINIATURES PUBLICATIONS

Little Things
P.O. Box 1588
Stouffville
Ontario, Canada LOH 1LO

Miniature Collector Magazine
Acquire Publishing Co., Inc.
170 5th Avenue
New York, New York 10010

The Miniature Magazine
Carstens Publications, Inc.
P. O. Box 700
Newton, New Jersey 07860

Miniature Patterns & Products Magazine
P.O. Box 406
Jean Dickey Publications
Westmont, Illinois 60559

NAME Gazette
National Association of Miniature Enthusiasts
Box 2621
Anaheim, California 92804

Nutshell News
Boynton and Associates
Clifton House
Clifton, Virginia 22024

Rocky Mountain Miniature Journal
Box 3315
Littleton, Colorado 80161

The Scale Cabinetmaker
Dorsett Publications, Inc.
P. O. Box 87
Pembroke, Virginia 24136

APPENDIX

ARTISANS AND SUPPLIERS

Following is a list of the names and addresses of artisans, dealers, and manufacturers whose work appears in the book (except for those who prefer their addresses not to be included). It is customary when writing artisans to enclose a self-addressed, stamped envelope. Some artisans, dealers and manufacturers offer catalogues or lists for which there is usually a fee.

Acquisto Silver Company
Pete Acquisto
3504 Delamar N.E.
Albuquerque, N. Mex. 87107

Ferenc Albert
Albert Custom Glassblowing
587 Rte. 1 Lake Shore
Putnam Valley, N.Y. 10579

E.W. Allen, Jr.
Artists' Workshop
Box 476
Montclair, N.J. 07042

Andrews Miniatures
Patrick and Center Streets
Ashland, Va. 23005

Hermania Anslinger
320 South Ralph Street
Spokane, Wash. 99202
p. 95

Al Atkins
The Village Smithy
204 Hulbert Hollow Road
Spencer, N.Y. 14883

Lionel and Ann Barnard
The Mulberry Bush
10 Firgrove Hill
Farnham, Surrey
England

Herbert and Jennifer Bennett
P.O. Box 1072
Mt. Vernon, Ill. 62864

Jane Bernier
Borrower's Press
2543 Queenstone Road
Cleveland Heights, Ohio 44118

The Bird House
Roberta Partridge
18 East High Street
Ballston Spa, N.Y. 12020

Birkemeier
see Studio B

Blackham's Studio
Mittsy and Jack Blackham
8534 Lakeshore Road
Clay, N.Y. 13041

Ellen Krucker Blauer
John M. Blauer
see The Miniature Mart®

Dusty Boynton
Country Rooms
Clay Court North
Locust, N.J. 07760

Renée Bowen
see The Tin Feather

Mary Brady
see The Original House
of Miniatures

268

Thomas C.T. Brokaw
100 Twaddell Mill Road
Greenville, Del. 19807

Don Buckley
Box 736 Main Street
Salisbury, Conn. 06068
p. 35

Barbara Bunce
Butterflies & Buttercups
315 East Second Street
Gaylord, Mich. 49735

Bill Burkey
The Burkey Place
Arnot Mall P.O. Box 5047
Horseheads, N.Y. 14844

Butt Hinge Pottery
see Phyllis Howard

Donald C. Buttfield
Old Port Road R.D. I
Kennebunk, Maine 04043
COLOR PG.

C.J. Originals
P.O. Box 155-KDK
Mendham, N.J. 07945
P. 56

Robert Carlisle
Carlisle Miniatures
703 N. Elm
Creston, Iowa 50801

Lee-Ann Chellis Wessel
Demi-Tasse Miniatures
4 Edgewood Terrace
Northampton, Mass. 01060

Chrysnbon, Inc.
Hobart, Ind. 46342

Clare-Bell Brass Works
P.O. Box 369
Southington, Conn. 06489

Mary Frances Cochran
H. Preston Cochran
1 Dutton Court
Catonsville, Md. 21228

Harry Cooke
c/o Dearring-Tracy Ltd.
Box 220 Rte. 29
South Montrose, Pa. 18843

Copper Corner
see Harry Littwin

T.C. Cottrell, Jr.
Cottrell Limited Editions
P.O. Box 1244
Plattsburgh, N.Y. 12901

Marj Creuger
P.O. Box 342
Reedsport, Oreg. 97467

Carolyn Nygren Curran
CNC Pottery
8 Pershing Road
Glens Falls, N.Y. 12801

Barbara Davis
Country Cottage Miniatures
3485 North Main Street
Soquel, Calif. 95073

Dearring-Tracy, Ltd.
Mary Lee Dearring-Tracy/
W. Foster Tracy
Box 220 Rte. 29
South Montrose, Pa. 18843

Demi-Tasse Miniatures
see Lee-Ann Chellis-Wessel

Warren Dick
1749 Sawmill Road
Rte. 2 Box 123
Cottonwood, Ariz. 86326

Dollhouse Antics
1308 Madison Avenue
New York, N.Y. 10028

The Dolls' Cobbler
Sylvia Rountree
P.O. Box 906
Berlin, Md. 21811

Dolphin Originals
Bob Bernard
P.O. Box 295
Dresher, Pa. 19025

Helen and Jim Dorsett
Dorsett Publications, Inc.
P.O. Box 506
Christiansburg, Va. 24073

Donald Dube
see Wexler-Dube Miniatures

Rosemary Dyke
1908 North Spruce
Little Rock, Ark. 72207

Barbara Epstein
Microbius
P.O. Box 1057
Crested Butte, Colo. 81224

Fantastic Merchandise
J.P. Ginsburg
465 Barneveld Street
San Francisco, Calif. 94124

Marie Friedman
13200 S.W. Glenn Court
Beaverton, Oreg. 97005

Ida Stearns Fritsche
Ipso Facto Studio
220 Farnham Road
Havertown, Pa. 19083

Sharon Garmize
27 Yorktown Road
Mountaintop, Pa. 18707

Susan Gentsch
139 Garden Court
Del Rio, Tex. 78840

Evelyn and Frank Gerratana
24 Chestnut Hill Road
Trumbull, Conn. 06611

Bill and Donna Gibbons
6333 Meridan Road
Jamesville, N.Y. 13078

Ginger Jar (one company
run by two artisans working
independently)
Ginger Jar
Jean Kirkwood
2506 King Arthur Drive
Monroe, N.C. 28110
and
Ginger Jar
Betsy Zorn
233 N. Franklin Street
Whitewater, Wis. 53190

Ibes and Annabell Gonzalez
Miniatures by Ibes
550 H Grand Street #8-A
New York, N.Y. 10002

p. 56, 96

Emily Good
Heirloom Replicas
2515 S. Solano Drive
Las Cruces, N. Mex. 88001

Grandmother Stover's, Inc.
P.O. Box 12225
1327 King Avenue
Columbus, Ohio 43212

Roger L. Gutheil, Inc.
510 English Road
Rochester, N.Y. 14616

Kent Halsted
c/o Mini-Fab
7701 S.E. 30th Avenue
Portland, Oreg. 97202

Handcraft Designs, Inc.
89 Commerce Drive
Telford, Pa. 18969

Rosemary Hansen
Mini-Fab
7701 S.E. 30th Avenue
Portland, Oreg. 97202

The Happy Unicorn
see Phyllis Tucker

Carol Hardy
Antiques in Miniature
17 Corrala Vista Drive
Watsonville, Calif. 95076

Howard Hartman
16 Ventosa Drive
Morristown, N.J. 07960

Jim Hastrich
see The Tin Feather

Joe Hermes
P.O. Box 4023
El Monte, Calif. 91734

John J. Hodgson
Elf Miniature Period Furniture
25 Sands Lane
Bridlington
North Humberside
YO15 2JG
England

George and Sally Hoffman
The Hoffman Collection
P.O. Box 531
Summit, N.J. 07901

Jim Holmes
P.O. Box 458
Foxboro, Mass. 02035

Phyllis Howard
Butt Hinge Pottery
One Butt Hinge Road
Chelmsford, Mass. 01824

Virginia Hultberg
Box 62
Erieville, N.Y. 13061

Miniatures by Ibes
see Ibes Gonzalez

Illinois Hobbycraft, Inc.
605 North Broadway
Aurora, Ill. 60505

Innovative Ideas
Barbara Jean Camp
2749 Costebelle Drive
La Jolla, Calif. 92037

Ipso Facto Studio
see Ida Stearns Fritsche

Jim Ison
Miniatures by Jim Ison
2509 East Jackson Boulevard
Elkhart, Ind. 46516

It's a Small World
Mary Jane Graham
555 Lincoln Avenue
Winnetka, Ill. 60093

Keshishian Collection
Box 3002
San Clemente, Calif. 92672

Brant Keyes
c/o Derek Perkins
14811 D Clark Avenue
Hacienda Heights, Calif. 91745

Douglas Kirtland
91 Canandaigua Avenue
Canandaigua, N.Y. 14424

Elena Lamb Designs
11 Hartley Road
Great Neck, N.Y. 11023

Thayer Langworthy
c/o Enchanted Dollhouse
Rte. 7
Manchester Center, Vt. 05255

Linda LaRoche
156 Westminster Avenue
Arlington, Mass. 02174

Thomas Latané
Latané Miniatures
P.O. Box 62
Pepin, Wis. 54759

Lawbre Company
888 Tower Road
Unit J
Mundelein, Ill. 60060

Ivan Lawson
c/o Shuttle Hill Herb Shop
243 Delaware Avenue
Delmar, N.Y. 12054

Ernie Levy
Box 348
Liberty, N.Y. 12754

Stan Lewis
1012 Todd Farm #203
Elgin, Ill. 60103

Betty Libo
see The Original House
of Miniatures

Harry Littwin
Copper Corner
8707 51 Avenue West
Bradenton, Fla. 33507

Allen Martin
Martin's Miniatures
6809 Knightswood Drive
Charlotte, N.C. 28211

Don and Cindy Massie
Rte. 2
Blacksburg, Va. 24060

Paul McNeely
Rte. 2 Box 453
Liberty, Mo. 64068

Fran and Don Meehan
793 Twin Rivers Drive North
East Windsor, N.J. 08520

Microbius
see Barbara Epstein

Millie August Miniatures
Plaid Enterprises, Inc.
P.O. Drawer E
Norcross, Ga. 30091

Robert S. Milne
Milne Miniatures
106 Prince Street
New York, N.Y. 10012

Mini-Fab
see Rosemary Hansen

Mini-Magic Carpet
3675 Reed Road
Columbus, Ohio 43220

The Miniature Mart ®
Ellen Krucker Blauer
John M. Blauer
1807 Octavia Street
San Francisco, Calif. 94109

Miniatures of Merritt
see J. S. Powel

Franklyn Morley
Morley Miniatures
16752 Cooper Lane
Huntington Beach, Calif. 92647

Lou Murter
c/o Tiny Treasures
Vivian Stoddard
328 Bear-Christiana Road
Bear, Del. 19701

Nic and Linda Nichols
Nic's Creative Workshop
P.O. Box 1292
Pt. Pleasant, N.J. 08742

Edward G. Norton
98 Wesley Avenue
Westbrook, Conn. 06498

Dan Nyberg
133 Onondaga Street
Corning, N.Y. 14830

Mary Grady O'Brien
Yankee Notions
726 Glen Avenue
Westfield, N.J. 07090

Robert Olszewski
Goebel Miniatures
Camarillo Studio
4820 Adhor Lane
Camarillo, Calif. 93010

Open House
see Noel and Pat Thomas

The Original House of Miniatures
Betty Libo and Mary Brady
Don Gaspar Patio
116 Don Gaspar P.O. Box 1816
Santa Fe, N. Mex. 87501

Originals by Tag
see Jean and Elmer Tag

Roberta Partridge
see The Bird House

George Passwaters
P.O. Box 761
Camden, N.J. 08101

Braxton Payne
Box 54431
Atlanta, Ga. 30308

Derek Perkins
14811 D Clark Avenue
Hacienda Heights, Calif. 91745

Tom Poitras
Thomas Creations in Wood
15911 5th Avenue N.E.
Seattle, Wash. 98155

Posy Patch Originals
Mary Payne
P.O. Box 52173
Atlanta, Ga. 30355

J. S. Powel
Miniatures of Merritt
1655 Sykes Creek Drive
Merritt Island, Fla. 32952

Lesli Rahmatulla
37 Willow
Guilderland, N.Y. 12084

Reminiscence, Inc.
3206 Old Coach Drive
Camarillo, Calif. 93010

José Rodriguez
c/o Washington Dolls'
House and Toy Museum
5236 44th Street N.W.
Washington, D.C. 20015

Terry Rogal
c/o Dearring-Tracy, Ltd.
Box 220 Rte. 29
South Montrose, Pa. 18843

APPENDIX

Ipheginia Rose
c/o Dearring-Tracy, Ltd.
Box 220 Rte. 29
South Montrose, Pa. 18843

Sylvia Rountree
see The Dolls' Cobbler

Susanne Russo
Memory Makers Shop—Brasses
305 North 5th Street
Clarksburg, W Va. 26301

Sherwood Interiors
Mary Sternberg
682 61st Street
Des Moines, Iowa 50312

Shuttle Hill Herb Shop
243 Delaware Avenue
Delmar, N.Y. 12054

Simms Miniatures
111 Edgewood Lane
Williamsburg, Va. 23185

Harry W. Smith
Coe-Kerr Gallery
49 East 82nd Street
New York, N.Y. 10028

Chet Spacher
Spacher's
5026 Tangerine Avenue
Orlando, Fla. 32807

Laurence St. Leger
c/o Steak Family Miniatures
2020 East Ocean Boulevard
Newport Beach, Calif. 92661

Steak Family Miniatures
2020 East Ocean Boulevard
Newport Beach, Calif. 92661

Suzanne R. Strickland
14 Albin Road
Delmar, N.Y. 12054

Studio B Miniatures
Margaret and Bill Birkemeier
(tinware)
46 Duck Woods Drive
Kitty Hawk, N.C. 27949
P. 81,115

Bob and Millie Birkemeier
(furniture)
976 Dartmouth
Wheaton, Ill. 60187

Sussex Crafts
Peter Warwick
26 Brighton Road
Crawley, Sussex RH10 6AA
England

Jean and Elmer Tag
Originals by Tag
R.D. 6 Box 171
Newton, N.J. 07860

Noel and Pat Thomas
Open House
Box 213
Seaview, Wash. 98644

Wilma Thomas
1430 Harlton Court
Columbus, Ohio 43221

Thomas Creations in Wood
see Tom Poitras

Tom Thumb Bricks
Binghamton Brick Co., Inc.
P.O. Box 1256
Binghamton, N.Y. 13902

The Tin Feather
Renée Bowen and Jim Hastrich
Rte. 1 South
Kennebunk, Maine 04043

W. Foster Tracy
c/o Dearring-Tracy, Ltd.
Box 220 Rte. 29
South Montrose, Pa. 18843

Phyllis Tucker
The Happy Unicorn
22825 Mastick Road
Fairview Park, Ohio 44126

David Frederick Usher
C. 1770 Flyer House
Old Newfield (Torrington)
Sawmill Hill Road R.R. 3
Winsted, Conn. 06098

Joan C. Vaber
2607 Columbia Drive
Endwell, N.Y. 13760

Betty Valentine
114-E New State Road
Manchester, Conn. 06040

Cheryl Vilbert
7516 Tudor Road
Colorado Springs, Colo. 80919

Pierre Wallack
P.O. Box 485
Beaver Falls, N.Y. 13305

Wee Treasures
see Jean Yingling

J. Weinberg
c/o Dollhouse Antics
1308 Madison Avenue
New York, N.Y. 10028

Theresa Welch-Stalbaum
c/o It's a Small World
Mary Jane Graham
555 Lincoln Avenue
Winnetka, Ill. 60093

Wexler-Dube Miniatures
Donald Dube and
Linda Wexler-Dube
P.O. Box 63
Woodmere, N.Y. 11598

David White
White Mountain Woodworking
Sawmill Lane
Franconia, N.H. 03580

Francis Whittemore
Box 1416
North Wales, Pa. 19454
P. 110 GLASS

Wise Miniatures
61 Knickerbocker Road
Demarest, N.J. 07627

Jean Yingling
Wee Treasures
Box 323 R.D. #1
Howard, Pa. 16841

Betsy Zorn
see Ginger Jar

MUSEUM COLLECTIONS REPRESENTED IN THIS BOOK

The Art Institute of Chicago
Michigan Avenue at Adams Street
Chicago, Ill. 60603

The Children's Museum
P.O. Box 3000
Indianapolis, Ind. 46206

Dulin Gallery of Art
3100 Kingston Pike
Knoxville, Tenn. 37919-4695

Miniature Museum of Kansas City
5235 Oak Street
Kansas City, Mo. 64112

Phoenix Art Museum
1625 North Central Avenue
Phoenix, Ariz. 85004

Washington Doll's House and Toy Museum
5236 44th Street N.W.
Washington, D.C. 20015

The Henry Francis DuPont Winterthur Museum
Winterthur, Del. 19735

MINIATURE ORGANIZATIONS

The International Guild of Miniature Artisans, Ltd.
P. O. Box 842
Summit, N.J. 07901

National Association of Miniature Enthusiasts
P. O. Box 2621
Anaheim, Calif. 92804

INDEX

Page numbers in italics refer to illustrations

A

accessories, general: colonial period, *60, 64,* 65, 68–82, *89;* early settlement, 20–25; early twentieth century, *229, 233,* 241; early West, *243,* 244; farmhouses, 258; Federal period, *85, 93, 96, 98, 100, 101, 108, 117,* 120–31; Shaker, 251, *253,* 255; Southwest and California, *246,* 247, 248, 250; Victorian period, 135, *137, 142, 147, 153, 154,* 159, *162, 163, 165,* 167–68, *175, 176,* 177–92

architectural style: colonial period, 27–29, 34–35; early settlement, 4; early twentieth century, 229–30; early West, 242–44; Federal period, 84; Southwest and California, 246; Victorian period, 144–49, 152

arrangement of furniture: colonial period, 66–67; Federal period, 92, 104–5, 116–20,

126–27; Victorian period, 153–55

Art Nouveau furniture: about, 236–37; beds, *158;* chairs, 157–59; cupboards/dressers, *158, 160;* tables, *158, 159*

Arts and Crafts furniture, 156–57, *176, 233,* 236–37

B

bath accessories: about, 217–24; colonial period, 45, 59, 61, *69;* early twentieth century, *231;* Federal period, *108,* 110; Victorian period, 133, 138, 166

bathrooms, 220–24

bathtubs, *217, 220,* 221, *223*

bed accessories: colonial period, 39, 77; early settlement, 24, 25; early twentieth century, *231;* early West, 244; Federal period, *114,* 115, 128–29; Victorian period, 169

beds: brass and iron, *158, 171,* 236; cannonball, 170; canopy, 53, 169; closet, 40; cradle, 19–20, 53; crib, *116, 171, 172;* cupboard, 20, *20;* daybed, *30,* 40, 46, 53; field,

53, 115, *115;* four-poster, 19, *114,* 170, *170, 172;* half-tester, 169; high headboard, 170; high-post, *108,* 115; low-post, 53, 115; one-post, 20; pencil post, 53; press, 40; single, 170; sleigh, 116, *117,* 170; spool and Jenny Lind, 170, *172;* tall-post, *169,* 170; tester, 19, 39, 53; three-quarter-size, 170; trundle, 19, *19;* twin, 116, 170; wainscot, 19

bidets, 218

C

candle-making, 21

ceilings: colonial period, 27, 29, *32;* early settlement, 7; early twentieth century, *233,* 234; Federal period, 88–89, *89;* Victorian period, 138, 170

ceramics: colonial period, *28, 37, 49, 50,* 61, *62,* 65, *69,* 71–72, *76, 81;* early settlement, 22–24, *23;* early twentieth century, *233;* Federal period, *89, 94, 108, 119,* 122–23, *122, 129;* Southwest and California,

246, 248; Victorian period, *152, 177, 179, 181,* 182–84, *183*

ceramics, kitchen: about, *204, 212, 213,* 214–17; creamware and pearlware, 216; delft, 216; earthenware, 214–15; modern pottery, 216; porcelain, 216; stoneware, 215–16, *216*

chairs: back stool, 45; balloon-back, *135,* 155–56; banister- or baluster-back, 35–36, *35, 42, 66;* bentwood, 159, 254; Boston, 36; Brewster, *9, 14;* Carver, 14, *14, 15, 17;* Charles II, 15; child's, *154, 165;* child's highchair, *49;* child's slat-back, *73;* cockfighting, 45–46; commode, 45; corner or roundabout, *16,* 36, 45, 65, 75; Cromwellian, 15; *curule, 87,* 101, 156; director's, 156; Duncan Phyfe, *94, 96, 100;* fancy (Hitchcock), 97–98, *99, 100,* 153, *160;* farthingale, 15; firehouse, 159; "Flemish," 36, *36;* gentleman's *152,* 155, *155;* gondola, 155; horn, 173, *173; klismos, 87,* 98, *100;* lady's, *152,* 155, *155;* Mackintosh, 156; Martha Washington, 45, *86, 89, 90, 101;* Morris, *157;* patent, *147,* 156; pressed-back, *235;* pretzelback, 56, *56, 102;* recliner, 101–2; Restoration, 15; rocker, 97, 98, 153, *153, 154, 157,* 229, 251, 254, *254,* 258; sabre-leg, *100;* settle *36,* 37; Sheraton side, *90;* shield-back, *85, 89, 96,* 97; side, *32,* 155–56; slat-back, 37; slipper, 45; "sloop," *113;* spade-foot, *96;* spindle-back, 254; splat-back, *41;* spoonback, 37; stool, *16,* 17, *17, 42,* 101, *188;* swivel, 156; tabouret, 155; tall-back, 36, 237; *taramitas,* 248; tilter, 254; tub (barrel-back), 101;

turned-spindle, *16;* turned triangular, *14;* vase-back, *73;* wainscot, 14–15, *30,* 36–37; wicker, 173–74, *174;* willow, 236; Windsor, 26, 42, *43,* 44–45, *44,* 97, *98,* 159, *198;* Windsor, modified, *243,* 244; wing or easy, *32,* 35, *47, 52,* 56–57, *60, 64,* 101, 155; writing-arm Windsor, *48*

chamber pots, 217, *217, 218,* 219

chests: Bible box, 10, *10;* blanket, 166; bow-front (commode), *90,* 113; cellarette, 61, 110, *110;* chest of drawers, 9, *45,* 46, 113, 166; chest-on-chest, 58; chest-on-frame, *59;* commode, 166, *168;* desk box, 10; dower, *117;* Guilford, 40, *41;* Hadley, 9, *10;* Hartford, 9, 26; highboy, *32,* 37, *37,* 38, 40, *41,* 46, *47, 51,* 58, *58,* 59; Ipswich, 9; lowboy, *32,* 37–38, 46, *47,* 58, 59, *60, 61;* slant-top box, 10; spice, 10, 50–52, *51;* sugar, *51,* 52, 110, 167; Taunton, 40; *varguña,* 248

Chippendale style furniture: about, 26, 53; beds, 53; chairs, *32,* 55–57, *56, 64, 65, 86, 149;* chests, *32, 45,* 57–58, *58, 59,* 61; cupboards/dressers, 61, *62;* desks, *57,* 58–59, *60;* Oriental influence in, 55, *64,* 65; regional differences in, 56–57, 65–66; sofas, 53–55, *54, 64;* tables, 59–63, *62, 63, 64;* woods used in, 53

clocks: colonial period, 70–71; early settlement, 24; Federal period, 121–22, *122;* Shaker, 255; Victorian period, *147, 176,* 180, *180*

closets: colonial period, 28–29; Victorian period, 133

colonial period, regional differences in, 29, 33, 34, 35, 80–81

colonial period furniture: beds, *30, 86;* chairs, *30, 32,* 36, *49,* 55, *60, 66, 73, 75, 76;* chests,

32, 60, 86; cupboards/ dressers, 29, 30, *30, 32,* 34, *49, 67;* regional differences in, 56–57, 65–66; sofas, *32;* tables, *32, 64, 66, 69, 79, 89. See also* Chippendale style furniture; Queen Anne style furniture; William and Mary style furniture

Corbit-Sharp House, 28–29, 31

cupboards/dressers: *alacena,* 247; armoire, 113, *113;* bookcase, 61, 110–11, 168; breakfront, 61, *62, 87,* 111; built-in, 29, 30, *32,* 34, 48; china cabinet, 111; commode, 219; corner, 48, *48, 149,* 166; court, 11–12, *11;* hall stand, *160,* 169; huntboard, 110; *kas, 12,* 13, *28;* linen press, 48; livery, 12–13; Pennsylvania, *49, 67;* pewter, *49;* press, 11–12, *12, 30;* settle, 13–14; sideboard, *85, 90, 95,* 109–10, 167, *167, 235; trastero, 249,* 250; washstand, 218–19, *218,* 232; water bench, *98;* Welsh dresser, 166

D

dairy operations, *193,* 199–200, *200, 202*

desks: child's, *165;* desk-on-frame, *37,* 38, *60;* drop-lid, *166;* kneehole, 58–59; lady's, *114,* 165; partners', 165; patent, *164;* secretary, 37, 38, 46, *57,* 58, *64, 85,* 111, *111, 112, 147,* 165; slant-front, 38; slant-top, *60;* slat-top, 165; Wooten (Wells Fargo), 165

doors: colonial period, 29; early settlement, 7; early twentieth century, 234, 236; Federal period, *85, 88,* 89, *91;* Shaker, 251, 252; Victorian period, 133, 138, 139, *147, 148,* 186

dumbwaiters: Federal period, 84; in kitchen, 209; Victorian period, 133

E

early settlement, regional differences in, 7
early settlement furniture: beds, 19–20; chairs, 14–17; chests, 8–10; cupboards/dressers, 10–13; tables, 13–14, 18–19
early twentieth century furniture: about, 236; beds, 236, *237;* built-in, 236; chairs, *229, 230, 235,* 236, 237; cupboards/dressers, 232, *235, 237;* desks, *237, 238;* sofas, *230;* tables, *229, 230.* *See also* Art Nouveau furniture; Arts and Crafts furniture; Golden Oak furniture; Mission furniture
early West: furniture, 242–45; interiors, 242
earth closet, 219–20
eglomisé, 94
Egyptian style: in Federal period, 103; in Victorian period, 156
elevators, Victorian period, 139
Elizabethan Revival furniture: about, 173, *186;* chairs, *137*
Elizabethan style: colonial period, *30;* early settlement, 18–19
Empire style furniture: about, 83, 84, 96; beds, 115–16, *115, 116, 117, 119;* chairs, *87, 96,* 98, *102, 113, 119;* cupboards/dressers, 110, 111, *113, 119;* in early West, 245; sofas, 102–5, *104;* tables, *87, 96,* 105, *105, 119*
étagère: about, 167, 177; curio cabinet, 168; hall stand, 169; hat rack, 169, *175;* whatnot, *152,* 167–68

F

farmhouses, 256–58
Federal period furniture: about, 83, 93, 97; beds, 97, *108, 114;* chairs, *96,* 97–98, *98, 99, 100,* 101–2, *101, 102;* chests, 110, *110,* 113, *117, 118, 126;* cupboards/

dressers, *87, 98,* 110–11, 113, *119, 125;* decorative techniques in, 92, 94, 97, 113, 116; desks, 111, *111, 112;* regional differences in, 94, 110; sofas, 97, *99,* 102; tables, *102,* 106–10, *106, 107, 108, 109, 119;* woods used in, 92, 115. *See also* Empire style furniture; Federal style furniture
Federal style furniture: about, 83, 94–96; chairs, *85, 86, 89, 90, 94, 99;* chests, *90;* cupboards/dressers, *85, 90, 95;* desks, *85, 114;* sofas, *87, 88, 90, 103;* tables, *85, 86, 89, 90, 94, 96, 101, 114*
fireplaces: colonial period, *30,* 32, *32,* 33–34, *64,* 74; early settlement, 4–6; early twentieth century, *229, 230, 235, 239;* early West, 242; in farmhouses, 257, 258; Federal period, 84–85, *85, 87, 89, 90, 130,* 131, *149;* kitchen, 192–95, *193,* 198, *210;* Southwest and California, 246; Victorian period, 139–42, *140, 141, 142,* 144, *148, 176, 183,* 186–87, *189*
floor coverings: colonial period, 76–77, *76;* early settlement, 24; early twentieth century, *229, 233,* 236, *238, 239,* 240; Federal period, *109, 119, 126,* 127–28, *128;* Shaker, 255; Southwest and California, 250; Victorian period, *135, 137,* 138, *147, 148, 149,* 187
floorplans: colonial period, 27–28, 52–53; early settlement, 4, 6, 7; early twentieth century, 229, 231, 232–33; early West, 242–43; farmhouses, 256–57; Federal period, 84, 91; kitchens, 201, 209; Shaker, 251, 252; Southwest and California, 246; Victorian period, 133–34, 144–48, *145*

floors: colonial period, *30,* 31; early settlement, 6–7; early twentieth century, 231, 234; Federal period, 89–91; kitchen, 209; Shaker, 251; Victorian period, 138
Franklin stove, 33, 84–85, 142, *143*

G

Georgian periods, 27
glassware: colonial period, 74; early twentieth century, 240–41; Federal period, 124; Victorian period, *140,* 184, *184*
Golden Oak furniture: about, 238–39; chairs, *235;* cupboards/dressers, *235;* dresser-desk-bed, *237;* tables, *235*
Gothic Revival furniture, 152
Greek Revival style: in Federal period, 91–92, 102–3, *119;* in Victorian period, 134, 162

H

heating systems: early twentieth century, 241; Federal period, 84–85; Shaker, 252; Victorian period, 142–43, *146*
Hepplewhite style furniture. *See* Federal style furniture
Hyland House, 202

I

interior appointments: colonial period, 27, 28, 29–31, *30, 32, 64;* early settlement, 7; Federal period, 87–88, *88, 89,* 91, 92; Victorian period, 134, 138, 144
Italianate style, 144
Italian Renaissance style, 8

J

Jacobean style: early settlement, *15*, 18–19; Victorian period, 156
Japanese influence, 174, 191
Jethro Coffin House, 202

K

kitchens: about, 192–217; colonial period, 34; decorating, 213–14; design of, 199, 209; early settlement, 4, 5–6; early twentieth century, 231; farmhouse, 257, 258; food storage in, 201, *204, 205*, 206–8, 209, 213; furniture in, *193, 195, 198, 200*. 201, 203, *205*, 207–8, *207, 208, 213, 214*; regional differences in, 201, 202, 205

L

Lagniappe dollhouse, *210*
laundry: about, 224–27; accessories, 224; ironing, 224–26, *225*; regional differences, 227; smoothing implements, 226; washing implements, 224, *225*, 226–27
lighting: colonial period, *50, 52, 64, 65*, 65, 69, *73*, 74, 75, *81*; early settlement, 4, *13, 16*, 21–22; early twentieth century, *229, 233, 238*, 239–40; early West, *243*; farmhouse, 258; Federal period, *88, 89, 90, 105*, 126–27, *126*; kitchen, *195*, 209–10; Shaker, 255; Southwest and California, 250; Victorian period, *136, 137*, 143–44, *147*, 151, 153, 155, *159, 176*, 180–82, *181, 183*, 189
Louis XV furniture, *151*, 156
Louis XVI furniture, 151, 156

M

machines, Victorian era, 187–91
meat smoking, 200–201
medieval style, 8, 14, *14*, 39
Megler Landing House, *215*
mirrors: colonial period, *60*, 68–70, *86*; early settlement, 24; Federal period, *87, 90*, 120–21, *120*; Shaker, 255; Victorian period, *140*
Mission furniture, *233*, 237

N

neoclassical style: Federal period, 83; Victorian period, 150

O

octagon house, 144–45, *145, 146*
Oriental style: colonial period, 55, *63, 64*, 65; Federal period, 83
outbuildings, colonial period, 34

P

pictures: colonial period, 70; early twentieth century, *231, 236, 239*, 240; Federal period, 121, *121, 128*; Victorian period, 136, *137*, 178–79, *179*
pillar-and-scroll style furniture, 150, *151, 229*
plumbing, indoor, 202, 219
privies (outhouses), 217, 219

Q

Queen Anne style furniture: about, 26, 41–42; beds, 46, 53; chairs, 41, 42–45, *43, 44, 47, 48, 52*, 56, *64*; chests, 46, *47*, 50–52, *51*; cupboards/dressers, *28*, 48, *48*; desks, 46, *60, 64*; regional differences in, 41–42; sofas, *45*, 46, *46*; tables, *28, 43, 44*, 48, 50, *50, 52*; woods used in, 53
quilt-making, colonial period, 77–78

R

Renaissance Revival furniture: about, 151–52, beds, *168, 171*; chairs, *152*, 156, *189*; chests, *168*; sofas, *189*
Rococo Revival furniture: about, *137*, 150–51; chairs, *155*, 156; sofas, 161, *161*; tables, *155*

S

seasonal changes: colonial period, 68, 74; in farmhouse, 258; Federal period, 115, 127; in kitchen, 209; Victorian period, 185–87
Shaker furniture: about, 251, 252–53, 254, 255; beds, *253*, 255; chairs, *243*, 254, *254*; chests, *253*, 255; cupboards/dressers, *253*, 255; decorative techniques in, 252–53, *254*; desks, 255; sofas, 254, tables, 254
Sheraton style furniture. *See* Federal style furniture
showers, 221–22
silver: colonial period, 72–73; early settlement, 23; Federal period, *105, 107*, 124, *125*; Southwest and California, 248–50; Victorian period, 184, 185
sinks: bathroom, *220*, 221; kitchen, 201–3, *202, 203*
sofas: bench, *99*; camel-back, 53–55, *54*; chairback settee, 46, *46*, 53, *88*, 161; Chesterfield, 162; cozy corner, 162–64; high-back settee, *32*; mammy bench, 104; medallion-back, 161, *161*; meridienne, 162;

ottoman, 162, 164; récamier, 103–4, *104;* settee, *45, 54, 64;* settle, 161; Sheraton, *103;* table/settee, *229;* tête-à-tête, 161; wagon-seat settee, *54,* 55, 104, 159–61; window seat, 55, *90;* Windsor settee (deacon's bench), 53, 159

Southwest and California, 245–51; decorative styles in, 245–46; furniture, 246–51, *247, 248, 249;* interiors, 246

stairs: colonial period, 28, 29; early twentieth century, 231–32; Federal period, 91; Victorian period, 134, 139, 187

storage: colonial period, 28–29; early settlement, 7; early West, 242; in farmhouse, 257–58; Shaker, 251, *253;* Victorian period, 133

stoves: colonial period, 33; farmhouse, 258; Federal period, 84–85; kitchen, 203–5, *204, 206, 215;* Shaker, 252, *252;* Victorian period, 142, 143, *143, 189*

T

table accessories: colonial period, *28, 39, 61, 63, 69,* 71–73, *72, 74, 76, 78, 81;* early settlement, 23–24, *23;* early twentieth century, *233;* early West, 244, *244;* Federal period, *85, 89, 105, 107, 109, 119,* 122–24, *123, 124, 125,* Victorian period, 182–84, *183,* 185

tables: basin stand, 59, 61, *89;* bedside, 164, 170; butler's tray, 50; butterfly, 38; candlestand, 38, *40, 43, 44, 52, 64, 107,* 254; center, *96, 105, 147, 151, 155,* 164; chair, 13; china, 63, *63;* circular pedestal, 164; dessert server (dumbwaiter), 50, *109;* draw, 19; dressing, 106, *106, 135;* drop-leaf, 48, *50,* 63, 254; drum, 63; extension, *90,* 106, *109;* gaming, 50, 63, *64, 107;* gateleg, *28,* 38, *39, 79;* handkerchief, 48, 50; harvest, 164; Hepplewhite, *94;* hunt, 110, *110;* hutch, 13; kettle stand, *52,* 63, 106, *107;* lazy-susan, 164; marble-top, 150, *155, 163,* 164, *166;* mixing, *37,* 50, 109; pedestal, *32, 87,* 164; Pembroke, 63, 105, *105;* pier, 106, *106, 137, 148,* 164; plant stand, *137,* 169; porringer, 63, *64;* refectory, 18–19, *198;* sawbuck, 18, *18, 66;* sectional dining, 106, 109, *109;* serving, 38, *109;* shaving stand, 61; side, 50, *89, 95, 96, 135,* 164; sideboard, 26, 38, *249;* snake-foot, *105;* sofa, 104–5; spider, 63; splayed-leg stand, *39;* stretcher, *10,* 18, *200;* tavern, 38, *39, 40, 69;* tea, *28, 32,* 38, 50, 61, *62,* 63, 164; teapoy, 63, 106; tiered, 164; trestle, *17,* 18, *18;* washstand, *86,* 106, *107, 108,* 166; worktable, *101, 102,* 106, *107,* 164, 248

telephones, *147,* 190, 233–34, 241, 258

toilets, 219, 220, *220*

Turkish influence, Victorian period, 162–64, *163,* 179

V

Van Cortlandt Baby House, *82*

Victorian period furniture: about, 132, 149–55, 173–74; beds, 169–73, *169, 170, 171, 172;* chairs, *135, 147, 154,* 156, *157,* 159, *160, 162, 165, 173, 176;* chests, 166; cupboards/dressers, *149,* 166, 167, *167, 218;* decorative techniques in, 155–56, 157, 159, 162, 167, 173–76; desks, *147, 164, 165, 165, 166;* étagère, *152,* 167–69; sofas, 159–64, *163,* 185; tables, *135, 137, 147, 148, 154, 162, 163,* 164, *166,* 169, 170, *173, 176;* woods used in, 150, 153, 173–74, 176. *See also* Art Nouveau furniture; Arts and Crafts furniture; Elizabethan Revival furniture; Gothic Revival furniture; Louis XV furniture; Louis XVI furniture; pillar-and-scroll style furniture; Renaissance Revival furniture; Rococo Revival furniture

Victorian period, regional differences in, 144, *165,* 169, 170, 174

W

walls: colonial period, 29–31, *30, 64;* early settlement, 4, 7; early twentieth century, *229,* 231, *231,* 234, 235; Federal period, 85–88, *86, 88,* 91–92; kitchen, 209, *215;* Shaker, 251; Victorian period, 134–38, *136, 148, 149, 176,* 179–80, *183*

Wanton-Lyman-Hazard House, 25

William and Mary style furniture: about, 26; beds, 38–40; chairs, 35–36, *35, 36,* 37, *42,* 56; chests, 37, *37,* 38, 40–41, *41;* decorative techniques in, 40–41; desks, 37, *37,* 38; tables, *35, 37,* 38, *40*

window accessories: colonial period, 31–32, *32,* 78–79; early settlement, 25; early twentieth century, *231, 239,* 240; Federal period, 131; Shaker, 252; Southwest and California, 250; Victorian period, 139, *148,* 185–86, *189*

windows: colonial period, *30,* 31–32; early settlement, 4, 6; early twentieth century, 234–35, *239;* Federal period, *88, 89,* 91; Victorian period, 138–39, 144, *147*